RORSCHACHIANA XXXII

Rorschachiana

Journal of the International Society for the Rorschach

Volume 32, Issues 1 & 2, 2011

Editor-in-Chief:
Sadegh Nashat, Tavistock Clinic, London, UK

Rorschachiana

Editorial Board Members

Publication

Rorschachiana is available as a book and as a journal (consisting of two online issues per year, an annual print compendium, and online access to back issues):

ISBN 978-0-88937-398-3 (Rorschachiana, Vol. 32)
ISSN 1192-5604 (journal)

Copyright Information

Rorschachiana, Volume 32, 2011 (book)

PUBLISHING OFFICES
USA: Hogrefe Publishing, 875 Massachusetts Avenue, 7th Floor, Cambridge, MA 02139,
Tel. (866) 823-4726, Fax (617) 354-6875, E-mail customerservice@hogrefe-publishing.com,
Web http://www.hogrefe.com
Europe: Hogrefe Publishing, Merkelstr. 3, 37085 Göttingen, Germany, Tel. +49 551 99950-0,
Fax +49 551 99950-111, E-mail publishing@hogrefe.com, Web http://www.hogrefe.com

SALES AND DISTRIBUTION
USA: Hogrefe Publishing, Customer Service Department, 30 Amberwood Parkway, Ashland,
OH 44805, Tel. (800) 228-3749, Fax (419) 281-6883, E-mail customerservice@hogrefe.com
Europe: Hogrefe Publishing, Merkelstr. 3 37085 Göttingen, Germany Tel. +49 551 99950-0,
Fax +49 551 99950-111, E-mail publishing@hogrefe.com

OTHER OFFICES
Canada: Hogrefe Publishing, 660 Eglinton Ave. East, Suite 119-514, Toronto, Ontario, M4G 2K2
Switzerland: Hogrefe Publishing, Länggass-Strasse 76, CH-3000 Bern 9

Hogrefe Publishing
Incorporated and registered in the Commonwealth of Massachusetts, USA, and in Göttingen,
Lower Saxony, Germany

Printed and bound in Germany

ISBN: 978-0-88937-398-3

Rorschachiana: Journal of the International Society for the Rorschach

Publisher: Hogrefe Publishing, Merkelstr. 3, D-37085 Göttingen, Germany, Tel. +49 551 99950-0, Fax +49 551 99950-111, E-mail publishing@hogrefe.com, Web http://www.hogrefe.com

Production: Juliane Munson, Hogrefe Publishing, Merkelstr. 3, D-37085 Göttingen, Germany, Tel. +49 551 99950-422, Fax +49 551 99950-111, E-mail juliane.munson@hogrefe.com

Subscriptions: Hogrefe Publishing, Herbert-Quandt-Str. 4, D-37079 Göttingen, Germany, Tel. +49 551 50 68 80, Fax +49 551 50 68 824

Advertising/Inserts: Melanie Beck, Hogrefe Publishing, Merkelstr. 3, D-37085 Göttingen, Germany, Tel. +49 551 99950-423, Fax +49 551 99950-111, E-mail marketing@hogrefe.com

Publication: Published in two online issues and a print compendium per annual volume.

Subscription Prices: Annual subscription (2011): Individuals: US $128.00 / € 92.00 / CHF 125.00; Institutions: US $195.00 / € 142.00 / CHF 192.00 (postage & handling: US $8.00 / € 6.00 / CHF 10.00). Single issue (online): US $132 / € 94.00.

Payment: Payment may be made by check, international money order, or credit card to Hogrefe Publishing, Merkelstr. 3, D-37085 Göttingen, Germany, or, for customers in North America, to Hogrefe Publishing, Inc., Journals Department, 875 Massachusetts Avenue, 7th Floor, Cambridge, MA 02139, USA.

Electronic Full Text: The full text of *Rorschachiana* is available online at http://www.psycontent.com/content/1192-5604 and also in PsycARTICLES®.

Abstracting/Indexing Services: *Rorschachiana* is abstracted/indexed in PsycINFO and PSYNDEX.

ISSN: 1192-5604

Contents

Advice for Authors

Rorschachiana 32, 1–4
© 2011 Hogrefe Publishing

DOI: 10.1027/1192-5604/a000012

Editorial

Grasping Complexity

Sadegh Nashat

Tavistock Clinic, London, UK

One quickly realizes that, beyond the task of reviewing several manuscripts a year, the role of Editor of an international journal such as *Rorschachiana* also implies keeping up to date with other publications. This means reading original contributions in the field of projective methods and in social sciences in general. The task remains herculean in nature and has its limits. However, you get some idea about current theories, research, and opinions that are discussed in the field.

What has struck me over the years is how the production of knowledge has increased and how it is being disseminated. A new study showing the effectiveness of some treatment might be proven ineffective by another study only a few months later. This seems to be the case not only in psychology but also in the experimental sciences such as pharmacology (Begley, 2011). This can be daunting both for clinicians and researchers as well as for policymakers and the public in general. One explanation for this situation is that publishing the result of a study in a peer-reviewed journal can take several months, and that the knowledge generated in the meantime is not always included or even noticed. This isn't helped by the fact that some studies are never submitted for publication because they do not show the desired outcome and fall into the area of what is commonly called "grey publication" (which stays in the researcher's drawer).

However, another explanation has to do with the Cartesian scientific approach that involves simplifying the object of study in order to examine it. Many have voiced their concerns about the reductionist aspect of such an approach in psychology. Consequently, a new paradigm has emerged that is more interested in complexity. Bachelard (1934/2003) is probably one of the first epistemologists to consider a "science of complexity." He started by stating that there is no simple idea, because a simple idea, in order to be understood, is always inserted into a complex system of thoughts and experiences, which probably summarizes Bachelard's thinking of a non-Cartesian approach to science. He established the foundation of a new way of scientific explanation, which identifies simplicity as a specific provisional phenomenon (Alhadeff-Jones, 2008). The complexity paradigm became not only popular with social scientists, but it has had many applications in cybernetics, physics, or quantum mechanics.

More recently, the work of the French philosopher and sociologist Edgar Morin on complexity has had many applications and has generated fascinating interdisciplinary dialogs. As Alhadeff-Jones (2010) demonstrates, Morin advocates the emergence of a type of science that supports an "en-cyclo-paedic" process, which generates knowledge in a circular rather than linear way. He believes in an open network of concepts and in principles of thought that create a dialog between various scientific fields. Antagonism, contradictions, and complementarity tensions are to be expected and create complexity while shaping our understanding (Alhadeff-Jones, 2008).

I believe this notion of complexity is not foreign to us as clinicians, therapists, and researchers in projective psychology. We are well positioned to know that, as tempting as it might be, simplifying is not always the effective way to address the complexities of human functioning, where tinkering with any one aspect of a human system of interconnected elements inevitably impacts, and thus changes, the whole system. This is equally true for the various approaches available to us for scoring and interpretation. They are all systems based on the understanding that one element cannot be interpreted in isolation, but rather needs to be considered in combination with other elements.

Rorschach (1932) himself was aware that giving a response to the inkblots required a complex operation between various processes. In his *Psychodiagnostik*, he states that perception consists of three distinct but interconnected processes: sensation, memory, and association (Rorschach, 1932). It is the interplay between these that generates a thought or an idea that forms the subject's response. Rorschach adds that this is not merely the work of imagination, but requires a complex operation involving several processes.

Complexity is also acknowledged in the foundations of the scoring of the Rorschach Test, which takes into account three pivotal dimensions: location, determinant, and content. Many authors, such as Beck, Klopfer, Piotrowski, and Anzieu, to name a few, have enriched the scoring and interpretation of the Inkblot Test. But perhaps it is the work of

Exner (2003) that best reflects the notion of a "science of complexity" with the development of the Comprehensive System.

Whatever approach one might favor, the future of projective techniques lies in our capacity to collaborate at international and interdisciplinary levels. Isolation will only weaken our scientific position and expose us to more criticism. The Editorial Board of *Rorschachiana* hopes to modestly contribute to this endeavor by becoming a platform for interdisciplinary dialogs.

Volume 32 of *Rorschachiana* contains a variety of topics that are explored using different lenses. A study by Arnon, Maoz, Gazit, and Klein establishes key indicators for the Rorschach Comprehensive System which can contribute to the diagnosis of posttraumatic stress disorder. Guinzbourg demonstrates how the Rorschach can be useful in understanding various subtypes of eating disorders in her study comparing 106 eating disorder patients to a normative sample. Verdon's comprehensive review of the use of the Thematic Apperception Test with older adults is an elegant and thought-provoking contribution to a field that is gaining momentum. Ikiz narrates how the Rorschach Test was adopted in Turkey and discusses some of the challenges the use of the test has encountered over the years. Finally, Carstairs shows how projective methods can be an invaluable addition to the assessment of parents in cases of child neglect.

The Special Section of this volume is introduced by our Guest Editor Professor Latife Yazigi, who has collated a variety of contributions on the use of projective methods with children and adolescents.

References

Alhadeff-Jones, M. (2010). The reduction of critique in education: Perspectives from Morin's paradigm of complexity. In D. Osberg & G. Biesta (Eds.), *Complexity theory and the politics of education* (pp. 25–23). New York: Sense Publishers.

Alhadeff-Jones, M. (2008). Three generations of complexity theories: Nuances and ambiguities. *Educational Philosophy and Theory, 4*, 66–82.

Bachelard, G. (1934/2003). *Le nouvel esprit scientifique* [The new scientific spirit]. Paris, France: Presses Universitaires de France.

Begley, S. (2011, January 23). Why almost everything you hear about medicine is wrong, *Newsweek*. Retrieved from http://www.newsweek.com/2011/01/23/why-almost-everything-you-hear-about-medicine-is-wrong.html

Exner, J. (2003). *The Rorschach: A comprehensive system*. New York: Wiley.

Rorschach, H. (1932). *Psychodiagnostik* [Psychodiagnostics]. Bern, Switzerland: Hans Huber.

Rorschachiana 32, 5–26
© 2011 Hogrefe Publishing

DOI: 10.1027/1192-5604/a000013

Original Article

Rorschach Indicators of PTSD

A Retrospective Study

Zahi Arnon[1], Gadi Maoz[2], Tali Gazit[1], and Ehud Klein[3]

[1]*Department of Behavioral Sciences, The Max Stern Academic College of Emek Yezreel, Emek Yesreel,* [2]*Tachanat Ha'amakim Community Mental Health Center and Faculty for Advanced Studies, Oranim Academic College, Tivon,* [3]*Rambam Medical Center, Haifa, all Israel*

Abstract. The complexity of posttraumatic stress disorder (PTSD) makes it difficult to assess and diagnose the syndrome. Most diagnostic tools are based on self-report questionnaires and are thus susceptible to both conscious and unconscious biases. Projective techniques, including the Rorschach inkblot test, might overcome these shortcomings. This retrospective study analyzed 187 Rorschach protocols, 4 or more years after the diagnosis (PTSD vs. non-PTSD) had been determined. The protocols were coded into the computer version of Exner's Comprehensive System (RIAP5) (Exner, 2005) and then analyzed statistically, using linear regression. A 13-item model was found to significantly predict 36.6% of PTSD patients.

Keywords: Rorschach, posttraumatic stress disorder (PTSD), assessment

Introduction

The term posttraumatic stress disorder (PTSD) was introduced into the third edition of the *Diagnostic and Statistical Manual of Mental Disorders* (DSM-III) in 1980 (APA, 1980). Today, 28 years later, professional interest in this topic still continues to grow, and the term has entered the mainstream of medicine, law, social sciences, and academic research (Wilson, 2004). A brief search for the term PTSD in the CSA Illumina international database (April 2008) found 19,830 publications, including peer-reviewed and other journals, books, and book chapters.

Although trauma may seem a simple concept, it is more than merely an unpleasant occurrence or even a terrible event that continues to agitate even after it is over. PTSD is a complex phenomenon due to the diversity of traumatic events as well as to the differences in human reactions to these events (Herman, 1999). Wilson (2004) also emphasizes the impact of PTSD on personality functioning and biology. Hence, the syndrome can be construed as "complex PTSD," involving five clusters of symptoms: Three are mentioned in the DSM-IV (APA, 1994) – re-experiencing, avoidance and arousal – and two others have been added: impaired self-functioning and effect thereof on interpersonal relations.

There is a growing need to develop an assessment tool to help understand and diagnose human responses to traumatic events beyond the content of the events themselves. Such a diagnostic tool would ideally provide information about the particular response of a specific person to a specific event as well as about the common denominator, i.e., the similarity among human responses to traumatic events.

Many diagnostic tools have been used to measure PTSD. Norris and Hamblen (2004) reviewed 24 standardized self-report questionnaires, seven of which assessed the traumatic event itself (criterion A) and 17 of which measured intrusion, avoidance, and arousal (criteria B, C, D). The major disadvantage of these questionnaires was that they were based on the client's self-report about the experience and the symptoms and are hence susceptible to changes in memory, subjectivity, and intentional manipulation (Luxenberg & Levin, 2004). Furthermore, their validity may be questioned when financial compensation is involved, or when secondary gains may encourage malingering. Structured clinical interviews, including the one used for DSM-IV (SCID), try to avoid these shortcomings, but the basic motivation of the interviewed patient (e.g., seeking relief versus compensation) influences the outcomes. "The accuracy, or sensitivity and specificity, of the structured interview is not necessarily a fixed attribute ..." (Weiss, 2004, p. 116).

Projective testing, being ambiguous, and having no clearcut "correct" answer may prevent the shortcomings. The client has no clue as to a specific or desirable answer and thus projects both content and processes onto the test stimuli. Unable to "guess" what answer will serve him best, he is compelled to project genuine content.

The Inkblot Test, developed in 1921 by Hermann Rorschach, is a projective test used extensively as a diagnostic tool. Since it consists of ten cards, the diagnosis is not based on a single response, but rather on the analysis of all ten or more responses. Thus, the examiner is able to gather information on several mental processes and contents. By using the Rorschach test for exposing diverse responses to trauma, we can avoid focusing on the usual PTSD clusters, i.e., re-experiencing, avoidance, and arousal reactions only. The Rorschach test makes it possible to analyze the client's complex response to the trauma, taking into account cognition, emotion, defenses, sense of self, interpersonal issues, perception, and content.

However, projective tests are not without disadvantages. Most projective tests have no standardized scales, thus making it more difficult to establish a diagnosis that is not based on subjective analysis of the projected data.

Since the Rorschach became popular, several approaches have been adopted to administer and analyze it. A standardized system was developed by Exner by the end of the 20th century (Levin & Reis, 1997). Since then, this system, known as the Comprehensive System, has been continually updated, including its latest version, the computer-based Rorschach Interpretation Assistance Program (RIAP5) (Exner, 2005). Exner's system of Rorschach scoring was developed following a survey of clinicians. The results indicated that most clinicians tended to integrate different features from the five major and popular approaches to Rorschach analysis, none of which had been systematically or empirically examined. The Comprehensive System was first published in 1974, reflecting an integrative, empirically demonstrable, and systematic approach for administering and analyzing the Rorschach test (Exner, 1986). The new scoring system integrates empirically supported coding with new coding systems that evolved during the development of the comprehensive system. Since then, numerous studies have standardized, refined, and improved the system's ability to diagnose psychiatric pathologies.

The first study of stress reactions using the Rorschach was published by Shalit (1965). Since then, nearly 20 other studies were published which used the Rorschach to assess posttraumatic responses. Most of these did not use samples exceeding 50 subjects, and not all used Exner's Comprehensive System (CS). Still, during the last two decades more researchers have tended to use the CS in studies concerning Rorschach and PTSD (Hartman et al., 1990; Kroch & Shahar, 2002; Sloan, Arsenault, Hilsenroth, Harvill, & Handler, 1995; Swanson, Blout, & Bruno, 1990). These studies, based on a computerized system, have deepened our understanding of PTSD by means of empirical as well as to theoretical research.

The RIAP5 adheres to interpretive strategies in which the hypotheses are arranged in major clusters, among them depression, suicide potential, obsessive style, hypervigilance index, perceptual thinking, and coping deficit. But, so far, no cluster to help diagnose PTSD is available.

7

While the assessment of traumatic responses should not be based on a single test, the Rorschach can add important information to help refine a diagnosis. Evidently, more research may be needed to enhance the ability of the test to assess PTSD – and to provide eventual PTSD typical clusters that may lead to a better understanding of the human response to trauma.

A review of the research on the use of Rorschach for the assessment of PTSD reveals that some Rorschach indicators are correlated to PTSD. Levin and Reis (1997) noted that "The single most consistent finding across Rorschach studies of various traumatized population ... is the presence of elevation in the number of inanimate movement responses (m)" (Levin & Reis, 1997, p. 538). Another determinant found to be consistently elevated is diffuse shading (Y). Unstructured color (FC < CF + F) is also used extensively. Goldfinger, Amdur, and Liberson (1998) compared the Rorschach protocols of 16 PTSD-diagnosed combat Vietnam veterans to 9 combat controls and 12 noncombat subjects. Of the many Rorschach indicators, only EB (relation between human movement and weighted sum of chromatic color responses) was able to differentiate PTSD subjects from controls.

Sloan, Arsenault, and Hilsenroth (2002) reported findings based on 30 U.S. marines who served in the Gulf War. Rorschach protocols administered 3–5 months after the reservists returned indicated a valid cluster of 10 Rorschach variables related to PTSD: X+% (conventional form use); Xu% (unusual form use); EA (adding human movement and weighted sum of chromatic color responses); es (adding nonhuman movements and shading and achromatic color determinants); m (inanimate movement responses); FC (form-color determinants); CF + C (color-form and color determinants); D (relation between EA and es, reflecting stress tolerance); AdjD (subtracting situational stress from D); and Lambda (ratio between pure form responses to all record answers). A few years later, Rorschach tests were administered again. This time only five variables were found to differentiate the PTSD group: X+%, es, D, AdjD, and Lambda. Armstrong and Kaser-Boyd (2004) reviewed the Rorschach indicators for trauma and concluded that traumatized clients displayed the following variables: low R (number of responses); pure F; low Afr (Affective Ratio: internalization of affect); low blends (responses that use more than one determinant); low EB, indicating avoidance; CF + C > FC; and traumatic content. These traumatized clients also showed high Y & V (Y-answers based on the light dark feature of the blot, like fog; V-depth or dimensionality based only on shading characteristics of the blot), indicating intrusion in thoughts and emotions; high m; high HVI (hypervigilance index), indicating arousal; low X+; high Xu; and high WSum6 (weighted Sum of six special scores), indicating impaired reality testing.

Luxenberg and Levin (2004, p. 208) summarized the Rorschach variables that may be related to complex trauma in a detailed table. These variables are similar to indicators found in previous studies, with additional indicators that may reflect the complex nature of some traumas. However, as mentioned earlier, no cluster (group of determinants or indexes) was specified for PTSD.

The present study made the attempt to define an index – a cluster of Rorschach indicators – for diagnosing PTSD, bearing in mind that no single test is sufficient to determine a diagnosis.

Method

The study group consisted of subjects who had submitted claims to the Israel Ministry of Defense for recognition of mental disability, allegedly caused by exposure to traumatic events during service in the security forces (army, police, and prison services). They were all referred to the Rambam Medical Center for evaluation and diagnosis of possible PTSD, performed by a team representing four different disciplines: psychiatry, clinical psychology, social work, and occupational therapy. Each team member met the subjects individually and submitted his/her findings to the psychiatrist, who added them to his own and summarized them in a final report. In this way the diagnosis regarding the presence of PTSD was determined by the psychiatrist. Of all subjects referred to the Rambam evaluation center during the years 1998–2003, 205 were met by the same clinical psychologist and underwent a battery of diagnostic tests including the Rorschach, Bender Gestalt, projective drawings, and Thematic Apperception Test (TAT). These tests were administered in one session that took 1 to 2 h. The final diagnoses and demographic details were collected retrospectively from the evaluation center's files, blind to the Rorschach protocols and its analysis. Of the 205 original subjects, 18 were excluded due to lack of diagnosis or refusal to respond to the Rorschach test. The Rorschach responses of 187 remaining subjects included in the study were then entered into the RIAP5 by the psychologist who had originally administered the tests. In order to check interrater reliability, randomly selected protocols (about 10%) were coded by a second clinical psychologist familiar with the RIAP5. Although interrater reliability was not statistically analyzed due to technical-methodological problems, the manual comparison revealed no significant differences. Finally, the diagnoses, demographic details, and structural summary produced by the RIAP5 program were statistically analyzed using the SPSS 14 software.

It should be emphasized that originally the Rorschach was administered as a part of a battery of tests in order to compose a psychodiagnostic report: It was one of four reports that led to the PTSD diagnosis. The Rorschach protocols were analyzed by RIAP5 only some years later, when the present study began. The study is thus retrospective, aimed at finding Rorschach scores that correlate to the previous diagnosis.

Results

Of the 187 subjects included in the study, 116 met the diagnostic criteria of PTSD and 71 did not (non-PTSD). The diagnosis was confirmed by the psychiatrist of the evaluation center as described earlier.

Table 1 shows the distribution of co-morbid diagnoses for PTSD and non-PTSD groups.

Table 1. Other (co-morbid) disorders distribution

	PTSD N (%)	Non-PTSD N (%)	χ^2
Personality disorder	4 (3.4)	6 (8.5)	$\chi^2(2) = 2.75$
Mood disorder	11 (9.5)	18 (25.4)	$\chi^2(2) = 8.46, p > .004**$
Anxiety	8 (6.9)	24 (33.8)	$\chi^2(2) = 22.47\, p < .001**$
Schizophrenia and psychotic state	3 (2.6)	7 (9.9)	$\chi^2(2) = 4.60, p > .03*$
Narcissistic damage	8 (6.9)	6 (8.5)	$\chi^2(2) = 0.154, p > .69$
Dissociation	6 (5.2)	3 (4.2)	$\chi^2(2) = 0.08, p > .76$
Malingering	12 (10.3)	14 (19.7)	$\chi^2(2) = 6.67, p > .01*$

Note. $*p < .05$, $**p < .01$.

As seen from Table 1, the non-PTSD patients displayed more mood, anxiety, schizophrenia, and psychotic disorders than the PTSD group.

Table 2 shows the background and demographic data, analyzed for determining the relevance to PTSD.

Table 2. Background and demographic data of PTSD/non-PTSD groups

		PTSD	Non-PTSD	
Age	mean	33.2	36.2	$t(122) = 1.564\ p > .12$
	SD	10.8	13.7	
	range	19–62	19–68	
Gender	male	104	62	$\chi^2(1) = 0.24, p > .62$
	female	12	9	
Marital status	married	63	35	$\chi^2(3) = 4.23, p > .23$
	single	44	26	
	divorced	7	3	
	separated	1	4	
	unknown	1	3	
Education	mean	11.7	11.4	$t(179) = 1.016, p > .31$
	SD	2.0	1.5	
	range	5–20	6–15	
Religion	Jew	83	54	$\chi^2 (3) = 0.96, p > .80$
	Druze	23	10	
	Moslem (Bedouin)	8	5	
	unknown	2	2	
Origin	Israel	86	55	$\chi^2(6) = 8.37, p > .21$
	Africa	3	10	
	America	10	1	
	Russia	9	2	
	Middle East	5	1	
	unknown	3	2	
Economic status	below average	63	38	$\chi^2(2) = 0.27, p > .98$
	average	51	30	
	above average	2	1	
	unknown	2		
Physically wounded during traumatic event	no	50	32	$\chi^2(1) = 0.12, p > .91$
	yes	63	39	
	unknown	3		
Previous trauma	no	82	56	$\chi^2(1) = 1.52, p > .21$
	yes	34	15	
Type of service	soldiers	89	57	$\chi^2(5) = 3.88, p > .56$
	prison guards	4	3	
	border guards	7	5	
	policemen	15	5	
	unknown	1		

		PTSD	Non-PTSD	
On psychiatric medication at time of Rorschach test	no	49	30	$\chi^2(1) = 0.09, p > .76$
	yes	55	37	
	unknown	12	4	
Years elapsed since traumatic event	mean	7.4	10.4	$t(119) = 1.888, p > .06$ *
	SD	8.8	11.4	
	range	1–36	1–46	
Employment status	unemployed	66	42	$\chi^2(2) = 5.98\ p < .05$ **
	employed	48	22	
	retired	2	6	
	unknown	1		

Note. *As seen from the above table, the time elapsed between exposure to the traumatic event and the evaluation date (in years) almost reached statistical significance between PTSD and non-PTSD groups. This may indicate that the PTSD syndrome changes over the years. **The only detail found to statistically differentiate between the groups was the ability to work. Subjects diagnosed as PTSD were less able to work than subjects from the non-PTSD group.

Rorschach Analysis

Formally, to be valid a Rorschach test should include 14 or more responses. Out of the 187 protocols in the study, 121 met this requirement, while the remaining 66 protocols included 13 or fewer responses (min 6, max 53, mean 16.65, SD 7.47) (Table 3).

The two groups differed statistically in the number of responses $[t(106) = 2.476, p > .01]$, indicating that the PTSD group had fewer responses (mean R = 15.5) than the non-PTSD group (mean R = 18.5).

For determining whether the 66 incomplete protocols differ from the complete ones, all background and demographic data (specified in Table 2) were analyzed. No statistically significant differences were found among any of these variables.

The issue of short protocols among PTSD patients has been treated in several studies. Van der Kolk and Ducey (1989) analyzed 13 Rorschach protocols of PTSD diagnosed patient, including 4 short protocols (R <

Table 3. Descriptive statistics comparing groups in (R) number of responses

	PTSD (N = 116)	Non-PTSD (N = 71)
R ≤ 13	N = 47	N = 19
R ≥ 14	N = 69	N = 52

14), assuming they express the patients' inability to incorporate emotional experiences into their inner world, resulting in regression and avoidance. Cohen and de Ruiter (1991) criticized this procedure, arguing that these invalid protocols should not be included in the analysis. Their critique is in line with Weiner (1998), who also defined such protocols as invalid. However, Ducey and Van der Kolk (1991) disagree, contending that although Exner determined a cut-off of 14 responses to a valid protocol, he also suggested that short protocols reflected a basic coping style, which, if analyzed, could add important understanding of mental functioning. Hartman et al. (1990) included short protocols in their study explaining that they reflected emotional numbing of PTSD patients, and thus should not be ruled out. Kroch and Shahar (2002) analyzed 90 Rorschach protocols, of which 51 (57%) had less than 14 responses. After reviewing recent studies they concluded that short protocols were characteristic of posttraumatic stress disorder and should be included in the study analysis.

Based on the above studies and on the statistical analysis that found no differences between characteristics of complete and incomplete protocols, the analysis was carried out on all 187 subjects, regardless of the number of responses.

RIAP5 provides 220 variables in its structural summary. In order to determine those relevant to PTSD, a stepwise linear regression analysis was carried out. All 220 variables were analyzed and a 13-item model was proposed by the computed analysis, being able to significantly predict 36.6% (R square) of PTSD cases ($F[13, 173] = 7.673, p < .001$).

The regression equation for predicting PTSD was:

0.768 (constant)

–0.715 VF (Vista-Form: The answer was primarily based on the shading features to represent depth or dimensionality, while the form features were secondary)

–0.182 Hh (Household content)

–0.040 Id* (Idiographic content)

–0.427 FV* (Form-Vista: The answer was primarily based on the form features to represent depth or dimensionality, while the shading features were secondary)

+0.077 An* (Anatomy content)

13

−0.109 FM   (Animal movement)

+0.287 INC1   (Incongruous combination into a single object, level 1)

−0.461 T   (Texture: shading components represented as texture)

−0.283 Food   (Food content)

+0.148 Bt **   (Botany content)

−0.096 C'   (achromatic color-based response)

+0.086 Fi***   (Fire content)

−0.199 Cn   (Color Naming: the response is the name of the color)

[*Primary content; **Secondary content; ***Total content (primary & secondary)].

Using this regression equation a new variable was defined: PPS: PTSD Predictive Score, calculated as PPS = 0.768 − (0.715 VF) − (0.182 Hh) − (0.040 Id) − (0.427 FV) + (0.077 An) − (0.109 FM) + (0.287 INC1) − (0.461 T) − (0.283 Food) + (0.148 Bt) − (0.096 C) + (0.086 Fi) − (0.199 Cn).

PPS was calculated for each subject of the two groups, PTSD and non-PTSD, as presented in Table 4.

Table 4. PTSD predictor score (PPS) for PTSD/non-PTSD groups

	N	minimum	maximum	mean	SD
PTSD	116	−0.51	1.25	0.6584	0.2660
Non-PTSD	71	−0.81	0.91	0.3035	0.3302

The two groups were compared by t-test and were found to differ significantly: $t(124) = 7.661$, $p < .001$. Specifity and sensitivity of PPS in PTSD and non-PTST groups is presented in Table 5.

Table 5. PPS specificity and sensitivity using the mean as a cut-off score

	Using mean as cutoff	Correct diagnosis	Incorrect diagnosis	Wrongly diagnosed
PTSD N = 116	above 0.6584	sensitivity N = 65 (56%)	false negative N = 51 (44%)	N = 9 (12%)
Non-PTSD N = 71	below 0.3035	specificity N = 32 (45%)	false positive N = 39 (55%)	N = 9 (0.8%)

Figures 1 and 2 display the PPS distribution for PTSD and non-PTSD groups.

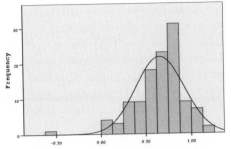

Figure 1. PPS distribution for PTSD group.

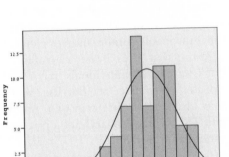

Figure 2. PPS distribution for the non-PTSD group.

Discussion

The present study identified 13 Rorschach indicators differentiating between subjects meeting PTSD diagnostic criterion and subjects that did not. The indicators consisted of four groups:

1. Determinants (VF, FV, FM, T)
2. Content (Hh, Id, An, Food, Bt, Fi)
3. Color (C', cn)
4. Special score (INC1).

The (+) components (marked by +) reflect positive correlation to PTSD, while the (–) components (marked by –) reflect negative correlation to PTSD.

Anatomy (An) was the first (+) component selected by the analysis. This component probably reflects the type of traumatic event: Military/combat events in which the patient was injured or exposed to friends who were injured. Much of the anatomy content included inter-

15

nal organs exposed due to injury. Anatomy responses did appear in PTSD patients (Levin & Reis, 1997). Surprisingly, Bl (Blood) was not found in the present study to discern between PTSD and non-PTSD patients, contrary to findings by Levin and Reis (1997) and Luxenberg and Levin (2004). A possible explanation is that blood responses are found in non-PTSD patients' protocols, as the red color does appear in some cards. Thus, a blood response might indicate a reality-based response more than an internal/intrusive thinking process.

INC 1 (Incongruous combination, level 1) was the second (+) component. INC reflects a causal or benign combination of implausible or impossible features that are attributed to a single object (Exner, 2003). Luxenberg and Levin (2004) defined INCOM as the improbable combination of elements that do not actually fit together, suggesting that "the elevated rate of incongruous combination in protocols of traumatized individuals may reflect responses to the implausible, unsuspected occurrence of a horrific event in their own life." This component may also reflect the integration process following dissociative aspects of the PTSD syndrome, and not a psychotic state, which might be coded more adequately as INC 2.

Bt (botany content) was the third (+) component likely to reflect human relationship avoidance characteristic of PTSD subjects. The last (+) component was Fi (fire content) which, like anatomy, was often part of military traumatic events. Many patients recalled and mentioned fire caused by explosion, and not the explosion itself. Neither Bt nor Fi are mentioned in previous studies as characteristic of PTSD responses.

Studies dealing with the ability of the Rorschach test to assess PTSD do not usually analyze the data in order to find negatively correlated components. The (–) components may add a significant contribution to this ability.

VF (Vista-Form) is the first (–) component, and FV (Form-Vista) is the fourth. Both reflect depth or dimensionality, based on shading characteristics of the blot, indicating an introspective process (Exner, 2003). The (–) sign shows that most patients diagnosed with PTSD were not involved in self-introspection and were rather more occupied with traumatic content such as anatomy and fire. On the other hand, vista responses may reflect the survivor's guilt and shame, which accompanies many PTSD patients (Luxenberg & Levin, 2004). Yet, the present study found a negative correlation between PTSD and vista responses. Another (–) determinant is FM (animal movement), related to mental activity not directly provoked by the focus of attention. Instead, it is regarded as a more peripheral process, the ability to alter the focus of attention

(Exner, 2003). The (-) sign indicates that PTSD-diagnosed patients show less flexibility and need to alter the focus of attention, which may reflect the intrusive and rigid style of their thinking processes. Yet another (-) determinant is T (Texture), in which shading features are interpreted as representing a tactual impression, with no form involved (Exner, 2003). One T response in a protocol was found consistently among nonpatients (between 75-80% according to Exner, 2003). Thus, the absence of T responses might be an apt indicator of PTSD pathology.

Other (-) content components include Hh (Household content), Id (idiographic content), and Fd (Food content). These findings may indicate that while posttraumatic patients are less occupied with trivial issues of daily life (compared to nonpatients), they do not necessarily have mediation disturbances such as idiographic content.

C' (achromatic color) and Cn (color naming) are the least negatively correlated to PTSD. C' indicates a response based on the achromatic color of the blot, regardless of the form. Cn is a response in which the chromatic response acknowledges only the presence of color. Exner (2003) found limited studies on color naming, and these responses were not correlated to specific diagnoses. Achromatic (C') answers are assumed to relate to affective constraint, typical to depressed patients and those with other affective disorders (Exner, 2003), thus helping to differentiate PTSD from other affective disorders.

Interestingly, R (total number of responses) was not one of the equation's components, although when standing alone it was found to be significantly lower in the PTSD group. It seems that the usual cutoff for a valid protocol (R ≥ 14) should be reconsidered due to the low R in PTSD patients' protocols. Since less than 14 responses seem to be characteristic to this disorder, they should be included in empirical studies (Van der Kolk & Ducey, 1989; but see Ducey & Van der Kolk, 1991; Hartman et al., 1990; Kroch & Shahar, 2002). Hartman et al. (1990) suggested that low R "were signs of the emotional numbing inherent in PTSD."

The PTSD Predictor Score (PPS) formulated by means of stepwise linear regression analysis offers limited sensitivity and specificity, even though two different cutoff numbers were used: above PTSD mean or below non-PTSD mean. Despite expectations of finding a distinct numerical criterion using the RIAP5 system for analyzing the Rorschach test and diagnosing PTSD, it seems we are still far from reaching this goal. Nevertheless, the results of the present study may provide additional insights into the components of PTSD through the analyses of PPS Contents.

17

References

American Psychiatric Association. (1980). *Diagnostic and Statistical Manual of Mental Disorders DSM-III-R* (3rd edition). Washington, DC: Author.

American Psychiatric Association. (1994). *Diagnostic and Statistical Manual of Mental Disorders DSM-IV* (4th edition). Washington, DC: Author.

Armstrong, J., & Kaser-Boyd, N. (2003). Projective assessment of psychological trauma. In M. Hilsenroth & D. Segal (Eds.), *Comprehensive handbook of psychological assessment, Vol. 2. Objective and prospective assessment of personality and psychology* (pp. 500–512). New York: Wiley.

Cohen, L., & de Ruiter, C. (1991). The Rorschach & PTSD revisited: Critique of Van Der Kolk & Ducey's (1989). The psychological processing of traumatic experience: Rorschach patterns in PTSD. *Journal of Traumatic Stress, 4,* 407–417.

CSA Illumina International Database. (April 15, 2008). Retrieved from http://www-md2.csa.com/ids70/quick_search.php?SID=83ce41606a c2ac9a5b07ca283edcb b7b

Ducey, C. P., & Van der Kolk, B. A. (1991). The psychological processing of traumatic experience: A reply to Cohen & de Ruiter. *Journal of Traumatic Stress, 4,* 425–432.

Exner, J. E. (1986). *The Rorschach: A comprehensive system* (2nd edition, Vol. 1). New York, NY: Wiley.

Exner, J. E. (2003). *The Rorschach: A comprehensive system* (4th edition, Vol. 1). New York, NY: Wiley.

Exner, J. E., Weiner, I. B., & PAR Staff. (2005). *RIAP5. Rorschach Interpretation Assistance Program* (Verion 5) [Computer software]. Lutz, FL: PAR Psychological Assessment Resources.

Goldfinger, D. A., Amdur, R. L., & Liberson, I. (1998). Rorschach patterns of response in Vietnam veterans with posttraumatic stress disorder versus combat and normal controls. *Depression and Anxiety, 8,* 104–111.

Hartman, W. L., Clark, M. E., Morgan, M. K., Dunn, V. K., Fine, A. D., Perry, G. G., & Zinsch, D. L. (1990). Rorschach structure of a hospitalized sample of Vietnam veterans with PTSD. *Journal of Personality Assessment, 54*(1&2), 149–159.

Herman, J. (1999). Complex PTSD. In M. Horowitz (Ed.), *Essential papers on posttraumatic stress disorder*. New York: New York University Press.

Kroch, R., & Shahar, I. (2002). Diagnostic evaluation of mental disability among military related PTSD. In A. Bleich & Z. Solomon (Eds.), *Mental disability. Medical, research, social, legal and rehabilitative aspects* (pp. 102–144, published in Hebrew). Israel: The Ministry of Defense.

Levin, P., & Reis, B. (1997). Use of the Rorschach in assessing trauma. In J. P. Wilson & T. M. Keane (Eds.), *Assessing psychological trauma and PTSD* (pp. 529–543). New York: Guilford.

Luxenberg, T., & Levin, P. (2004). The role of Rorschach in the assessment and treatment of trauma. In J. P. Wilson & T. M. Keane (Eds.), *Assessing psychological trauma and PTSD* (pp. 190–225). New York: Guilford.

18

Norris, F. H., & Hamblen, J. L. (2004). Standardized self-report measures of civilian trauma and PTSD. In J. P. Wilson & T. M. Keane (Eds.), *Assessing psychological trauma and PTSD* (pp. 63–102). New York: Guilford.

Shalit, B. (1965). Effects of environmental stimulation of the M, FM and m responses in the Rorschach. *Journal of Projective Techniques and Personality Assessment, 29,* 228–231.

Sloan, P., Arsenault, L., & Hilsenroth, M. (2002). Use of the Rorschach in the assessment of war-related stress in military personnel. *Rorschachiana. Yearbook of International Rorschach Society, 25,* 86–122.

Sloan, P., Arsenault, L., Hilsenroth, M., Harvill, L., & Handler, L. (1995). Rorschach measures of posttraumatic stress in Persian Gulf War veterans. *Journal of Personality Assessment, 64,* 397–414.

Swanson, G. S., Blout, J., & Bruno, R. (1990). Comprehensive System Rorschach Data on Vietnam Combat Veterans. *Journal of Personality Assessment, 54*(1&2), 160–169.

Van der Kolk, B. A., & Ducey, C. P. (1989). The psychological processing of traumatic experience: Rorschach patterns in PTSD. *Journal of Traumatic Stress, 2,* 259–274.

Weiner, I. B. (1998). *Principles of Rorschach interpretation.* Mahwah, NJ: Erlbaum.

Weiss, D. S. (2004). Structured clinical interview techniques for PTSD. In J. P. Wilson & T. M. Keane (Eds.), *Assessing psychological trauma and PTSD* (2nd ed., pp. 103–121). New York: Guilford.

Wilson, J. P. (2004). PTSD and Complex PTSD. Symptoms, syndromes, and diagnoses. In J. P. Wilson & T. M. Keane (Eds.), *Assessing psychological trauma and PTSD* (2nd edition, pp. 7–44.). New York: Guilford.

Zahi Arnon
Department of Behavioral Sciences
The Max Stern Academic College of Emek Yezreel
19300, Israel
Tel. office +972 4 642-3542
Tel. home +972 4 654-6570
Fax office +972 4 642-3512
Fax home +972 4 654-6570
E-mail zahia@yvc.ac.il

Summary

Posttraumatic stress disorder (PTSD) is a complex psychological phenomenon in which witnessing a threatening event and experiencing intense fear, helplessness, or horror are necessary, yet not sufficient, to define the disorder. Many diagnostic tools have been developed to assess PTSD, mostly based on self-report questionnaires and thus susceptible to both conscious and unconscious bias. By using projective testing, in which the client is exposed to ambiguous stimulus with no clue to a specific or desirable answer, these shortcoming may be attenuated. The Rorschach inkblot test is widely used as a diagnostic tool in combination with other tests. Several attempts were made to develop standardized scales for its administration and analysis, among them the Exner Comprehensive System, including its latest computer-based version, the Rorschach Interpretation Assistance Program (RIAP-5). This system analyzes Rorschach responses both through a structural summary of the responses, including ratios, percentages, and derivations, and through constellation tables that are clusters of previously documented responses according to major disturbances. No such cluster has been defined and published for PTSD, and the present study aimed to empirically define a cluster of Rorschach indicators for PTSD. The study group consisted of 187 subjects, who were clinically assessed following claims submitted to the Israel Ministry of Defense for recognition of mental disability. Every patient was interviewed and assessed by a team of professionals, comprising a psychiatrist, a clinical psychologist, a social worker, and an occupational therapist. The diagnosis of PTSD was determined by the psychiatrist based on the team's assessment. The clinical psychologist used for his assessment a battery of diagnostic tests including the Rorschach. Some 4 years later, the diagnoses and demographic data were collected from the medical charts, and the Rorschach responses were entered into the RIAP-5 by the psychologist who originally administered the tests. Of the 187 subjects included in the study, 116 met diagnostic criteria of PTSD and 71 did not (non-PTSD). Exner's Comprehensive System defines a valid protocol as having 14 or more responses, and 121 subjects met this requirement. The remaining 66 protocols included 13 or fewer responses. The issue of insufficient responses among PTSD patients has been addressed in several studies; most agree that short protocols reflects physical numbing and avoidance characteristic in PTSD patients. Since the statistical analysis of all background and demographic data revealed no differences between complete and incomplete protocols, all of these protocols were included. A stepwise linear regression analysis was carried out on all 220 variables derived from the RIAP5 and a 13-item model was proposed by means of computed analysis. This model was able to correctly predict 36.6% (R^2) of PTSD cases, and was named PTSD Predictor Score (PPS). The indicators comprised the following groups: (1) Determinants (VF, FV, FM, T), (2) Content (Hh, Id, An, Food, Bt, Fi), (3) Color (C', cn), (4) Special score (INC1). These indicators are in line with results of other studies using the RIAP5 to diagnose PTSD, contributing additional insights into the components of PTSD through the analyses of PPS Contents, and are useful for building a cluster of Rorschach indicators positively and negatively correlated to PTSD.

התסמונת הפוסט טראומתית (PTSD) היא תופעה פסיכולוגית מורכבת, שאינה מסתכמת רק באירוע מסוכן הכולל חווית פחד, חוסר אונים ואימה. כלים אבחוניים רבים פותחו לצורך הערכת התסמונת, רובם ככולם מבוססים על שאלוני דיווח עצמי, ובכך רגישים להטיות מודעות ובלתי מודעות. שימוש במבחנים השלכתיים, בהם הנבדק נחשף לגירויי מעורפל ללא רמז לתשובה הנכונה המבוקשת, יכול לעקוף מכשלה זו. מבחן כתמי הדיו של רורשאך מהווה כלי אבחוני נפוץ כחלק מבטריית מבחנים. במסגרת פיתוח סטנדרטיזציה של העברת המבחן וניתוחו פותחה גישתו האמפירית של אקסנר (Exner) הכוללת גם גרסה ממוחשבת עדכנית (RIAP5). מערכת ניתוח המבחן כוללת הן ציונים לתגובות, יחסים, ואחוזים, והן מערכי תגובות המהווה צבר ספציפי מתוך הקודמים וממוקדות בהפרעות נפשיות עיקריות. עד היום לא הוגדר ולא פורסם מערך תגובות האופייני לתסמונת הפוסט טראומתית, וזו מטרת המחקר הנוכחי: לנתח רטרוספקטיבית מבחני רורשאך במטרה לזהות מערך המתקשר לתסמונת. קבוצת המחקר כללה 187 נבדקים שהגישו תביעה למשרד הביטחון בישראל להכרה כנפגעי טראומה צבאית. הנבדקים עברו הערכה רב מקצועית שכללה פגישות נפרדות עם פסיכיאטרית, פסיכולוג קליני, עובדת סוציאלית ומרפאה בעיסוק. האבחנה נקבעה ע"י הפסיכיאטרית על סמך דווחי ארבעת אנשי המקצוע הנ"ל. כחלק מסוללת המבחנים העביר הפסיכולוג הקליני גם את מבחן הרורשאך. ארבע שנים מאוחר יותר לוקטו האבחנה והנתונים הדמוגרפיים מהארכיון, ותגובות הרורשאך הוקלדו לתוכנת RIAP5. 116 מתוך 187 הנבדקים אובחנו כסובלים מהתסמונת, ו-71 ללא התסמונת. גישת אקסנר מגדירה פרוטוקול רורשאך תקף רק מעל 14 תגובות, אלא שרק 121 מהנבדקים עמדו בדרישה זו, בעוד 66 פרוטוקולים נוספים הניבו 13 תגובות ומטה. שאלת הפרוטוקולים הקצרים עולה במחקרים נוספים, שרובם מציעים להתייחס אליהם כתקפים שכן הפרוטוקול הקצר משקף את דפוס התגובה הנמנע והרדוד רגישת של הסובלים מהתסמונת. בהשוואה סטטיסטית של נתוני הרקע והנתונים הדמוגרפיים של קבוצת הפרוטוקולים הארוכים והקצרים לא נמצא הבדל, ולפיכך הוחלט להכניס אותם למחקר. על כלל 220 המשתנים שמפיקה תוכנת RIAP5 נערך מבחן רגרסיה ליניארית שהניב מודל בעל 13 פריטים המסוגל לנבא 36.6% מהנבדקים שאובחנו כבעלי התסמונת. המשתנים נחלקים לארבע קבוצות: 1. דטרמיננטים (VF, FV, FM, T) 2. תוכן (Zn, Food, Bt, Fi) 3. צבע (C', cn) 4. ציונים חריגים (INC1). משתנים אלה עולים בקנה אחד עם מחקרים נוספים המשתמשים בתוכנת RIAP5 לצורך אבחון התסמונת הפוסט טראומתית, תורמים בכך להבנת ההפרעה, ולבניית מערך תגובות רורשאך אופייניות להפרעה הפוסט טראומתית.

Résumé

Le syndrome posttraumatique (SPT) est un phénomène psychologique compliqué qui ne se résume pas qu'à un événement risqué engendrant une expérience de peur, d'impuissance et de frayeur. De multiples outils diagnostiques ont été développés pour évaluer le syndrome, dont la plupart se basent sur des questionnaires du rapport personnel. Ainsi, ceux-ci sont sensibles aux inclinations conscientes et inconscientes. Or, l'utilisation des tests projectifs, où la personne examinée est soumise à des stimuli ambigus sans avoir aucun indice pour la réponse correcte requise, peut surmonter cet obstacle. Le test de Rorschach (ou test des tâches d'encre) constitue un outil diagnostique répandu employé dans une série de tests. Dans le cadre d'une mise en place d'une standardisation de l'administration et de l'analyse d'un test, l'approche empirique d'Exner, offrant en plus une version informatisée moderne (RIAP5), a été introduite. Ce système d'analyse du test comprend des évaluations des comportements, des rapports et des pourcentages, aussi bien que des ensembles de réactions, fondées spécifiquement sur les facteurs mentionnés ci-avant, et se focalisant sur des troubles mentaux principaux. Jusqu'à présent, aucun ensemble de réactions, propre au syndrome posttraumatique, n'était ni défini ni mis au jour. De ce fait, c'est le but de la présente étude: analyser rétrospectivement les tests de Rorschach pour pouvoir identifier un ensemble caractéristique de ce syndrome. Le groupe de l'étude comportait 187 patients, ayant présenté une revendication au ministère de la défense israélien pour se faire reconnaître comme atteints du stress posttraumatique résultant du service militaire. Les patients avaient donc fait l'objet d'une évaluation multidisciplinaire effectuée au moyen des rencontres avec un psychiatre, un psychologue clinicien, un assistant social et un ergothérapeute. Le diagnostic avait été établi par le psychiatre sur la base des rapports de ces quatre professionnels. + noter que le test de Rorschach avait été inclus dans la série de tests administrés par le psychologue clinicien. Après quatre ans, lors du recueil du diagnostic et des données démographiques tirés des archives, les réactions de Rorschach ont été saisies dans le logiciel RIAP5. 116 personnes parmi les 187 patients ont été diagnostiquées comme souffrant du syndrome posttraumatique, alors que 71 personnes n'ont pas reçu ce diagnostic. En fait, l'approche d'Exner met en vigueur le protocole de Rorschach, à condition qu'il y ait plus de 14 réactions. Pourtant, dans ce cas, seulement 121 patients ont répondu à ce critère, tandis que 66 protocoles supplémentaires ont entrainé13 réactions et au-dessous. La question de protocoles courts est soulevée dans d'autres études, dont la majorité proposent de les considérer comme valables, du fait que ce type de protocoles reflète la manière de réaction empêchée et superficielle au niveau sentimental des personnes porteuses de ce syndrome. Une comparaison statistique des données de base et des données démographiques du groupe de protocoles longs et du groupe de protocoles courts n'a révélé aucune différence, et c'est pourquoi il a été décidé d'intégrer ces derniers dans la recherche. Un test de régression linéaire, sur l'ensemble de 220 variants créés par le logiciel RIAP5, a produit un modèle disposant de 13 éléments, qui peut prédire 36.6% des patients diagnostiqués comme ayant le syndrome posttraumatique. Les variants se repartissent dans quatre groupes: 1. Déterminants (VF, FV, FM, T) 2. Contenu (Zn, Food, Bt, Fi, Hh, Id) 3. Couleur (C', cn) 4. Évaluations exceptionnelles (INC1). Ces variants s'accordent avec d'autres recherches qui utilisent le logiciel RIAP5 pour diagnostiquer le syndrome posttraumatique, en contribuant ainsi à la compréhension de ce trouble et à la formation d'un ensemble de réactions de Rorschach propres au syndrome posttraumatique.

Resumen

El trastorno de estrés postraumático (PTSD) es un fenómeno psicológico complejo en el cual experimentar un evento amenazante, miedo intenso, desamparo u horror son experiencias necesarias pero no suficientes para definir el trastorno. Muchos instrumentos diagnósticos se han desarrollado para evaluar el PTSD, casi todos basados en cuestionarios auto-informativos, y por lo tanto susceptibles a todo tipo de predisposicion consciente e inconsciente.

Mediante el uso de las pruebas proyectivas, en la que el cliente es expuesto a estímulos ambiguos, sin ninguna referencia a una respuesta específica o deseable, estas deficiencias pueden ser atenuadas. El test de Rorschach es ampliamente utilizado como instrumento diagnóstico en combinación con otros tests. Se han hecho varios intentos para desarrollar escalas estandarizadas para su administración y análisis, entre ellos el Sistema Integral de Exner, incluyendo su última versión para computadora: Interpretación del Programa de Asistencia para el Rorchach (RIAP5). El sistema analiza las respuestas del Rorschach, incluyendo el resumen de las respuestas estructurales, sus proporciones, porcentajes y derivaciones, junto con las constelaciónes que son grupos de respuestas previamente documentadas con relacion a problemas importantes. Hasta el presente no se ha definido o publicado un grupo especifico para el PTSD.

El presente estudio tenia como objetivo definir empíricamente un conjunto de indicadores Rorschach para el PTSD. El grupo de estudio consiste de 187 sujetos, que fueron evaluados clínicamente después de haber presentado reclamaciones ante el Ministerio de Defensa de Israel para recibir el reconocimiento de discapacidad mental. Todos los pacientes fueron entrevistados y evaluados por un equipo profesionales que incluyo un psiquiatra, un psicólogo clínico, trabajador social y terapeuta ocupacional. El diagnóstico de PTSD fue determinado por el psiquiatra, en base a las conclusiones de estos profesionales. El psicólogo clínico utilizo para su evaluación una serie de pruebas diagnósticas empleando el test de Rorschach. Cuatro años más tarde, el diagnóstico y los datos demográficos de las historias clínicas, junto con las respuestas del Rorschach fueron codificadas en la RIAP5 por el mismo psicólogo que administro el test en el principio. De los 187 sujetos incluidos en el estudio, 116 cumplíeron con los criterios diagnósticos del trastorno de estrés postraumático (PTSD) y 71 no lo hicieron (no PTSD). EL Sistema Integral Exner define valido un protocolo si contiene 14 respuestas o más, y 121 participantes cumplieron con este requisito. Los restantes 66 protocolos incluyeron 13 respuestas o menos. El tema de insuficiencia de respuestas entre los pacientes con PTSD se ha tratado en varios estudios, la mayoría esta de acuerdo en que los protocolos cortos reflejan un estado de entumecimiento físico adormecedor y evasivo, ambas característica en pacientes con PTSD. En el presente estudio un análisis estadístico de todos los antecedentes y datos demográficos no reveló diferencias entre los protocolos completos e incompletos, por lo tanto todos los protocolos fueron incluidos. Un análisis de regresión lineal se llevó a cabo en todas las 220 variables derivadas de la RIAP5, y un modelo de 13 elementos fue propuesto por el análisis calculado. Este modelo ha sido capaz de predecir correctamente el 36.6% (R cuadrado) de casos de estrés postraumático y trastornos de estrés postraumático, y fue denominado PTSD Predictor Score (PPS). Los indicadores consisten en 4 grupos: 1. Determinantes (VF, FV, FM, T). 2. Contenido (Hh, Id, An, Food, Bt, Fi) 3. Color (C ', cn) 4. Special Score (INC1).

Estos indicadores concuerdan con los resultados de otros estudios que han utilizado el RIAP5 para diagnosticar trastornos de estrés postraumático, aportan nuevos datos sobre los componentes del trastorno de estrés postraumático a través del análisis de contenido de PPS, y ayudan a construir un conjunto de indicadores Rorschach correlados positiva y negativamente con el trastorno de estrés postraumático.

25

トラウマとそれに対する心理学的反応は、ひとつの検査では十分にアセスメントし、診断を行えない、非常に複雑な現象である。主な困難さは外傷を受けた患者なのか、別の障害に苦しんでいるのか区別をすることである。ロールシャッハ法は、情緒の機能に加えて、認知的操作の過程と内容の両方を反映しているので有効である。

この研究ではロールシャッハを介しての PTSD の診断を予測しようとするのではなく、むしろ、すでに診断のついた患者のロールシャッハプロトコルを回顧的に分析することである。しかし、コンピュータ化されたシステムの利用には限界がある。我々は RIAP 5 のみを使用し、他のコンピュータ化されたシステムとの比較を行わなかった。もうひとつの限界はコンピュータによる結果はロールシャッハの分析の非コンピュータによる方法と比較されないことであろう。これらの限界もかかわらず、本研究は増大している全般的な PTSD に関する多数の研究、および PTSD を診断する際のロールシャッハインクブロットテストの役割に関する多数の研究に貢献するものであった。本研究に参加している比較的同質で大きな数のグループは、すべて軍隊の戦闘にさらされた後になんらかの外傷的反応を体験したと主張されている被験者であるが、外傷にたいするロールシャッハ指標の概観を提供することに役立っている。ここに記述された分析方法（直線回帰）は、外傷と正の相関、負の相関のあるロールシャッハの指標のクラスターを構築する道のさらなる一歩となるであろう。

Rorschachiana 32, 27–45
© 2011 Hogrefe Publishing

DOI: 10.1027/1192-5604/a000014

Original Article

Eating Disorders – A Current Concern

Similarities and Differences Among the Anorexia, Bulimia, and EDNOS Categories

Mónica Guinzbourg

Psychiatry Department, Italian Hospital of Buenos Aires, Argentina

Abstract. Epidemiological data shows that Eating Disorders (ED) have been increasing over the past decades and have become one of the most common categories seen in outpatient settings. The EDNOS category – Eating Disorder Not Otherwise Specified – was included in DSM-IV, joining the traditional Anorexia and Bulimia categories. However, some controversy still exists about whether this inclusion is justified. For this reason we decided to examine the differences between ED groups and a population sample, and to compare the three subgroups using data from the Rorschach Comprehensive System. We compared 106 patients suffering from Eating Disorders with a population of 60 nonpatient subjects from a similar demographic subjects background. The ED group consists of 25 Anorexia, 27 Bulimia, and 54 EDNOS cases. We found that the three groups differ significantly from the nonpatient sample, and while they share some features, Anorexia differs from Bulimia and EDNOS. This last group presents differences in regard to introspective capacities. These differences may have an impact on therapy planning.

Keywords: Rorschach Comprehensive System, Eating Disorders subgroups

Introduction

The interest in Eating Disorders (ED) has grown in view of the steady increase of eating disorders over the past decades. ED still remains a current concern in the young urban female population.

These young people are usually found in Western countries where the incidence of ED is higher in the industrialized and postindustrialized cities. Other characteristics are gender (female), age, in particular those

27

individuals between 16–23 years old (Vega & Quiroga, 2003), the socio-economic status (middle class and upper class), and a history of high educational performance (including university students).

The three eating disorder categories, Anorexia, Bulimia, and Eating Disorders Not Specified (EDNOS), are multidetermined syndromes. They include a combination of physiological predispositions with particular psychological factors that, if associated with social demands, may cause the onset of ED.

DSM-IV includes three groups: Anorexia (F50.0), Bulimia (F50.2), and EDNOS (F50.9).

With the publication of DSM-III (American Psychiatric Association, 1980), the American Psychiatric Association's *Diagnostic and Statistical Manual of Mental Disorders* first included EDNOS as an "atypical" disorder in DSM-III and later as a "not otherwise specified" category in DSM-III-R (1987) and in DSM-IV (1990).

While anorexia usually appears during the first years of adolescence and in midteenage years, bulimia has a later age of onset; the data available on EDNOS are in comparison quite limited (Turón Gil, 1997).

Epidemiological studies indicate that the Anorexia criterion is met in 1% to 5% of people aged 14 to 18, with an increasingly younger age of onset. The criteria for this syndrome were outlined in DSM-IV (for both forms, restrictive and purging).

With Anorexia a biological perspective must be adopted because of the medical conditions of emaciation, endocrinological changes, including amenorrhea (Hypotalamo Hypophisiario axis), and the risk of death. In the majority of cases the illness has a chronic course, and most anorexic and bulimic patients require hospitalization due to medical complications. Suicide is also a risk.

According to Turon Gil (1997) epidemiological studies of bulimia exhibit varying data. Meanwhile for Garner, Olmstead, and Polivy (1983), bulimics represent 4% to 8% of the total population with ED, other authors mention far more alarming figures (Pope, 14%, Hart and Ollendick, 18%, and Halmi, 19%).

As far as EDNOS is concerned, the epidemiological information available is still limited and controversial. Some authors even mention that, like any other residual category, EDNOS is quantitatively limited and a clinically less relevant group of subjects in relation to the two main diagnostic entities, anorexia and bulimia (Ricca et al., 2001).

For other authors, like Nielsen and Palmer (2003), EDNOS is more common than might be expected. Many people suffer from this eating disorder without meeting the criteria for either anorexia or bulimia. The literature dealing with eating disorders indicates a remarkable prevalence of EDNOS among ED patients, with estimates ranging from 13% to 25% (Fairburn & Harrison, 2003), to 50.3% (Ricca et al. 2001), to 57% (Martin, Williamson, & Thaw, 2000), or even 70.5% (Turner & Bryant Waugh, 2004). According to Fairburn and Bohn (2005) EDNOS "attracts highly specialist referrals and it was the most common diagnosis made, its weighed average prevalence being 60%" (p. 693).

Nevertheless, the prevalence of EDNOS in the community is not clear. This is because there are no positive criteria for diagnosis, so "there is no agreement as to determine what constitutes a case" (Fairburn & Bohn, 2005, p. 694).

Despite this prevalence – and although clinicians mainly use this diagnosis – there is little literature about this syndrome because it has been "largely ignored by researchers" (Fairburn & Bohn, 2005, p. 691). Then, it is also reasonable to find that information about the treatment outcomes for this subgroup of patients is not available.

EDNOS: A Controversial Diagnosis

EDNOS appears in the DSM-III as an "atypical" eating disorder, but it was awarded its own category in the DSM-IV. There are different opinions about whether this inclusion is justified or not.

In 2005, Fairburn and Bohn noted that there had been few attempts to characterize the clinical features of patients with EDNOS and compare them with those seen in Anorexia nervosa and Bulimia nervosa. Concerning response to treatment, nothing is known since there have been no studies of the treatment of these patients (p. 695). There have been only three recent studies about EDNOS, all of which confirmed that the clinical features of Anorexia nervosa and Bulimia nervosa are present (Ricca et al., 2001; Turner & Bryant-Waugh, 2004; Wales, Fairburn, & Palmer, 2009). The duration, severity, and secondary psychosocial impairment also appears to be the same, especially when Bulimia and EDNOS are compared.

Some EDNOS patients' symptoms diminish progressively over time, and some of their eating habits cease to be problematic. Whereas for other patients their difficulties with eating intensify and their diagnosis changes to Anorexia or Bulimia (Fairburn & Harrison, 2003).

A characteristic of EDNOS is that any of the eating disorders show a considerable crossdiagnostic flux with the patients moving from one eating disorder to another. (Milos, Spindler, Schnyder, & Fairburn, 2005).

Fairburn and Bohn (2005) offer a solution to the problem of EDNOS by reformulating the Anorexia and Bulimia criteria in order to make them less rigid. They expand the criteria to encompass the subthreshold cases within not specified eating disorders (EDNOS) and the remaining cases as "mixed disorders." All eating disorders need a "transdiagnostic" unitary category embracing the three actual subgroups (Anorexia, Bulimia, and EDNOS). In this case it would be necessary to restart longitudinal studies and to recategorize the clinical problems currently included as EDNOS.

Marino and Zanarini (2001) adopt a different point of view in relation to EDNOS. In their article about the "Relationship Between EDNOS and its Subtypes and Borderline Personality Disorders," they mention that in their sample "the EDNOS patients have never met the criteria for anorexia or bulimia nervosa" (p. 349). These findings suggest that the majority of EDNOS cases reported do not present prodromal or residual forms of ED symptoms, but "rather form a cluster of separate disorders." Marino and Zanarini (2001) argue that EDNOS may be seen as a different sub group with distinguishable traits.

The difficulties in solving current controversies are that ED patients evolve and change their diagnosis. As the patients with anorexia, bulimia, and EDNOS basically share common traits, this condition suggest that common mechanisms are involved in the development of these ED and maintenance. For that reason it is pertinent to examine the consequences of these conditions in their diagnosis, therapy, and prognosis.

At the same time, another problem is that there have been few attempts to study these differences between the subgroups with standardized instruments.

Our aim is to examine the differences between a nonpatient group and an eating disorder sample as well as the differences within the subgroups, using data from the Rorschach Comprehensive System (CS).

Method

To achieve this, the schema of analyzing the variables by clusters suggested by Exner was followed (Exner, 2003). The protocols were coded in both groups in accordance with the CS, and average deviations and median in quantitative variables were calculated, using the Student Test and ANOVA. Chi-square was used to compare the relationship between qualitative variables. For cases in which these variables would not adjust to a normal distribution and show high asymmetry, we used nonparametric statistical tests (Mann-Whitney, Kruskal-Wallis).

The Rorschach protocols were coded according to Exner's norms, the interscorer correlation lying between 80.4 and 97.5 (kappa index). The results take into account only the variables that qualify as significant after the statistical procedures.

The statistical program SPSS was used for data analysis (descriptive correlational study of group differences).

Sample

Both samples are composed of women, inasmuch as eating disorder pathology has a greater incidence in females between 18 and 30 years of age.

Demographically speaking, ED patients and controls were similar in terms of age ($m = 23.6$ for the control group and 22.4 for the ED group), marital status, socioeconomic status, and educational level. As far as age is concerned (Table 1), there were no significant differences between the nonconsulting group and ED patients, even though subjects with anorexia were younger than the other groups. The majority were students (students still at the university: 64.2% in the control sample and 70% in ED patients; students who had finished their university careers: 16% of the nonpatient group and 30% in the ED sample). With respect to marital status, 89.6% women of the nonconsulting group and 85% of ED patients were single.

Table 1. Demographic data

Age	Media	N	Desv.tip.	Media	Minimum	Maximum
EDNOS	22.7	54	4.6	22.0	17	32
Bulimia	24.3	27	4.8	24.0	18	35
Anorexia	19.8	25	3.2	19.0	16	32
Control	23.6	60	2.9	24.0	19	30
Total	22.9	166	4.1	22.5	16	35

Nonpatient subjects include 60 women from the Argentinean normative data sample (Lunazzi et al., 2006), the 106 ED patients stemming from the Eating Disorders Center of the Italian Hospital of Buenos Aires (25 Anorexics, 29 Bulimics, and 52 EDNOS). Each patient was screened by a multidisciplinary team with extensive experience in Eating Disorders (a nutritionist, a gynecologist, an endocrinologist, a family therapist, a psychiatrist, and a psychologist trained in personality assessment and in the Rorschach Comprehensive System). Patients were not in treatment and the diagnosis was made following the DSM-IV criteria (see Table 2, Table 3, and Table 4).

Table 2. Anorexia

ANOREXIA (F 50.9)

A) Fear of becoming fat or obese even when weight is normal.

B) Rejection of normal weight in relation to age and weight.

C) Perception disturbances in relation to body self-image.

D) Amenorrhea.

Table 3. Bulimia

BULIMIA (50.2)

A) Binge eating: (frequent episodes)

   1) In short periods (less than 2 h) or in more quantity of food than desirable.

   2) Feeling of losing control over eating.

B) Compensatory behaviors such as excessive exercise, vomits, and the use of diuretics or medicines.

C) Both, binge eating and compensatory behaviors at least during 3 months and no less than twice per week.

D) Self-concept or evaluation depends extremely on body image and weight. These behaviors not only occur during an anorectic episode or disorder.

Table 4. EDNOS

EDNOS (50.9)

1) All criteria for anorexia are present, but amenorrhea is absent.

2) Weight responds to normal expectations.

3) All criteria for bulimia are present, but not at the same frequency.

4) The patients effect compensatory behaviors even if weight is normal but they do not have binge eating.

5) They chew and spit the food, they do not swallow.

6) Binge eating is present, but compensatory behaviors are not present.

Results

Differences Between the Nonconsulting Group and the ED Patient Sample

Differences were observed (Table 5) between the nonconsulting women and ED sample. With regard to the ED patients, the results show that:

- They were different with respect to their coping style (introversive style 45.3% versus 28.3% in normal sample, χ^2 p = .001),
- Usually they processed information as well as other young people (L = 70%) being able to understand information coming from the environment but,
- They avoided complexity when dealing with stimuli (L higher, Blends lower),
- They showed less personality resources (EA lower) when confronted with experiences and particularly with new situations or a problem,
- Presented less ability to process sensations and emotions (FM, m, C', and Y lower) neglecting to register of needs, distress, and helplessness and to constrain their emotions, which they did not not express openly (C'),
- Had less expressive resources (FC, CF and C lower),

Table 5. Differences between the nonconsulting sample and ED groups

Variables	Control	ED	p	Statistical test
R	20.52	18.10	0.015	Mann-Whitney
L	0.46	0.82	.000	Mann-Whitney
Blends/R	0.20	0.14	.002	Mann-Whitney
EA	6.83	5.21	.000	*T*-test
FM	3.87	2.05	.001	Mann-Whitney
FM + m	5.13	3.97	.001	Mann-Whitney
C'	2.13	1.41	.001	*T*-test
Y	1.47	0.57	.000	*T*-test
FC	2.33	1.17	.000	*T*-test
CF + C	2.01	1.50	.009	Mann-Whitney
Fr + rF	0.18	0.54	.001	*T*-test
H	2.93	2.15	.006	*T*-test
COP	1.00	0.37	.000	Mann-Whitney
GHR	3.87	0.35	.000	Mann-Whitney
PHR	2.58	0.27	.000	Mann-Whitney

- Showed less interest in people and social ties (H low) being avoidant or indifferent with others,
- Had limited expectations about human relationships (H, COP, GHP and PHR lower),
- Presented more self-centeredness that other young people with narcissistic focus investment (Fr higher).

Differences Between ED Categories

Although the subgroups shared common traits, according to our data they exhibited different coping styles.

While anorexics showed a more consistent introversive-extratensive style (48% introversive, 26% extratensive, and 24% ambitent), bulimics (41% ambitent, 11% extratensive, and 48% introversive) and EDNOS (46% ambitent, 11% extratensive, and 43% introversive) included a more ambitent style.

Table 6. Differences between anorexia and bulimia categories or patients

Variables	Anorexia	Bulimia	*p*	Statistical test
			0.002	ANOVA
Zd	-3.34	0.72	.001	ANOVA
Human Cont	2.04	4.33	.003	K-W
Pure H	0.76	2.37	.001	K-W
2	5.56	2.26	.004	ANOVA
Sum6	1.60	0.59	.024	ANOVA
INC	0.68	0.19	.026	ANOVA
MOR	1.44	0.44	.001	K-W
DEPI	3.08	1.44	.022	ANOVA
CDI	2.28	0.63	.000	ANOVA
S-CON	3.04	0.41	.000	ANOVA

A look at the the comparison between anorexics and bulimics (Table 6) specifically shows that anorexics:
- Presented a significant proportion of introversive style (48%) using ideational patterns to control their behaviors,
- Their perception adjustment was as conventional as expected, but they did not understand the complexity of reality stimuli (W + D higher but H + DA% lower),

- Showed less motivation with respect to environment stimuli (Zd lower) with a tendency to use a simplifying and neglecting style,
- Exhibited less interest in other people (H and H Cont low),
- Were more self-centered with egocentricity personality traits (pairs higher),
- Their comprehension of social behaviors was sometimes inefficient and distorted (M–),
- Presented ideational slippages that affect their logical thinking (INC, Sum 6 higher),
- Depressive emotions sometimes underlay their symptoms and thinking, with less confidence in their resources (DEPI higher),
- Presented more pessimistic and morbid perceptions of situations (MOR higher),
- Were more vulnerable to suffer emotional turmoil and to involve themselves in harmful behaviors (S-CON higher).

Table 7. Differences between anorexia and EDNOS categories

Variables	Anorexia	EDNOS	p	Statistical test
W + D	18.08	14.57	.027	K-W
DQv	1.52	0.76	.024	K-W
F	8.6	5.15	.001	ANOVA
2	5.56	3.22	.008	ANOVA
INC	0.68	0.15	.002	ANOVA
MOR	1.44	0.63	0	K-W
L	1.02	0.78	.028	K-W
Pure H	0.76	1.8	.001	K-W
Sum6	5.08	2	.028	ANOVA
M–	0.80	0.28	.003	K-W
WDA%	0.16	0.48	.001	ANOVA
XU%	0.17	0.25	.021	K-W
Zd	–3.34	0.43	.001	ANOVA
DEPI	3.08	1.15	.001	ANOVA
CDI	2.28	0.83	0	ANOVA
S-CON	3.04	0.69	0	ANOVA

With respect to anorexics and EDNOS (Table 7), anorexics tended to:
- Use a more introversive style (48%) with a consistency in ideational patterns to control their emotions. Ambitent (24%) or extratensive (28%) styles are less significant.

- Show less motivation to deal with stimuli (Zd lower) especially in relation to conventional social demands,
- Be more immature (Dv higher),
- Present more control but be less effective in their behavior (L and F higher) because they processed information with impulsiveness, negligent to register stimuli and concrete thinking. Their perception adjustment was quite precarious and did not allow them to understand situations in their entire complexity (W + DA% lower),
- Introduce thoughts that are slightly distorted (M-) with an excessive degree of autocentricity (Xu%),
- Show cognitive slippage affecting their perception and ideation negatively,
- Are influenced by pessimistic ideas and morbid perceptions (MOR higher),
- Have more difficulties dealing with dysphoric emotions (DEPI higher); their behaviors could expose them to risk of harmful behaviors (S-CON higher),
- Show more self-centeredness and egocentricity traits (pairs), and
- Have less interest in people (H low) with unsuccessful social coping abilities and are vulnerable to losing control (CDI higher).

Table 8. Differences between bulimia and EDNOS categories

Variable	Bulimia	EDNOS	p	Statistical test
D	9.00	8.22	.020	ANOVA
F	6.85	5.15	.016	ANOVA
C'F	0.30	0.04	.022	ANOVA
CP	0.11	0.00	.013	ANOVA
$p > a + 1$	1.89	1.65	.022	Brown-Forsythe
FD	0.30	0.85	.005	Brown-Forsythe

In comparison, bulimics and EDNOS were more similar (Table 8): Both showed a significant ambitent style (bulimics 41% and EDNOS 46%) with more unpredictable behaviors being more unstable and emotionally vulnerable. The other half presented an introversive style (48% and 43%, respectively). In this case they showed more consistency in using ideational patterns.

In relation to EDNOS, bulimics patients had
- better practical skills and formal control over responses (D and F higher),

36

– a tendency to constrain their emotional expressions; they tended to internalize their distress with much more risk of losing control (C'F higher),
– a maniacal style of confronting anxiety (CP), helplessness, and insecurity caused by unpleasant and harming experiences in the past,
– more passive behaviors geared toward the search for solutions; they seemed to be dependent and fanciful, with ($p > a + 1$),
– no introspective capacities (FD absent).

Discussion

This study compares ED groups with a population sample of nonconsulting women. The results suggest that ED young women develop eating disorders as symptoms of their difficulties in conventional adjustment. Significant changes in different domains, particularly body image and self-esteem, were affected.

The first significant difference between the ED patients and the nonconsulting group was that women from the control sample were more extratensive in contrast to the ED categories with a significant introversive style (45.3% versus 28.3% χ^2 $p = .001$). While young women were commonly more involved with emotions, ED patients preferred an ideational method of solving problems.

Although the subgroups shared common traits, according our data they showed different coping styles.

Introversive anorexics as well as some of bulimics and EDNOS tend to be more ideational to make decisions, and the majority of the latter showed an ambitent style, which explains some of their changing and unpredictable behaviors.

With respect to Rorschach CS results, in our sample we did not find the significant presence of ambitent style in anorexic patients, as in Garcia Alba's sample (38%) (2005, p. 200). At least half of our patients were introversive (48%), and the other half were either ambitent or extratensive. Also, they did not have the ability to deliberately start and end their behaviors, probably because they had insufficient psychological resources available to them (Garcia Alba, 2005, p. 203).

Anorexics also presented ideational slippages and morbid, pessimistic, and distorted thinking, which negatively influenced their self-esteem and social ties. In accordance with the conclusions from other samples evaluated with Rorschach CS, they showed problems when grasping and translating information from the environment (Garcia Alba, 2005, p. 204), which affected their adjustment to social conventions. Whereas the anorexia group differed not only from the nonpatient group, but also from that with bulimia and EDNOS, it seems that "primary anorexia nervosa is a separate entity when compared with other disorders or mental illnesses, with their own psychophysical characteristics" (King, 1963). Anorexics can be recognized as different, with a particular and unique own status in relation to the other subgroups (Bulimia and ED-NOS), though they can evolve to any other of the ED is not very clear yet.

Bulimia and EDNOS groups clearly differed from anorexics and shared more common features. Although we did not find many differences between EDNOS and bulimics, the latter group showed more control over their emotional expressions and were usually more passive and dependent when interacting with other people. However, under other conditions they could be more impulsive and lose control of their behavior. Also bulimics seemed to be less introspective than EDNOS patients.

In the last decade, many somatic disorders have been associated with poorly differentiated expressions of emotions affecting patients, especially in relation to symbolic and verbal expressions.

Some of the traits that we found in our ED patients are similar to those of patients who present with alexithymia: They have difficulty describing symptoms, and they tend to be defensive, trying to remain unaware of their emotions and bodily sensations (FM low). Their thinking and processing styles are simplified, and they avoid emotional stimuli (R. low, Lambda high, low Blends).

In the present sample our anorexic patients exhibited poorly integrated aspects of self; they avoided emotions and could not register or express their sensations. They also showed certain perceptual stereotypes and concrete cognition without introspective skills. It seems that these patients are much like other somatic patients with similar complaints and alexithymic traits.

Troop, Schmidt, and Treasure (1995) found that anorexics are more affected by alexithymia than are bulimics. While anorexics try to suppress and avoid their emotions, bulimics show deficits in emotional control.

According to our results, patients with EDNOS were neither as alexithymic as anorexics nor as depressive as bulimics. They could express their feelings and emotional states, they were not as impulsive, and they could make an introspective analysis of their behaviors.

With regard to the controversial inclusion of EDNOS, Fairburn and Bohn (2005) proposed a reconceptualization of clinical features; they used a "transdiagnostic" solution and, at least for the time being, eliminated the EDNOS category until more specific criteria appear.

For Fairburn et al. (2007), their clinical experience and knowledge about ED supports the proposal to characterize these disorders as "mixed," because the clinical features are present and combined in subtle different ways with those seen in the anorexia and bulimia syndromes.

With regard to this hypothesis, Fairburn et al. (2007) studied 170 consecutive patients with an eating disorder using standardized instruments. Operational diagnoses were made, and EDNOS cases were compared with anorexia and bulimia cases. The EDNOS cases represented 60% of the sample. The authors found that almost a quarter (22.5%) of EDNOS patients had a history of anorexia nervosa, and 38.2% had a history of bulimia nervosa. The EDNOS patients in this study resembled those with bulimia nervosa in many ways. They even displayed the psychopathologic characteristics of anorexia and bulimia, and their severity was comparable to that seen in bulimia nervosa.

But even though EDNOS patients share the eating habits and attitudes toward shape and weight that characterize the other two disorders, few cases could be reclassified into the other categories.

In addition, a low prevalence of binge eating was found in this research, which is consistent with data from other samples. However, the high prevalence of EDNOS was not due to the presence of the latter syndrome. In conclusion, "the high prevalence of EDNOS is not attributable to the existence within the diagnosis of cases closely resembling anorexia nervosa nor bulimia nervosa, nor is it due to the presence of cases of binge eating disorder" (Fairburn et al., 2007, p. 1713).

According to our data, EDNOS patients differ from anorexics and share more common features with bulimics. Nevertheless, compared with patients of this latter group, they have more psychological resources available, and particularly the presence of introspective capacity demonstrates that EDNOS patients could benefit from a different therapeutic approach.

The results, in this case using standardized measurement instruments, are similar to those of Marino and Zanarini (2001) who studied a sample of female borderline patients. For these authors, EDNOS is a separate cluster of ED among the studied women "rather than a prodromal or residual category of a more clear cut case of anorexia or bulimia nervosa" (p. 349).

Regarding treatment, Nielsen and Palmer (2003) wonder whether there is a different treatment for EDNOS patients because, to date, we know very little about the appropriate treatment for those patients as demonstrated in their response: "Nothing is known, for there have been no studies of the treatment of these patients" (Fairburn & Bohn, 2005).

Our findings suggest that EDNOS patients have more psychological resources available for treatment and more introspective behaviors. The differences found with respect to the other two groups seem important for creating a prevention and therapeutic approach. It could be possible to design different strategies of treatment for this subgroup.

Conclusion

One criticism of our work is that we took a sample from only one center. It is therefore necessary to look for larger and broader samples from different ED centers. The findings allow us to continue with the research, examination, and consideration of the possibility of going deeper into the differences between the categories. No doubt these conditions will have an impact on therapy planning.

Acknowledgment

I would like to thank Julie Smith, Honorary Treasurer of the PSAD Study Group, for proofreading the present article.

References

American Psychiatric Association. (1980). *American Psychiatric Diagnosis Statistical Manual of Mental Disorders DSM-III*. Washington, DC: Author.

American Psychiatric Association. (1987). *American Psychiatric Diagnosis Statistical Manual of Mental Disorders DSM-III-R*. Washington, DC: Author.

American Psychiatric Association. (1990). *American Psychiatric Diagnosis Statistical Manual of Mental Disorders DSM-IV*. Washington, DC: Author.

Exner, J. E. (2003). *Manual de codification del Rorschach para el Sistema Comprehensivo*

[Rorschach coding manual for the comprehensive system] (5th ed.). Madrid, Spain: Psimática.

Fairburn, C., & Harrison, P. (2003). Eating disorders seminar. *The Lancet, 361,* 407–414.

Fairburn, C. G., & Bohn, K. (2005). Eating Disorders NOS (EDNOS) an example of the troublesome "not otherwise specified" NOS category of the DSM-IV. *Behavior Research and Therapy, 43,* 691–701.

Fairburn, C. G., Cooper, Z., Bohn, C., O'Connor, E., Doll, H. A., Palmer, L. R. (2007). The severity and status of eating disorder NOS: Implications for DSM-V. *Behavior Research and Therapy, 45,* 1705–1715.

Garcia Alba, G. (2005). Cognitive functioning and other discriminatory variables in anorexic patients. *Rorschachiana, 27,* 191–206.

Garner, D. M., Olmstead, M. P., & Polivy, J. (1983). Development and validation of a multidimensional eating disorder inventory for anorexia nervosa and bulimia. *International Journal of Eating Disorders, 2,* 25–34.

King, A. (1963). Primary and secondary Anorexia Nervosa syndromes. *British Journal of Psychiatry, 109,* 470–479.

Lunazzi, H., Urrutia, M. I., De La Fuente, M. G., Elias, D., Fernandez, F., & De La Fuente, S. (2006). *Rorschach of nonpatient subjects: Normative data.* Madrid: Psimática.

Marino, M. F., & Zanarini, M. C. (2001). Relation between EDNOS and its subtypes and borderline personality disorders. *International Journal of Eating Disorders, 29,* 349–353.

Martin, C. K., Williamson, D. A., & Thaw, J. M. (2000). Criterion validity of the multiaxial assessment of eating disorders symptoms *International Journal of Eating Disorders, 28,* 303–310.

Milos, G., Spindler, A., Schnyder, U., & Fairburn, C. G. (2005). Instability of eating disorder diagnoses: Prospective study. *British Journal of Psychiatry, 187,* 573–578.

Nielsen, S., & Palmer, B. (2003). Diagnosing eating disorders-AN, BN and the others. *Acta Psychiatrica Scandinavica, 108,* 161–162.

Ricca, V., Mannucci, E., Mazzani, B., Di Bernardo, M., Zucchi, T., Paionni, A., ... Faravelli, C. (2001). Psychopathological and clinical features of outpatients with an eating disorder not otherwise specified. *Eating and Weight Disorders, 6,* 157–165.

Troop, N. A., Smith, N. H., & Treasure, J. L. (1995). Feelings and fantasy in eating disorders: Factor analysis of the Toronto Alexithymia Scale. *International Journal of Eating Disorders, 198,* 151–157.

Turner, H., & Bryant-Waugh, R. (2004). Eating Disorder not Otherwise Specified (EDNOS): Profiles of clients presenting at a community eating disorder service. *European Eating Disorders Review, 12,* 18–26.

Turón Gil, V. (1997). *Eating disorders.* Madrid: Masson, S. A.

Vega, V., & Quiroga, S. (2003). Eating behavior in adolescents. Memories of the research meeting at the university. Buenos Aires University, School of Psychology. *Tomo, 1,* 113–115.

M. Guinzbourg

Mónica Guinzbourg
Psychiatry Department
Italian Hospital of Buenos Aires
Argentina
E-mail monica.guinzbourg@gmail.com

Summary

Eating Disorders (ED) have been increasing over the past decades and have become one of the most common categories seen in outpatient settings. The EDNOS category – Eating Disorder Not Otherwise Specified – was included in the DSM-IV, joining the traditional Anorexia and Bulimia categories. There has been great controversy as to whether this inclusion was justified.

Since there have been only few systematic approaches to the subject, with small samples and especially relying on nonstandardized instruments, we decided to examine the differences between ED groups and a nonconsulting sample, comparing the three subgroups using data from Rorschach Comprehensive System.

We compared 106 patients (25 Anorexia, 27 Bulimia, and 54 EDNOS) with a population of 60 nonpatient subjects of similar demographic background.

We found that ED patients differ from the general population with regard to their coping style, complexity, and resources. They had less ability to deal with experiences and feelings. They also had more difficulties in their social ties and appeared to be more self-centered than women from the nonconsulting group.

Among the subgroups, anorexics were as introversive as the bulimics and EDNOS but less ambitent than both of them. They tended to use a neglecting style when processing information and showed less motivation when dealing with environmental stimuli. They also present more ideational slippages and morbid perceptions. They were more self-centered and less interested in other people. Clearly, they were more vulnerable to suffering emotional turmoil, and probably for this reason they tend to avoid interpersonal relations.

In comparison, bulimics and EDNOS were more alike. Both were as introversive as they were ambitent. Also, they were emotional unstable and vulnerable. Nevertheless, bulimics had the tendency to constrain more their emotional expressions, and they tend to internalize their distress with much risk of losing control, with a maniacal style to control anxiety and insecurity. In their relationships to other people bulimics tended to be more passive and could not have introspective capacities. No doubt these conditions will have an impact on therapy planning.

Resumen

Los Trastornos Alimenticios se han incrementado en las últimas décadas y constituyen uno de los más frecuentes motivos de la consulta ambulatoria actual. La incorporación de la categoría EDNOS (Trastornos Alimenticios No especificados) en el DSM-IV, junto a las ya tradicionales Anorexia y Bulimia, ha generado opiniones controversiales respecto a su inclusión.

Teniendo en cuenta que los estudios sistemáticos respecto al tema se han producido en general con muestras poco representativas y en base al uso de instrumentos poco estandarizados, decidimos estudiar los datos obtenidos a través de la aplicación del Rorschach Sistema Comprehensivo comparando una población de 60 no pacientes con 106 pacientes con trastornos alimenticios (25 anorexias, 29 bulímicas y 54 EDNOS), teniendo ambos grupos similar constitución demográfica. Luego hemos comparado los subgrupos entre sí.

Encontramos que la muestra de las pacientes con trastornos alimenticios se diferenció de la población no consultante por el estilo vivencial, la complejidad y los recursos. Las pacientes disponen de menos recursos para manejar sus experiencias y sentimientos. También presentan mayor autocentración y más dificultades en sus vínculos interpersonales.

Entre los distintos subgrupos las anoréxicas resultaron tan introversivas pero menos ambitendentes que las bulímicas y que las EDNOS. Presentaron menor motivación para el tratamiento de los estímulos. También evidenciaron algunas distorsiones ideativas y contenidos mórbidos afectaron sus percepciones. Se las observó con mayor tendencia al retraimiento y autocentración en desmedro de la capacidad de establecer vínculos. Resultaron más vulnerables a padecer estados de inestabilidad emocional y por ende presentaron mayor evitación de las relaciones con los otros.

Tanto las bulímicas como las EDNOS parecen compartir más rasgos en común. Suelen proporcionalmente ser tanto introvertidas como ambitendentes. También parecen emocionalmente inestables y por ende vulnerables a este tipo de situaciones. Sin embargo, las bulímicas presentan mayor tendencia a restringir la expresión de sus emociones con el consecuente riesgo de descontrol y con intentos maniacos de controlar la ansiedad e inseguridad. En las relaciones interpersonales parecen adoptar actitudes más pasivas y no disponen de posibilidades para realizar registros introspectivos acerca de sus comportamientos.

Es probable que estas diferencias ejerzan influencia en la programación de los abordajes terapéuticos.

Résumé

Au cours des dernières décennies, les troubles alimentaires se sont développés et les patients qui en souffrent constituent une part importante de la demande de consultation ambulatoire. L'inclusion de la catégorie de l'EDNOS dans le DSM-IV a engendré des controverses. La plupart des études sur ce sujet ont été réalisées avec des groupes peu représentatifs et avec des instruments non standardisés. Notre travail a comparé une population de femmes non patientes (69) à un groupe de 106 jeunes femmes atteintes de troubles alimentaires (25 anorexiques, 29 boulimiques et 54 EDNOS). Nous avons ensuite étudié les différences entre les trois sous-groupes.

Nous avons utilisé le Rorschach System Comprehensive d' Exner en analysant les variables qu'il propose.

Les résultats montrent que le groupe souffrant de troubles alimentaires est différent de celui des femmes de la population. Les patientes sont moins complexes et elles ont moins de ressources disponibles. Elles ont beaucoup plus de mal à faire face aux expériences et à l'affectivité. La plupart de ces femmes sont plus égocentriques et accordent moins d'intérêt aux autres.

Les anorexiques sont différentes des autres groupes. La plupart ont des personnalités introverties. Elles présentent des troubles quant à l'idéation et ont une vision pessimiste de l'expérience. Elles préfèrent être loin des autres et se réfugient en elles-mêmes. Les boulimiques et les EDNOS se ressemblent plus. Elles sont instables et émotionnellement vulnérables Mais les boulimiques sont moins expressives quant à leurs émotions et elles courent le risque de devenir plus impulsives et plus incontrôlées. Les boulimiques sont plus maniaques face au manque d'assurance et à l'anxiété. Elles ont aussi des difficultés dans les relations interpersonnelles et sont incapables d'introspection vis-à-vis de leur conduite.

Ces différences ne manqueront pas d'influencer le choix de la stratégie thérapeutique.

　摂食障害はここ数十年の間増加し続けており、外来という設定では最もよく出会う疾病カテゴリーとなってきた。EDNOS（特定不能の摂食障害）という診断カテゴリーがやせ症と大食症のカテゴリーに加えて DSM-IV に導入されたが、この導入が正当であるかどうかについては議論が生じている。

　このテーマに対する系統的な接近法がほとんど見当たらないこと、サンプル数が少ないこと、標準化されていない手段に頼っていることを考慮して、我々は ED の 3 つのグループと非臨床群の間の違いを検討することを決心し、さらに包括システムによるロールシャッハ法のデータをもちいて 3 つのサブ・グループを比較した。我々は 106 名の患者（やせ症 25 名、大食症 27 名、EDNOS54 名）をこれらの被験者と類似した人口統計学的な背景を持つ 60 名の非患者群と比較した。ED の患者は非患者群に比較して、対処スタイル、複雑さ、資質において異なっていることを我々は発見した。ED 群は体験や感情を扱うのにより低い能力を有していた。彼らはまた社会的なつながりにおいてもより困難を有しており、非患者群の女性より自己中心的な見方をしていた。

　サブ・グループの比較においては、やせ症は、大食症と EDNOS と同程度に内向であったが、不定型が両群よりも少なかった。やせ症は情報処理に際して無視をするスタイルをもちいる傾向があり、環境の刺激を扱う際には動機づけが低いようであった。さらに、思考の飛躍や不快な反応もより多く認められた。彼らは自己中心的であり、他者への関心がより少ない傾向にあった。明らかにやせ症は情緒的混乱によって苦悩することに脆弱であり、そしておそらくこの理由によって対人関係を回避する傾向にある。

　比較してみると、大食症と EDNOS はより類似していた。内向型、不定型も両群とも同じ程度であった。また、彼らは情緒的に安定しておらず、傷つきやすかった。それでもやはり、大食症は彼らの情緒的な表出をより抑制する傾向にあり、不安や不安定をコントロールするのに躁的なスタイルをもちいて、統制を失う危険の高い彼らの苦悩を内在化する傾向にあった。他の群に比較して大食症はより受け身的な傾向があり、内省する力を持つことができなかった。このような条件が心理療法に影響を与えるであろうことは疑いのないことである。

Rorschachiana 32, 46–71
© 2011 Hogrefe Publishing

DOI: 10.1027/1192-5604/a000015

Original Article

The Case of Thematic Tests Adapted to Older Adults

On the Importance of Differentiating Latent and Manifest Contents in Projective Tests

Benoît Verdon

Laboratoire de Psychologie Clinique et de Psychopathologie (EA 4056), Université Paris Descartes – Institut de Psychologie, Boulogne-Billancourt, France

Abstract. Since the 1950s, the growing interest of clinicians in using projective tests to study normal or pathological aging processes has led to the creation of several thematic tests for older adults. This development reflects their authors' belief that the TAT is not suitable to the concerns and anxieties of elderly persons. The new material thus refers explicitly to situations related to age; it aims to enable older persons to express needs they cannot verbalize during consultations. The psychodynamic approach to thematic testing is based on the differentiation between the pictures' manifest and latent content, eliciting responses linked to mental processes and issues the respondent is unaware of. The cards do not necessarily have to show aging characters to elicit identification: The situations shown in the pictures are linked to loss, rivalry, helplessness, and renunciation, all issues elderly respondents can identify with and that lead them to express their mental fragilities and resources. The article first explains the principles underlying four of these thematic tests, then develops several examples of stories told for card 3BM of the TAT, thus showing the effectiveness of this tool for the understanding and differentiation of loss-related issues facing older men and women.

Keywords: aging, thematic tests, TAT, psychodynamic, projective techniques, manifest content, latent content

In his concluding lecture given at the 13th International Congress of Rorschach and Other Projective Techniques, held in Paris in 1990, Leopold Bellak spoke of "the amazing increase in the longevity of the general population," underscoring the importance, in his view, of adapting thematic tests to the growing population of aging adults. In the early 1970s, Bellak, together with Sonia Bellak, had already created the Senior Apperception

46

Technique (SAT). He concluded his speech in these terms: "Let us hope that we continue to have to revise the tables of senectitude to reflect increasing improvement in the quality and length of life" (1990, p. 363). Now, 20 years later, we cannot but sadly observe that research on thematic tests with older adults has remained quite scarce. Thus, at the 16th International Congress of Rorschach and Projective methods in Leuven in 2008, only one paper was devoted to the SAT (Tardivo, 2008). Conversely, for many years now, a great deal of research has been conducted with the Rorschach on older populations (Ames, 1960, 1966; Ames, Learned, Metraux, & Walker, 1954; Baudin, 1998, 2001, 2005; Caldwell, 1954; Eisdorfer, 1963; Ferreira Novo & Silva, 2002; Grossman, Warshawsky, & Hertz 1951; Klopfer, 1946, 1974; Light & Amick, 1956; Mattlar, Carlsson, Forsander, Karppi, & Helenius 1992; Mattlar, Knuts, & Virtanen, 1985; Péruchon, 2002; Poitrenaud & Moreaux, 1975; Prados & Fried, 1947; Shimonaka & Nakazato, 1991; Vazquez & Osuna, 2002; Verdon, 2003, 2007a,b, 2009; Verdon & Duplant, 2006).

Much of the research devoted to the psychological evaluation of older adults focuses on the creation of neuropsychological tests for the screening of pathologies linked to dementia, and projective method specialists have studied the input of the Rorschach in this area (Kökenek, Degirmenci, Kübra Kanar, & Ikiz 2008; Muzio, 1999, 2002; Muzio & Luperto, 1999; Nihashi & Kosaka, 2002; Orme, 1955; Overall & Gorham, 1972; Péruchon, 1990, 1994; Vazquez, Hierro, & Tomas 1999; Viala & Chu, 1999). Foote and Kahn (1979) have used the SAT for discriminating aging patients with brain disorders.

Some research has also been conducted on normal or pathological aging with the Holtzman Inkblot Technique (Hayslip 1981, 1982), the Hand Test (Panek, Wagner, & Avolio 1978), figure drawing techniques (Gilbert & Hall, 1962; Oberleder, 1967; Plutchik, Conte, Weiner, & Teresi 1978), a story-telling test based on a plot suggested by the psychologist (Bouisson, 2003), or techniques using tales (Lavallée, 1999). Lawton, Whelihan, and Belsky (1980), Panek, Wagner, and Kennedy-Zwergel (1983), Hayslip and Lowman (1986) conducted a detailed review of existing techniques, their various uses, and the different results observed.

Thematic Tests Adapted to a Geriatric Population

According to Danon-Boileau (2000, p. 9), "aging is a dangerous exercise and we all know how it ends." As we grow old, we are confronted with cognitive, social, and physical losses, together with the death of friends or relatives – anticipatory announcements of our own death, in fact, which requires intense mental adjustment. Whether the aging process is normal or pathological, it is important to understand the nature of the mental processes at hand in order to ensure that the therapeutic program is adapted to the person's needs. In some cases, one consultation may be enough to determine the patient' mental needs and resources. In others, however, a projective test may be necessary. According to some, the TAT material does not sufficiently address the concerns and anxieties of old age, since only few pictures show older persons. As a result, new tests were designed to fill the gap.

The Gerontological Apperception Test (GAT)

Wolk and Wolk (1971) as well as Wolk, Rustin, and Seiden (1966) designed the GAT to assess the mental responses of patients when viewing representations of specific situations linked to aging, illness, invalidity, and loneliness. Some research has been devoted to verifying its validity (Mercer, 1973; Pasewark, Fitzgerald, Dexter, & Gangemi, 1976). Traxler, Swiener, and Rogers (1974) concluded that the GAT revealed only superficial aspects of the individual's personality. Fitzgerald, Pasewark, and Fleisher (1974) compared TAT and GAT protocols for specific themes such as loss of sexuality, loss of attractiveness, family difficulties, and dependency. According to their findings, the results obtained through the GAT did not yield a more sensitive understanding of the patient's issues than those obtained thanks to the TAT, except for the dimension of physical limitation.

The Senior Apperception Technique (SAT)

The SAT was developed following the creation of the Children Apperception Test (CAT) in the 1950s. The CAT is a valuable thematic test designed for children, which takes into account their specific defense mechanisms, eliciting identifications and projections onto animal figures placed in anthropomorphic situations. The SAT was created with a view toward adapting the pictures to the specificities of an older population. "We had to produce images that were sufficiently ambiguous to allow freedom of imagination, while at the same time reflecting the situations and issues that aging persons have to cope with on a daily basis (loneliness, illness, happiness at being grandparents, pleasure of a ball-room dancing event, of a game)" (Bellak & Bellak, 1973, pp. 5f.). One of the reasons given for creating this test was that the support material enables the person to speak about issues that are difficult to verbalize during a consultation. But as Bellak and Bellak themselves recognized, "compared to the TAT or the CAT, the SAT seems both more widely usable and more restrictive" (ibid.). More widely usable, because it can be used by persons who are not clinical psychologists "to deepen their investigation by considering the responses to certain cards as additional information, on a conscious level" (ibid., p. 11); more restrictive, because the images and stories remain limited to concrete situations experienced in reality.

> "The additional information brought by the SAT concerns on one hand the specificity of the forms taken by these different states for a given individual, and on the other hand the factors that trigger this situation. Does this elderly woman feel depressed because she feels abandoned by her eldest daughter? By her younger daughter or her son? Or is she depressed because she is becoming aware of the deterioration of her abilities, or is she experiencing a narcissistic wound tied to the fact that she is no longer sexually desirable?" (ibid. p. 7).

The SAT thus has "specific and modest" aims (ibid.). It allows elderly adults who are weakened by illness, suffering from inhibition due to a traumatic event, burdened by the routine of institutional life, or by depression, to express their own concerns and needs through displacement onto the characters and concrete situations represented on the cards (Schroth, 1978; Stock & Kantner, 1980).

Laforestrie – Missoum Personnes Agées (Laforestie-Missoum Aged Persons – LMPA)

Laforestrie and Missoum developed a projective test which "unlike the GAT and the SAT, tends to elicit among elderly persons, thanks to the choice of themes and the graphic design and layout, the projection of fantasies" (1977, p. 4). These graphic techniques are in fact a set of pictures that are strikingly crude (emaciated bodies, a corpse on a bed, someone falling in the street, a visit to the cemetery), with blurry outlines and out-of-focus images that are certainly not suited to the eyesight difficulties of many elderly persons.

The 13 cards intend to recreate a concrete environment of the elderly person which can be a source of stress. They are analyzed according to the presence of themes such as death, sexuality, communication, loss of work, isolation, physical deterioration, or living in a group. The scoring is performed according to different "classes," a positive class ("positive value attributed to the situation or the characters, positive affects") and a negative or pathological class ("failure to adapt to the situation, delirious content") (ibid., pp. 10f.). Both the material and the mode of interpretation are puzzling. Here is a brief example. One of the first cards shows a "very thin old man sitting on a bed, his legs bent and spread out, his arms also spread. On another bed, a character with a sheet in his mouth. In front of them, the shadow of a third character who is standing up. Behind the man, a human form" (ibid. p. 7). According to the authors, the representation of a sports activity, a sexual activity, whether alone or in a group, or of childbirth is to be interpreted positively, because the patient is in control of the stressful situation and reverses it. Conversely, stories dealing with illness, loneliness, and deterioration are to be scored negatively. We are very critical of this model of interpretation. Speaking of illness or poverty concerning this card would be in harmony with the actual content of the image; a "positive" response in this case is more likely to correspond to a manic defense (in particular the forced sexualization of a morbid situation).

In the manual explaining how to use the test, the authors provide only four succinct clinical illustrations and no synthetic conclusion. The only observation commented upon concerns a 79-year-old woman with severe behavioral disorders due to a degenerative and vascular disease she has been suffering from for several years. This thematic test thus seems quite difficult to use for clinical or research purposes.

The Projective Assessment of Aging Method (PAAM)

Starr and Weiner (1979, 1993) created the Projective Assessment of Aging Method (PAAM). Although the 31 pictures depict themes and situations exclusively related to aging (loneliness, impairment, disease, couple relationships, sexuality, suicide and death, work and retirement), the authors believe that the PAAM material is

"relatively ambiguous so that a theme is suggested but the specifics of what is happening and what the people are thinking or feeling must be supplied by the respondent. In making up stories to these pictures the respondent reveals important needs, concerns, anxieties, styles of coping, and other dynamics related to aging. (. . .) The PAAM has advantages over an interview that would directly probe the various areas of interest. People generally enjoy making up stories and they are usually nondefensive since they feel they are talking about a picture and not themselves. Direct interviews generally require more time to build up a trusting relationship before the client will let go of defenses to be more open and revealing" (Starr & Weiner 1993, pp. 69f.).

Even though the authors defend the idea that this test "can very quickly provide a strong sense of knowing the respondent, which can be very useful in many situations with elderly clients" (ibid, p. 70), we must remember the warning formulated by Bellak and Bellak concerning material that remains very suggestive, and as such does not permit a deep understanding of the patient's mental functioning. Indeed, telling a story based on a PAAM card is interpreted by the authors as telling one's own story, in the here and now of a concrete situation perceived solely on a conscious level. "For example, one resident's response to card 1 indicated a great deal of loneliness: she has to eat alone now. She is lonely. She remembers how there always was someone she could eat with and talk to now." It seemed clear to the staff that a compatible roommate would be beneficial. But more importantly, the awareness of her loneliness prompted the staff to observe her more actively and to seize opportunities for encouraging socialization" (1993, p. 77). Panek et al. (1983) mention the lack of research conducted on this tool, which has not been used much. Hayslip and Lowman (1986) do not mention it in their review of existing techniques published 3 years later.

Manifest Content and Latent Content in Psychoanalysis

The terms "manifest content" and "latent content" were introduced by Freud in *The Interpretation of Dreams* (1900). Freud believed that artistic productions were reflections of the artist's personality. He applied this principle to another and much more widespread type of production, namely, dreams. He thus developed a theory explaining the construction of dreams, along with a method to understand and even interpret them. According to Freud, the manifest content of a dream is the result of dream work, i.e., the "descriptive narrative of the dream as told by the subject" (Laplanche & Pontalis, 1967, p. 101), whereas its latent content is the

"group of meanings revealed upon the completion of an analysis of a production of the unconscious, particularly dreams. Once it has been deciphered, the dream

51

no longer appears as a story told through images but as an organization of thoughts, a narrative expressing one or more wishes" (Laplanche & Pontalis, ibid., p. 100).

The latent content – an intricate web of childhood memories, daily experiences, and transference elements – thus precedes the manifest content. This is an essential differentiation, since it marks the presence of two levels of understanding,

> "two versions of the same subject-matter in two different languages. Or more properly, the dream-content seems like a transcript of the dream-thoughts into another mode of expression, whose characters and syntactic laws it is our business to discover by comparing the original and the translation" (Freud, 1900, p. 277).

> "By extension, write Laplanche and Pontalis, we speak of the manifest content of any verbal product – from fantasies to literary works – which we wish to interpret according to the analytical method" (op. cit., p. 101).

This model was also used by Freud to explain the complex construction of many symptoms: Something that is expressed in a given way on the manifest level (anxieties, disorders, functional deficits) but which can, and must, be heard on another level: that of underlying conflicts and wishes. Thus, psychologists who use projective techniques work on distinguishing manifest content from latent content in subjects' responses to the Rorschach and thematic tests in general, but they are also careful to make a distinction between the manifest content of the cards (the visible content, easily grasped by the subject) and their latent content (the hidden, disguised, ambiguous content) of the projective material itself.

Manifest Content and Latent Content in Projective Tests

In his work *Psychodiagnostics* (1921), Rorschach explains that the shapes and the way they are presented can elicit certain types of responses rather than others. Nina Rausch de Traubenberg (1970) studied the "privileged latent symbolic suggestions" of the different cards, while Murray (1943) developed a method, partly inspired by Freud, for the passing and interpretation of the TAT: The subjects were asked to lie down in a dimly lighted room, suggesting confidentiality, and imagine stories based on the pictures shown on the cards. Unknowingly, through their identification with one of the characters on the card, they would express their own needs (whose relationships with the other characters portrayed are more or less conflictual). Significant material concerning the subjects' conflicts, of which they themselves might have been unaware, could thus be obtained. The psychologist's task was to bring these conflicts to light thanks to the analysis of the stories. Although the TAT is a test in which certain specific "themes" are submitted to the subject, Murray believed that the stories made up by the persons taking the test were disguised descriptions of their own behavior and motivations in real life, such as the need for domination or submission, sexual needs, the need to be helped, the need to defend oneself, feelings of guilt, ideals, narcissism, etc.

The advantage of projective tests over objective tests is that they solicit the respondent on several levels, which are more or less explicitly stated. In addition, unlike the Rorschach, thematic tests present figurative material, suggesting a story. Even though the material does show persons or situations, it remains relatively ambiguous, making it possible for the respondents to express their own fantasies inspired by the picture and represent them verbally. This perception of projective tests is partly shared by the authors of thematic tests for aging adults. Following in Murray's steps (1943), they support the persons' identification with the central character, who expresses their needs, the relationships they wish to entertain or not, with the other characters portrayed in the pictures, who supposedly represent the patient's immediate, real, concrete environment.

Bellak (1954), Schafer (1958, 1967), and Holt (1961), who all received psychoanalytic training, underscored the importance of paying attention not only to the content of the story, but also to the way the story is told. They further developed Murray's approach, which was to perform a rigorous formal analysis of the imagined story (accuracy of perception, coherence of the narrative, tendency to describe, imagination, quality of syntax, etc.). They were particularly intent on observing how the fluidity and construction of the narrative were either enhanced or disorganized, not by the events of the subject's daily life, but by the *unconscious* conflicts mobilized by the material. In addition, they addressed the question of the status of the story's content – neither an uncontrolled product of the imagination, like daytime dreaming or even a nighttime dream, nor is it a purely cognitive product devoid of emotional and unconscious content.

In 1960, Shentoub and Shentoub conducted a widespread research to determine the ordinary responses to the different TAT cards. They suggested the hypothesis that "certain themes are prominent, given the degree of structure of the TAT images." The test was administered to 100 persons with no psychopathological disorders, recruited in the context of career counseling, and to 60 persons with various psychopathological disorders (depression, anxiety, obsessive ideas, schizophrenia, etc.). Thanks to this comparative study, they found that certain themes were repeatedly brought up by most subjects, both with and without disorders. For example, for card 3BM, several themes were frequently addressed (sadness, punishment, suicidal thoughts, physical fatigue, guilt, despair, poverty, prison). Over the years, Shentoub (1973, 1987, 1990) and Shentoub and Debray (1970–71) further worked on this question and consolidated these various themes as a "privileged latent content of the card": "facing the elaboration of the depressive position." Following Freudian theory, they highlighted the variety of manners in which this theme was addressed by the patients (work of mourning, guilt, narcissistic vulnerability, bodily expression of depressive affects). In addition to this research, which was carried out for each of the TAT cards, Shentoub suggested the term "induced conscious fantasy" to describe the production generated by thematic tests. The story is a conscious elaboration based on a relatively structured and figurative material; it reveals the mental elaboration of latent content, of which the viewer is not aware, and which trigger unconscious processes. This approach, based on Freudian theory, was also developed by Anzieu and Chabert (1987), Chabert (1998), and Brelet and Chabert (2003). The latent content reactivates mental issues, potentially shared by all and at the same time apprehended by each patient in his or her own unique way (Brelet, 1986). As Golse wrote, primal fantasies "can be seen as large basic containers of fantasy (general containers) which are represented within each subject thanks to specific and private mental representations (specific contents)" (2009, p. 84).

The notion of latent content of TAT material should be understood in this sense. Murray suggested that the TAT images represented typical human situations, while Shentoub believed that these situations refer to universal conflicts whose underlying issues remain unconscious for the subject (management of libido and aggressiveness, difference between sexes and generations, "oedipal conflicts, processing of loss and depression). Indeed, as we have seen, Freud (1900) left behind the earlier conception of the "latent content" of a dream, whereby the meaning and symbolism of dream images were universal and automatically applicable to all, emphasizing instead that the latent content of a dream could only be found within the patient, and that this content could only be understood in relationship to the patient's own, specific mental issues. The use of the term "latent content" in projective psychology is somewhere in the middle ground: As Shentoub (1973, 1987, 1990) showed, the fantasies produced through the TAT do not have the same status as dreams; they are based on a preset image and are not purely spontaneous, nor are they based only on the sole fantasy of the subject. However, it is true that certain themes appear more frequently with some cards; the frequency of these themes being sufficiently high, projective test specialists have considered the possibility that the themes may be induced by the material, which may seem neutral but is not. As we will see below in the analysis of card 3BM of the TAT, even though the latent content of the card seems to refer to depression – which some subjects may fail to recognize – what is important is the specific, individual way in which this issue is reflected in the subject's psyche, and his or her ability not only to recognize it, but also to process it. As pointed out by Chabert, each card calls forth representations, affects that "follow a relatively homogeneous direction of fantasy while preserving the conflicts that are specific to each subject" (1983, p. 57).

This approach to the analysis and interpretation of projective test protocols raises several questions concerning thematic tests adapted to older adults which show scenes explicitly involving old persons in situations deemed typical for that age. Indeed, the use of such explicitly oriented material can lead to two main stumbling blocks. On the one hand, if the material does match real life situations too closely, little room is left for fantasy, and the persons' discourse can be taken literally, as supposedly reflecting actual problems of their daily lives. On the other hand, what the persons say is understood as referring to themselves; if both actor and narrator of the scene are one, we run the risk of attributing a positive value to a story that is in fact conventional, where conflicts are avoided or minimized, or that is given a false happy end as a result of manic defense mechanisms. Similarly, a sad story can be interpreted as a sign of depression, when in fact its being able to represent loss and attach an affect of sadness to it is an important part of mental life and has nothing to do with pathology.

The latent content is interesting precisely because it is unknown to the person inventing the story. The pictures on the cards are productive if they offer a framework in which to play, where one can use and interpret the material or conversely choose to avoid a given dimension, due to the apparent neutrality of the cards. For this reason, the TAT remains a very interesting projective test for elderly adults. Although only three cards show aging persons (6BM, 7BM, and 12F), the test overall refers to mental issues such as object loss, depression, narcissistic fragility, adjustments of desire and aggressiveness, renunciation, and powerlessness. Owing to the variety of scenes and protagonists, the persons can fantasize, with the possibility of displacement onto characters that are apparently far removed from their immediate concerns. Thus, the first card showing a child, a boy, can evoke different fantasies among men and women, young and old. The latent content of the card, "identification with a young individual in a situation of functional immaturity" (Shentoub, 1990, p. 45), which elicits a feeling of powerlessness in front of an object which is not mastered, on the other hand, is a mental issue that can be shared by everyone regardless of age and sex. Furthermore, the defense mechanisms, their nature and quality, still remain specific to each person, according to age, sex, and mental reality seen in the context of their own life events and experience.

Several studies based on the TAT with elderly adults have been conducted to investigate certain mental aspects of aging, in particular the complex issue of sexuality and sexual identifications, the processing of loss, depression, and renunciation (Baudin, 1998, 2001, 2005; Péruchon, 2002; Verdon, 2004a,b, 2005, 2007a, 2007b; Verdon & Duplant, 2006). Though we cannot provide in this article a detailed review of these researches, we chose to give an example of the wealth of information produced by the TAT, following our approach based on the differentiation between manifest content and latent content. For the purpose of this article, we selected several stories pertaining to card 3BM. We chose to focus on this card and its interpretation separately from the global analysis of the protocol only for the sake of precision; it goes without saying that such a selection does not correspond to usual clinical practice.

Illustration with TAT Card 3 BM

For clinicians working in the framework of Shentoub's school of interpretation (Brelet, 1986; Brelet-Foulard & Chabert, 2003; Chabert, 1987, 1998; Shentoub, 1990), card 3BM is given to all persons, not only to boys and men as Murray indicated (1943). This is because card 3GF elicits feelings that are too obviously and too exclusively tied to depression. Card 3BM, on the other hand, is more ambiguous. Indeed, the manifest content of this card represents a person of indeterminate age and gender, prostrated and leaning on a couch; next to the person, on the floor, lies a blurry object. The latent content of this card is the recognition of the character's depressive feelings, the linking of affect to a representation, specifically a representation of loss, absence, and guilt. Depending on their mental organization, the respondents are more or less able to work through the depressive stimuli: The affect will be either repressed and isolated, displaced onto another representation within another sequence of associations, or transformed into its opposite; there can be inhibition, discharge of unqualified anxiety, sometimes in association with crude, violent, morbid representations; or the depressive affect can be translated into a somatic state (exhaustion, fatigue) or concealed under a mask of social hyperconformism, where feelings seem to be dictated by propriety and external considerations. In some cases there are no representations, or the patient cannot tell a story and presents instead autonomic manifestations linked to emotions experienced in the here and now of the testing session. Furthermore, because of its ambiguous nature, this card potentially gives rise to a rich and dense fantasy content pertaining to the question of sexual identification (and the issue of loss is closely tied to this question – is it a man, a woman, a child?), or even the question of narcissistic integrity (indeed, some subjects are sensitive to the perception that the character's body may be deformed), whereas card 3GF does not call forth this type of response.

The persons whose stories were selected for this article were seen in the framework of a consultation for memory complaints. Their ages range from 63 to 91. Their concern was that they might have Alzheimer's disease, but their neuropsychological evaluations did not confirm this. These persons are not suffering from incipient dementia nor even mild cognitive impairment (MCI). They underwent a global medical checkup and are in good physical health, they do not have eyesight problems nor any background of psychiatric disorders. They do not take psychotropic drugs.

Here are several examples of stories told for card 3BM. A global comment will describe their richness and variety as well as their contrasts, thus reflecting the diversity and specificity of ways in which loss can be processed, depending on the subject's form of mental functioning.

B. Verdon

Alyson, 82 years old

A prisoner is half-sitting on his knees, he's crying in front of his cot. It's sad. I have nothing else to say.

Joyce, 66

(Sighs, shakes her head, long silence). I can't tell a story about this scene ... It's ... it's ... maybe a young woman filled with pain, maybe in a cell, in a prison, in a desolate place, that expresses her feeling of desolation. I don't know why. She is back to us. We can't see anything. Title of this picture: "Desolation."

Jennifer, 91

Ah, there's great despair there, hm ... the ..., she, she or he, I think it's a "she," difficult to say, I think it's rather a "she," ... she's just suffered a great shock, probably a scene with someone she loves, and she is trying to return to a ... something more normal, she's trying to calm down emotionally, but she's very sad and I'm not sure she'll manage. She seems to have abandoned everything, her shoes, her ... I don't know what she has there with her ... She's really desperate.

Peter, 63

Dear me! This time, I imagine the story differently, that is ... I have a friend who's a painter, she's about my age, her painting is a little figurative but she studies movement mainly by studying the body. And I have one of her pictures at home, a picture representing, as I imagine, a woman who has fallen asleep in this way, but we don't see her entirely like this one, only the small of her back, she's sitting in the same position. I find that in painting, what is both easy and difficult is to have imagination, either to understand what the painter or the artist is representing, what he wants to say, or for yourself, what you understand of what you see, which is sometimes totally different.

Virginia, 69

Well, it's ... well a story ... I think it's an image of helplessness and abandonment, a woman, who's been, there's been a fight, she was hit and she's fallen under the blows, and ... well she stays in that position, she doesn't feel ... she doesn't feel like reacting, she keeps on crying and she's very discouraged ... and at that moment, ah .... she has the impression that ... well she's feeling very miserable and very ... very lonely and she wants to die and .... finally she hears her husband's steps, well yes, the steps of the man who hit her and ... he's coming back and he's trying to ... comfort her ... and after this moment of despair, she

58

once again wants to live and ... ah ... until the next ... fight. There's no end to it really.

Judith, 84

Oh ... oh ... oh ... I see a man crouching, his head ... his head is lying on his right arm ... and ... one can imagine, one can imagine that the box in the background is a ... what do you call it? a ... a coffin, and that he's crying over this coffin. That's what this makes me think of most.

Claire, 82

This picture reminds me of a Goya painting, maybe. I see a child, from behind, crouching.... leaning on what may be a grave ... His arm is folded, he lays his head on his arm and on the stone. Does the picture evoke mourning, the death of someone he loved?

Rachel, 85

Ah! Oh! I think it's, it's a woman, a man, in prison. I have the feeling he's a humpback, unfortunately, though it's difficult to say. He's a humpback. He's very unhappy, his attitude shows it ... he's discouraged, disappointed in life and has no hope for the time being. I hope he'll win his trial, that he'll be found not guilty and will be able to be happy again. It's not really ... What's it called? (Looks at the back of the card, sighs ...) ... not a very good interpretation (laughs). I don't have much imagination.

Paul, 76

(Long silence) There's ... this little boy was born in a difficult family ... He wanted to help his parents ... and perhaps, ah, sorry, he wanted to help his parents and then, maybe I'm wrong, he wanted to help them by carrying bottles, and he tripped and practically all the bottles of wine his family was keeping for the holidays were broken, and the father is a violent man and scolded him, maybe he even ... he scolded him, slapped him and put him in a cell, that is in a cellar to punish him, and the little boy seems very unhappy, he is very unhappy, he is very desperate but the parents, the mother in any case, it's always the mother in those cases, the mother intervened; she herself was very upset to see her little boy, her little boy so despondent, so she intervened, she brought him something to drink, something to eat, and then she went to see the daddy and told him that he could have realized that the little boy, even though he's clumsy, that the little guy (laughs), though clumsy, had good intentions, and that the punishment is too severe and she asked him if she could bring him back. Of course the mommy fetched the boy and took him to the kitchen where she gave him a ... snack to

make him feel better. It's difficult for me to ... to tell a story. I'm no longer used to it. I used to tell my children lots of stories.

Raymond, 65

Well, that's a young girl aged about 15 or 16, and well, her parents have just forbidden her to go out on a Friday night because she's too young, and her parents, of course, have learned about her little love affair with her boyfriend Jonathan and ... she's tried everything, everything to see him again; she invented something to be able to leave on Friday night without her parents knowing where she was going, but they found out of course, because parents always find out everything, at that age, so they forbade her to go out and locked her up a little, not really locked up because they didn't dare, she would've been too ... Anyway they forced her to stay in her room, so she's in her room and she's crying, crying, she thinks her life is over, that life isn't worth living, she's wondering, she really has dark thoughts, as dark as her hair, and ... for the time being that's where she is, she won't leave ... she'll fall asleep and tomorrow maybe, she'll feel better.

Helen, 63

Well I see a person ... who looks very sad. A woman sitting near a bed ... sitting on the floor ... alone in a room ... and she's thinking about when she wasn't alone. She's remembering her partner ... and their life together ... She feels discouraged ... So she's meditating, in her way. Not much to say about that, huh! (?) Well it can end in different ways ... Probably as usual ... after spending a lot of time thinking and suffering, because of his absence .... then she goes back to every day life, the things she has to do: Get up, wash up, do her work ... see her family and friends ... that's it.

Patricia, 80

(Takes the card) That, I don't know. Is it a homeless man? It's not a child, his feet are too big. A man who's a little dislocated, he seems to have a hump ... in a rather deserted place. He's sitting, leaning but ... not ... not really resting; maybe he's looking for something. He surely has problems. But he could have found a better place to ... to rest, to try and relax. He seems to be feeling really low. Even if he's sleepy, he's not feeling well. Not really joyful, these pictures of yours, huh!

As we can see, although the manifest content of the material is the same for all, the issue of loss suggested by the latent content varies and is different for each subject, even though we do observe some permanent features.

For some, the depressive affect is clearly identified, sometimes named in a rather dramatic fashion ("despair," "extreme sadness," "desperation," "unhappiness," "discouraged," "disappointed in life," "no hope for the time being"), and linked to a representation of loss, in a context of mourning (Judith, Helen, Claire), relational conflict (Jennifer, Virginia), guilt, punishment and powerlessness (Rachel, Paul, Raymond). However, for Jennifer and Judith, there seems to be no possibility for positive elaboration, nor can they find an object to support them. A slight tendency toward narcissistic self-deprecation can be observed in Rachel's final commentary, where she expresses feelings of inferiority and powerlessness, clearly echoing the latent content of the card and that of the story. On the other hand, Paul, Raymond, and Helen are able to construct stories showing an original and rich fantasy life, where sadness is expressed with emphasis and linked to loss, or even clearly linked to oedipal conflict, somewhere between desire and prohibition (Paul, Raymond). Helen, whose story offers the most positive mental elaboration, finds a solution thanks to a common reference: the work of grieving, which implies pain, renunciation, the possibility of positive elaboration and narcissistic and objectal recathexis. Conversely, the ending of Virginia's story, if one can call it an end, strikes us because of the impossibility of her elaborating a positive solution. The depressive affect is named and linked to a representation of physical pain ("hit," "fallen under the blows") as well as to a masochistic representation of loss of an object that cannot be given up. Virginia is locked in a circular conflict – it's better to suffer in a relationship than to break up – which bars all possibility of working through mourning and loss. Claire, on the other hand, can evoke a representation of loss, that of a love object, but she is unable to link it to an affect of sadness.

For others (Alyson, Joyce, Patricia, Peter), the depressive affect is expressed through a bodily function ("he's crying," "filled with pain") and with a comment, an intellectualized title that freezes the affect ("it's sad," title of this picture: "desolation," "a desolate place expressing her feeling of desolation," "not really joyful, these pictures of yours") and shows their difficulty in mobilizing inner representations to describe the suffering of the person on the card. The depressive content reveals Patricia's intense narcissistic fragility, a poor self-image ("homeless man," "dislocated," "hump") in a nonsupportive environment ("a rather deserted place," "he could have found a better place to rest"). Although the

61

depressive affect is linked to this negative narcissistic image, she cannot elaborate a positive outcome. Peter shows major inhibition: His story is restricted to an esthetic commentary, reflecting a narcissistic defense that is effective by helping him to avoid painful feelings.

Conclusion

Even though the material of card 3BM does not explicitly represent an elderly person in a situation specifically addressing the concerns of old age, nonetheless its nature, both figurative and ambiguous, gives rise to the expression of a variety of issues and defense mechanisms. The responses give us an insight into whether it is possible for these men and women to mentally elaborate the experience of loss, link a representation of loss with an affect of sadness, and to imagine – or not – a solution enabling them to withstand and elaborate this painful experience. Growing up, becoming mature, and aging are all experiences that over and over again, in new and different ways, compel us to use our mental capacity to relinquish the mastery of the object, to recognize the difference between self and other, and to accept the risk of loss that goes with this recognition.

We must never forget that these persons too were once children, adolescents, and young adults, and that their past experiences of pleasure and pain, hope and disenchantment are still present in their mental lives. For this reason, we must be careful not to consider the elderly population as a homogeneous clinical entity whose mental characteristics and concerns would have nothing more to do with those of their past. The TAT is a valuable asset revealing mental fragilities and resources that sometimes remain unsuspected. Though apparently neutral and far removed from present concerns, the material masks latent contents related to major existential issues. As such, the TAT aids in understanding the depth and specificity of a person's mental functioning when confronted with a painful external reality, marked by the experience of loss.

References

Ames, L. B. (1960). Age changes in the Rorschach responses of a group of elderly individuals. *Journal of Genetic Psychology, 97,* 257–285.

Ames, L. B. (1966). Changes in the Rorschach response throughout the human life-span. *Genetic Psychology Monographs, 74,* 89–125.

Ames, L. B., Learned, J., Metraux, R. W., & Walker, R. N. (1954). *Rorschach responses in old age.* New York: Hoeber-Harper.

Anzieu, D., & Chabert, C. (1987), *Les méthodes projectives* [The projective methods]. Paris: PUF.

Baudin, M. (1998). La psychologie projective et les âges du milieu de la vie [Projective psychology and middle age]. In V. Boucherat-Hue (Ed.), *La psychologie projective en pratique professionnelle* (pp. 145–152). Paris: In-Press.

Baudin, M. (2001). Ménopause, Syndrome Sec: Approche métapsychologique et méthodologie projective [Menopause and Sjögren's syndrome: Metapsychological approach and projective methodology]. *Bulletin de Psychologie, 54,* 455, 563–572.

Baudin, M. (2005). Vieillir au féminin [Aging as a woman]. *Psychologie Clinique et Projective, 11,* 277–288.

Bellak, L. (1954). *TAT, CAT and SAT in clinical use* (4th edition, 1986). New York: Allyn & Bacon.

Bellak, L. (1990). The CAT and other projective techniques: 50 years later. *Rorschachiana, XVII,* 361–364.

Bellak, L., & Bellak, S. S. (1973). *Manual for the Senior Apperception Technique* (revised 1985, Transl. fr., Paris, ECPA, 1992). New York: C. P. S..

Bouisson, J. (2003), Etude des stratégies de vieillissement [A study of aging strategies]. *Psychologie Clinique et Projective, 9,* 457–474.

Brelet, F. (1986). *Le TAT. Fantasme et situation projective* [The TAT: Fantasy and the projective situation]. Paris: Dunod.

Brelet, F., & Chabert, C. (2003). *Nouveau manuel du TAT. Approche psychanalytique* [New TAT manual. Psychoanalytic approach]. Paris: Dunod.

Caldwell, B. McD (1954). The use of the Rorschach in personality research with the aged. *Journal of Gerontology, 9,* 316–323.

Chabert, C. (1983). *Le Rorschach en clinique adulte. Interprétation psychanalytique* (2nd éd., 1997) [The Rorschach test in clinical work with adults. Psychoanalytic interpretation, 2nd ed.]. Paris: Dunod.

Chabert, C. (1987). Rorschach et TAT: Antinomie ou complémentarité [Rorschach and TAT: Are they compatible or incompatible?]. *Psychologie Française, 32,* 141–144.

Chabert, C. (1998). *Psychanalyse et méthodes projectives* [Psychoanalysis and projective methods]. Paris: Dunod, coll. Les Topos.

Danon-Boileau, H. (2000). *De la vieillesse à la mort. Point de vue d'un usager* [From old age to death: A user's point of view]. Paris: Calmann-Levy.

Eisdorfer, C. (1963). Rorschach performance and intellectual functioning in the aged. *Journal of Gerontology, 18,* 358–363.

B. Verdon

Ferreira Novo, R., & Silva, D. (2002, September). *The expression of the late adulthood in Rorschach; singularity of the personality or specificity of the age?* Paper presented at the 17th International Congress of Rorschach and Projective Methods, Rome, Italy.

Fitzgerald, B.J., Pasewark, R.A., & Fleisher, S. (1974). Responses of an aged population on the gerontological and thematic apperception tests. *Journal of Personality Assessment, 38,* 234–235.

Foote, J., & Kahn, M.W. (1979). Discriminative effectiveness of the Senior Apperception Test with impaired and non-impaired elderly persons. *Journal of Personality Assessment, 43,* 360–364.

Freud, S. (1900). The interpretation of Dreams. *The standard edition of the complete psychological works of Sigmund Freud* (Vol. IV and Vol. V). London: Vintage, Hogarth Press, and the Institute of Psycho-Analysis.

Gilbert, J., & Hall, M. (1962). Changes with age in human figure drawing. *Journal of Gerontology, 17,* 397–404.

Golse, B. (2009). Le concept de neuro-psychanalyse. Avantages, désavantages et problématiques [The concept of neuro-psychoanalysis. Advantages, drawbacks and issues]. In L. Ouss, B. Golse, N. Georgieff, & D. Widlöcher (Eds.), *Vers une neuropsychanalyse?* (pp. 79–128). Paris: Odile Jacob.

Grossman, C., Warshawsky, F., & Hertz, M. (1951). Rorschach studies of personality characteristics of a group of institutionalized old people, *Journal of Gerontology, 6*(Suppl. 97), 3 (abstract).

Hayslip, B. (1981). Verbosity and projective test performance in the aged. *Journal of Clinical Psychology, 37,* 662–666.

Hayslip, B. (1982). The Holtzman Inkblot technique and aging: Norms and factor structure. *Journal of Personality Assessment, 46,* 248–256.

Hayslip, B., & Lowman, R.L. (1986). The clinical use of projective techniques with the aged. A critical review and synthesis. *Clinical Gerontologist, 5,* 63–93.

Holt, R.R. (1961). The nature of TAT stories as a cognitive product. In J. Kagan & G.S. Lesser (Eds.), *Contemporary issues in thematic apperceptive methods* (pp. 3–43). New York: C.C. Thomas.

Klopfer, W.G. (1946). Personality patterns of old age. *Rorschach Research Exchange, 10,* 145–166.

Klopfer, W.G. (1974). The Rorschach and old age. *Journal of Personality Assessment, 38,* 420–422.

Kökenek, Y., Degirmenci, R., Kübra Kanar, H., & Ikiz, T. (2008, July). *Evaluation of Rorschach protocols of elderly with dementia.* Paper presented at the 19th International Congress of Rorschach and Projective Methods, Leuven, Belgium.

Laforestrie, R., & Missoum, G. (1977). *Test projectif pour personnes agées* [Projective Test for Old People]. (LMPA), Etablissements d'Applications Psychotechniques, Issy Les Moulineaux, France, 1983.

Laplanche, J., & Pontalis, J.B. (1967). *Vocabulaire de la psychanalyse* [The language of psychoanalysis]. Paris: PUF.

Lavallée, F. (1999, July). *Le conte comme moyen d'évaluation psychologique auprès d'une clientèle âgée. Une analyse exploratoire* [Tales used as a psychological test for older adults. An exploratory research]. Poster presented at the 16th International Congress of Rorschach and Projective Methods, Amsterdam, The Netherlands.

Lawton, M. P., Whelihan, W., & Belsky, J. (1980). Personality tests and their uses with older adults. In J. E. Birren & B. Floant (Eds.), *The handbook of mental health and aging* (pp. 537–553). New York: Printed Hall.

Light, B. H., & Amick, J. H. (1956). Rorschach responses of normal aged. *Journal of Projective Techniques, 20,* 185–195.

Mattlar, C. E., Carlsson, A., Forsander, C., Karppi, S. L., & Helenius, H. (1992) Rorschach and Old Age: Personality characteristics for a group of physically fit 80-year-old men. *British Journal of Projective Psychology, 37*(2), 41–51.

Mattlar, C. E., Knuts, L. R., & Virtanen, E. (1985). Personality structure of the Rorschach for a group of healthy 71-year-old females and males. *Projective Psychology, 30,* 3–8.

Mercer, M. (1973). Review of the Gerontological Apperception Test. *Journal of Personality Assessment, 37,* 396–397.

Murray, H. A. (1943). *Thematic Apperception Test.* Cambridge, MA: Harvard University Press. (Fr. transl., Paris, Centre de Psychologie Appliquée, 1950).

Muzio, E. (1999, July). *The utility of the Rorschach in the neuropsychological assessment of suspected dementia.* Paper presented at the 16th International Congress of Rorschach and Projective Methods, Amsterdam, The Netherlands.

Muzio, E. (2002, September). *Neuropsychological correlates of selected comprehensive system Rorschach variables in a geriatric population.* Paper presented at the 17th International Congress of Rorschach and Projective Methods, Rome, Italy.

Muzio, E., & Luperto, L. (1999). Démence et fonctionnement de la personnalité à travers le Rorschach chez un groupe de femmes âgées hospitalisées [Dementia and personality functioning through the Rorschach in a group of hospitalized elderly women]. *Revue Européenne de Psychologie Appliquée, 49,* 227–236.

Nihashi, N., & Kosaka, K. (2002, September). *A Rorschach test research in dementia of Alzheimer type.* Paper presented at the 17th International Congress of Rorschach and Projective Methods, Rome, Italy.

Oberleder, M. (1967). Adapting current psychological techniques for use in testing the aged, *The Gerontologist, 7,* 188–191.

Orme, J. E. (1955). Intellectual and Rorschach test performances of a group of senile dementia patients and a group of elderly depressives. *Journal of Mental Science, 202,* 863–870.

Overall, J. E., & Gorham, D. R. (1972). Organicity versus old age in objective and projective test performance. *Journal of Consulting and Clinical Psychology, 39,* 98–105.

Panek, P. E., Wagner, E. E., & Avolio B. J. (1978). Differences in hand test responses of healthy females across the life-span. *Journal of Personality Assessment, 42,* 139–142.

Panek, P. E., Wagner, E. E., & Kennedy-Zwergel, K. (1983). A review of projective test findings with older adults. *Journal of Personality Assessment, 47,* 562–582.

B. Verdon

Pasewark, R. A., Fitzgerald, B. J., Dexter, V., & Gangemi, A. (1976). Responses of adolescent, middle-aged, and aged females on the Gerontological and Thematic Apperception Tests. *Journal of Personality Assessment, 40,* 588–591.

Péruchon, M. (1990). Rorschach et TAT dans la maladie d'Alzheimer. Prolégomènes à une étude du processus démentiel [Rorschach and TAT in Alzheimer's disease. Introduction to a study of the dementia process]. *Bulletin de Psychologie, 44,* 398[?], 2–10.

Péruchon, M. (1994). *Le déclin de la vie psychique. Psychanalyse de la démence sénile* [The decline of mental life. A psychoanalytic view of senile dementia]. Paris: Dunod.

Péruchon, M. (2002). La névrose dans le grand âge à l'appui d'épreuves projectives [Neurosis among the very old, studied through projective tests]. *Cahiers de Psychologie Clinique, 18*(1), 45–56.

Plutchik, R., Conte, H., Weiner, M., & Teresi, J. (1978). Studies of body image: IV. Figure drawings in normal and abnormal geriatric and nongeriatric groups. *Journal of Gerontology, 33,* 68–75.

Poitrenaud, J., & Moreaux, C. (1975). Réponses données au test de Rorschach par un groupe de sujets âgés, cliniquement normaux. Analyse quantitative des protocoles en fonction de l'âge [Responses to the Rorschach test in a group of clinically normal elderly subjects]. *European Review of Applied Psychology, 25,* 267–284.

Prados, M., & Fried, E. G. (1947). Personality structure of the older age groups. *Journal of Clinical Psychology, 3,* 113–120.

Rausch de Traubenberg, N. (1970). *La pratique du Rorschach* [Using the Rorschach Test]. Paris: PUF.

Rorschach, H. (1921). *Psychodiagnostik* [Psychodiagnostics]. Bern: Huber.

Schafer, R. (1958). How was this story told?, *Journal of projective techniques, 22,* 181–210.

Schafer, R. (1967). *Projective testing and psychoanalysis.* New York: International University Press.

Schroth, M. (1978). Sex and generational differences in Senior Apperception Technique projections. *Perceptual and Motor Skills, 47,* 1299–1304.

Shentoub, V. (1973). A propos du normal et du pathologique dans le TAT [Study on the normal and pathological in the TAT]. *Psychologie Française, 18,* 251–259.

Shentoub, V. (1987). Thematic Apperception Test (TAT), théorie et méthode [The TAT, theory and method]. *Psychologie Française, 32,* 117–126.

Shentoub, V. (1990). *Manuel d'utilization du TAT - approche psychanalytique* [TAT Manual, a psychoanalytic approach]. Paris: Dunod.

Shentoub, V., & Debray, R. (1970–1971). Fondements théoriques du processus-TAT [Theoretical fundamentals of the TAT process]. *Bulletin de Psychologie, XXIV*(292), 12–15, 897–903.

Shentoub, V., & Shentoub, S. A. (1960). Recherche expérimentale et clinique du thème "banal" dans le TAT [Clinical and experimental research on the "common response" theme in the TAT]. *Psychiatrie de l'Enfant, 3,* 405–524.

Shimonaka, Y., & Nakazato, K. (1991). Aging and terminal changes in Rorschach responses among the Japanese elderly. *Journal of Personality Assessment, 57*(1), 10–18.

Starr, B. D., & Weiner, M. B. (1979). *The Projective Assessment of Aging Method (PAAM)*. New York: Springer Publishing.

Starr, B. D., & Weiner, M. B. (1993). The Projective Assessment of Aging Method (PAAM) in clinical practice. *Clinical Gerontologist, 12*(4), 69–80.

Stock, N. A., & Kantner, J. E. (1980). Themes elicited by the Senior Apperception Test in institutionalized older adults. *Journal of Personality Assessment, 44*, 600–602.

Tardivo, L. (2008, July). *Estudio de validez del Senior Apperception Test en ancianos de la ciudad de São Paulo: Datos iniciales* [Validation of the senior apperception test in older people of the city of Sao Paulo: First results]. Communication in the XVI International Congress of Rorschach and Projective Methods, Leuven, Belgium.

Traxler, A., Swiener, R., & Rogers, B. (1974). Use of the Gerontological Apperception Test (GAT) with community-dwelling and institutional aged. *The Gerontologist, 14*, 52 (abstract).

Vázquez, N., & Osuna, M. (2002, September). *Entendiendo los diferentes procesos de envejecimiento a través de los indices de Rorschach* [Different processes of aging through the Rorschach indices]. Paper presented at the 17th International Congress of Rorschach and Projective Methods, Rome, Italy.

Vázquez, N., Hierro, D., & Tomas, I. (1999, July). *El Rorschach en pacientes de Alzheimer: Peculiaridades del discurso y errores lingüísticos* [The Rorschach among patients with dementia of the Alzheimer type: Peculiarities of speech and linguistic errors]. Poster presented at the 16th International Congress of Rorschach and Projective Methods, Amsterdam, Netherlands.

Verdon, B. (2003). Le traitement des affects dépressifs dans le fonctionnement narcissique à l'épreuve du vieillissement. Apports de la méthodologie projective [The treatment of depressive affects in narcissistic functioning facing old age. The input of projective methods]. *Bulletin de Psychologie, LVI*, 467, 655–665.

Verdon, B. (2004a), Traitement narcissique de la perte dans la névrose. Observations dans la clinique projective de la femme vieillissante [Narcissistic treatment of loss in neurosis. Observations in projective clinical work with aging women]. *Psychologie Clinique et Projective, 10*, 315–337.

Verdon, B. (2004b), Souffrance névrotique chez le sujet vieillissant [Neurotic suffering in aging subjects]. *Cahiers de Psychologie Clinique, 23*(2), 35–57.

Verdon, B. (2005). Diversité de traitement des affects dépressifs chez l'adulte vieillissant rencontré en "consultation mémoire" [Diversity of processing of depressive affects among aging adults seen in the context of "Memory consultations"]. *Dementiæ, 15*, 186–192.

Verdon, B. (2007a). Diversité psychopathologique dans la clinique de la plainte mnésique de l'adulte vieillissant [Psychopathological diversity of memory complaints among aging adults]. *Psychologie et Neuropsychiatrie du Vieillissement, 5*, 209–223.

Verdon, B. (2007b). Actualité du sexuel chez l'adulte âgé. Réflexions à partir de la clinique projective [The current sexual reality of the aging adult. Reflections

B. Verdon

based on clinical practice with projective tests]. *Bulletin de Psychologie, LX*, 490, 309–321.

Verdon, B. (2009). Le corps âgé. Dynamisme et fragilité des destins pulsionnels à l'épreuve du vieillissement [The aging body. The dynamism and fragility of drives when confronted with aging]. *Psychologie Clinique et Projective, 15*, 119–143.

Verdon, B., & Duplant, N. (2006). Masochisme et angoisse de perte de l'objet. Figure de la psychopathologie de la plainte mnésique [Masochism and object-loss anxiety. An aspect of the psychopathology of memory complaints]. *Psychologie Clinique et Projective, 12*, 119–154.

Viala, F., & Chu, P. T. (1999, July). *Particularités du fonctionnement intellectuel chez les patients déments: Évaluation à l'aide du psychodiagnostic de Rorschach* [Specificity of the intellectual functions of patients suffering from dementia: Results of the Rorschach psychodiagnosis). Poster presented at the 16th International Congress of Rorschach and Projective Methods, Amsterdam, The Netherlands.

Wolk, R. L., & Wolk, R. B. (1971). *The Gerontological Apperception Test*. New York: Behavioral Publications.

Wolk, R. L., Rustin, S. L., & Seiden, R. A. (1966). A custom-made projective technique for the aged: The Gerontological Apperception Test. *Journal of the Long Island Consultation Center, 4*, 8–21.

Benoît Verdon
Laboratoire de Psychologie Clinique et de Psychopathologie (EA 4056)
Université Paris Descartes – Institut de Psychologie
71, avenue Edouard Vaillant
92100 Boulogne-Billancourt
France
Tel. +33 1 5520-5893
Fax +33 1 5520-5956
E-mail benoit.verdon@parisdescartes.fr

Summary

Since the 1950s, the growing interest among clinicians to use projective tests to study normal or pathological aging processes has led to the creation of several thematic tests for older adults, in addition to existing research based on the Rorschach. The creation of these tests reflects their authors' belief that the TAT is not adapted to the concerns and anxieties of elderly persons. The new material thus refers explicitly to situations related to age; it aims to enable older persons to express needs they cannot otherwise verbalize during consultations.

The psychodynamic approach to thematic testing is based on the differentiation between the manifest and latent contents of the pictures, eliciting a response linked to mental processes and issues of which the respondent is unaware. The cards do not necessarily have to show aging characters to elicit identification: The situations shown in the pictures are linked to loss, rivalry, helplessness, and renunciation, issues elderly respondents can identify with and which lead them to express their psychic fragilities and resources. The article first explains the principles underlying four of these thematic tests (GAT, SAT, LMPA, and PAAM), and then develops several examples of stories told for card 3BM of the Thematic Apperception Test by male and female respondents aged 63 to 93. This is meant to show the effectiveness of this tool for the understanding and differentiation of loss-related issues facing older people.

Résumé

Depuis les années 1950, plusieurs épreuves thématiques ont été créées pour la population des adultes âgés. Cela témoignait de l'attention portée par les cliniciens utilisant les épreuves projectives à la clinique du vieillissement normal et pathologique, en associant des tests thématiques aux recherches déjà existantes avec le Rorschach. Parce qu'ils jugent les images du TAT peu pertinentes pour appréhender les préoccupations et les angoisses inhérents à la vieillesse, les auteurs de ces tests ont établi un matériel montrant de façon répétée et explicite des images de personnes âgées placées dans des situations réelles que l'on sait être souvent attachées au grand âge. Les tests sont alors notamment envisagés comme permettant d'accéder à des besoins que les sujets ne verbalizent pas en entretien.

L'approche psychodynamique des tests thématiques veille à différencier le contenu manifeste des images et le contenu latent qui sollicite le sujet vis-à-vis de problématiques et de processus psychiques qui lui échappent. Ainsi, nul besoin d'images d'adultes âgés sur les planches pour que le sujet âgé puisse quand même s'identifier aux personnages et déployer les ressources et les fragilités psychiques qui sont les siennes face à des problématiques de perte, de rivalité, d'impuissance et de renoncement. Après avoir rappelé les principes de quatre tests thématiques (GAT, SAT, LMPA et PAAM), cet article expose diverses histoires racontées à la planche 3BM du TAT par des femmes et des hommes âgés de 63 à 93 ans, afin de montrer l'intérêt majeur de cet outil pour ap-

B. Verdon

préhender et différencier les problématiques de perte auxquelles peuvent être confrontées les personnes qui vieillissent.

Resumen

A partir de la década de los 50, varias pruebas temáticas han sido específicamente creadas para el adulto mayor, indicando el interés que representaba, para los clínicos que utilizan las pruebas proyectivas, la clínica del envejecimiento normal y patolügico y la asociaciün de tests temáticos a las investigaciones ya existentes respecto del Rorschach. Considerando las imágenes del TAT poco pertinentes cuando se trata de captar las "inquietudes y ansiedades" inherentes a la vejez, los autores de estos tests han establecido un material que muestra, de manera reiterativa y explícita, imágenes de personas de edad en situaciones reales que sabemos asociadas, a menudo, a la edad avanzada. Estos tests son así vislumbrados como una manera de acceder a las "necesidades" que los sujetos no verbalizan durante la entrevista.

La aproximaciün psicodinámica de los tests temáticos tiene especial cuidado en diferenciar el contenido manifiesto de las imágenes y el contenido latente que solicita el sujeto ante problemáticas y procesos psíquicos que le escapan. Las imágenes de adultos mayores en las láminas resultan así innecesarias a la identificaciün a los personajes representados, pudiendo un sujeto de edad desarrollar tanto sus recursos como las fragilidades psíquicas que le son propias ante problemáticas de pérdida, de rivalidad, de impotencia y de renuncia. Luego de una revisiün de los principales principios de los cuatro tests temáticos (GAT, SAT, LMPA, PAAM), el presente artículo expone las diversas historias relatadas ante la lámina 3BM del TAT por mujeres y hombres que tienen entre 63 y 93 años, con el propüsito de mostrar el interés mayor de esta herramienta al momento de captar y diferenciar las problemáticas de pérdida a las que se pueden ver confrontadas las personas que envejecen.

1950年代以降、正常なあるいは病的な老化を研究するのに投映法を利用するという臨床家の関心の高まりは、すでにあるロールシャッハをベースとする研究に加えて、高齢の成人のためのいくつかの主題検査の創作を導いた。これらの検査の創作はこれらの制作者がTAT を高齢の人々の心配事や不安に採用できないという考えを持っていることを反映している。こうして新しい検査素材は年齢に関連した場面にと明確に触れている；このことは高齢者が診察の間には言語化することができない欲求をあらわすことを可能にすることを目的としている。主題検査に対する精神力動的な接近法は絵画に顕在的な内容と潜在的な内容の区別に基づいており、反応者の気が付いていない心的過程と問題に結びついている反応が引き出される。同一化を引き出すために、図版は必ずしも年をとっている人物を示している必要はない；絵の中に、喪失や競争、無力さ、放棄、などの高齢者が同一化することができ、彼らの心的な脆さや資質が表現されることを導く可能性のある状況が描かれている。本論文ではこれらの4つの主題検査（GAT、SAT、LMPA,PAAM）にみられる原則を解説し、63歳から93歳の男女によって TAT の3BM カードにおいて話された物語の例を紹介し、高齢者を理解するこの手段の有効性と、高齢者が立ち向かっている喪失に関連した問題の分類を示した。

Rorschachiana 32, 72–90
© 2011 Hogrefe Publishing

DOI: 10.1027/1192-5604/a000016

Original Article

The History and Development of the Rorschach Test in Turkey

Tevfika İkiz

Psychology Department, Istanbul University, Turkey

Abstract. The history of Turkish psychology, the cultural changes, and the rise of psychoanalysis have accompanied the development of Rorschach in Turkey. Yani Anastasiadis, the Turkish Rorschach pioneer, perceived Rorschach as "the radiography of human spirit." So the history of the Rorschach begins in 1943, and it became widely utilized in hospitals and clinical settings. Although in the 1950s statistical evaluation ruled, Anastasiadis continued his research and presented several articles at conferences and published many written articles. Today other approaches such as Exner's Comprehensive System and the currently used psychoanalytically oriented Rorschach, highly influenced by French schools, have emerged. The psychoanalytically oriented Rorschach system and the development of psychoanalysis in Turkey in general occurred at the same time, which is not a coincidence. The spread of psychoanalysis as well as the Rorschach test has been helped by a number of associations. The Society of Rorschach and Projective Tests was formed in 2003. Today, there are standardized Turkish norms of adults and adolescents, and several books have been published.

Keywords: Rorschach, psychoanalysis, Turkish Rorschach Society

The development of the Rorschach test in Turkey can be best understood by defining certain important axes: the history of Turkish psychology as well as both the social and cultural changes in Turkish society including the growth of psychoanalysis within the country. Understanding these points enlightens the current situation of the Rorschach test in Turkey. This article aims at understanding the use and development of the Rorschach test in Turkey within a historical perspective.

Turkish History and the History of Psychology

The Turkish Republic holds a strategic location and has been a bridge between Asia and Europe for many centuries. This geographical location has also greatly influenced the history of the country. Turkey is the continuation of the Ottoman Empire, which ruled much of the region from the 12th century until the establishment of the Turkish Republic in 1923. The Ottoman Empire ended with the establishment of the Turkish Republic by Gazi Mustafa Kemal Atatürk (1881–1938). It was the first Moslem nation to become a republic (Tunaboylu-İkiz, Pirim Düşgör, Yavuz, & Ertem-Vehid, 2008).

Throughout the latter years of the Ottoman Empire, the need to import scientific knowledge and the progress from the Western world aroused much discussion and controversy. Experts from Europe implemented the modernization of the army, the medical schools, and the engineering faculties. Positivistic thinking began gaining influence particularly through the efforts of German scientists. In 1915, within the context of this school of thought, 20 professors were invited from Germany to provide instruction in botany, anatomy, chemistry, and, in the person of Professor Anschütz, psychology. Wundt had founded his laboratory in 1879, and 36 years later, in 1915, the first experimental psychology laboratory was established in Istanbul (Arkonaç, 1995). The same year psychology was first taught under the guise of other disciplines. In 1917, the laboratories and the experimental psychology courses were delegated to the Philosophy Department at Istanbul University to be organized as a course. Over the following years, the university staff began to pay special attention to this field. As one remarkable example of the development in this field, we can mention that the Binet-Simon Intelligence scale was translated into Turkish before there was an American version!

At the end of the First World War, the Entente (French, Russia, and Great Britain) occupied much of Turkey. Professor Anschütz returned to his native country of Germany, and an eminent Turkish psychologist, Şekip Tunç, who had been trained at the Jean-Jacques Rousseau Institute in Geneva, returned to Istanbul and became head of the Psychology Department. He worked with Clapèrede and can be considered as the first Turkish psychologist. He also translated Freud and James from French (Bolak Boratav, 2004). He continued to work until 1933. By this time, The Ottoman Empire had been dismantled and Atatürk had established the Turkish Republic. The Entente powers had now left the country, and in 1933 university reforms accelerated. With the rise of the Nazis in Europe, a group of scientists took refuge in Turkey – among them Professor Wilhelm Peters formerly of Jena University in Germany. He came to Istanbul and founded an Applied Psychology Department at Istanbul University in 1937. In those years, Rorschach cards were already being imported and a private psychotechnical laboratory opened in Istanbul. Turkey benefited greatly by granting refuge to a number of German Jewish professors from several disciplines who had escaped the Nazis. Professor Peters remained head of the Psychology Department until 1952. At the same time, a Turkish psychologist, Dr. Mümtaz Turhan, who had been sent to Germany by the Turkish government in 1936, had completed his PhD under the Gestalt psychologist, Professor Max Wertheimer, and returned to Turkey and began to work at Istanbul University. He had already done a PhD under Sir Frederick Bartlett in Cambridge on "Culture Changes." The Department of Applied Psychology was opened under Dr. Turhan (Toğrol, 1972) in 1939; another important psychologist, Muzaffer Sherif, had, upon returning from the United States, created the first social psychology department at Ankara University (Bolak Boratav, 2004). Thus, these years were very productive for psychology – still mostly European in origin – in Turkey. In the 1950s, with the help of Fulbright scholarships and psychologists trained in the USA who returned to Turkey to live and teach, the impact of American psychology increased. New psychology departments opened in addition to those already existing at Istanbul and Ankara Universities (Bolak Boratav, 2004)

From the beginning students completed their studies by obtaining a degree granted after the preparation of a dissertation, in the several fields of psychology. For example, at Istanbul University the Applied Psychology Department was divided into two sections: general and experimental psychology. This system changed after 1980, with the growth of psychology and the addition of universities both state and private. There were now approximately 20 psychology departments, which granted degrees in psychology after a 4-year basic education and were readily available to students wishing to continue on to Master's and PhD programs.

The History of Personality Testing

The history of personality testing is relatively recent in Turkey. The development and standardization of adequate testing began in the early 1970s, leading to the publication of various tests. Between the early 1970s and the mid-1990s there were several translations and adaptations characterized by small sample sizes, usually the outcome of theses and dissertations. Psychological tests were becoming commonly used. Some of them were standardized – such as the MMPI, the State-Trait Anxiety Inventory, the WISC-R, and the NEO-PI-R. Other nonstandardized tests, such as the CAT (Children Apperception Test), the TAT, and Louisa Duss, were also being used after having been translated and adapted. The Binet-Simon Intelligence Test was one of the very first tests to be translated and standardized in 1915. Since then, several scales had been systematically developed, nearly all of which were standardized by academics working in various psychology departments around Turkey. Öner provides an extensive review of several psychological tests used in Turkey (Öner, 1994). The Turkish Psychological Association offers several training programs for professionals focusing on the WISC-R and the MMPI scales.

Unfortunately, standardization is a slow process, basically because of a lack of interest, as the majority of psychologists in Turkey belong more to the field of clinical psychology. Indeed, only a few psychologists are involved with the standardization of tests and psychometrics in general. Although well-known and widely used projective tests for children, such as the CAT and TAT, have now been translated and are currently used in Turkey, they have not yet been standardized.

Where Does the Rorschach Test Stand?

"The Rorschach test is the radiography of the human spirit." This phrase stems from the first Turkish Rorschach pioneer, Yani Anastasiadis. The history of Rorschach begins with him, a Turkish citizen of Greek origin. He was a student at Istanbul University, and in one of the seminars on "character disorders" he heard about a projective test called the Rorschach. In 1943, he found Hermann Rorschach's book in the library, but nobody in the psychology department could understand or translate German. As he spoke French Loose-Usteri's book "Manuel Pratique du test du Rorschach" (Practice Manual of the Rorschach Test) served to acquaint him with the technique.

In the 1940s as well as currently, psychology students were obliged to have hospital training. Therefore, he worked in one of the most important Turkish psychiatric hospitals, Bakırköy State Mental Hospital, during the following years. A very well-known Turkish psychiatrist, Prof. Mazhar Osman, (1881–1951) the founder of contemporary Turkish psychiatry and of the best-known Turkish psychiatric hospital in Istanbul (3000 beds), asked him to use the Rorschach Test with his paranoid patients. This was the beginning of Rorschach and Anastasiadis ordered Rorschach cards from the Applied Psychology Center in Paris. He worked with Rorschach until 1990. Anastasiadis prepared the first Turkish dissertation on Rorschach: "The Application of Rorschach to Certain Psychopathological Cases" (Anastasiadis, 1948).

From 1955 to 1960, Anastasiadis gave twice-weekly Rorschach training for psychologists in hospitals. In his courses, he tried to present the several different interpretations of Palem, Bohm, Beck, and Nina Rausch de Traubenberg. He worked at St. Anne hospital in Paris to improve his clinical experience. According to Anastasiadis, like an EEG, Rorschach is an effective instrument for showing brain dysfunction. He was also loyal to Hermann Rorschach's book and principles. His PhD thesis was also on Rorschach: "The Comparison of Rorschach, Bernreuter Test and Kent-Rosanoff Free Association Test on 100 Subjects" (Anastasiadis, 1954).

Why Rorschach Is Not as Appreciated as Other Instruments

In the psychology department, the work of Anastasiadis was not rejected – nor was it greatly appreciated. In the beginning Turkish academic circles did not show much interest for the Rorschach test, though Sabri Esat Siyavuşgil became interested in the cards. He was a psychology professor at İstanbul University and was also a painter. Experimental Psychology was so dominant in the 1940s and 1950s in Turkey that everything had come to be evaluated according to numerical and statistical values. This did not stop Anastasiadis from continuing his research on psychopathology and presenting articles at conferences. During this time, he also translated many other tests such as the CAT, TAT, Louisa Duss psychoanalytical stories, and many questionnaires.

Rorschach entered into many areas also outside university circles. Until 1980, a number of dissertations were prepared based on the Rorschach technique. Some examples are as follows; "Comparison of Rorschach and Other Tests of Psychopathology," "Normative Studies, Detail and Banalities," "The Application of the Rorschach and the Stanford-Binet to Families," "Comparison of Paranoid and Nonparanoid Patients with the Rorschach test," etc. (Bakır, 1984; Ebadi, 1988; Erden, Özaydın, Kireçi, & Taneli, 1987; Erdener, 2002; Gücer, 1992; Gürel, 1985; İnceer, 1982; Oğuzkaya, 1991; Oran, 1986; Torun, 1994; Üge, 1993; Yücel et al., 1998).

Practitioners used the translated Beizmann form for the Rorschach and adapted the methods of Hermann Rorschach without standardization. Psychologists applied the Rorschach test to a minimum of 5 patients a day at the psychiatric hospitals where a large amount of Rorschach materials was available in the cupboards (Tunaboylu-İkiz, 2001). Although the students worked with this method and prepared their dissertations, in the beginning there were no Rorschach courses at Turkish universities. This situation has now changed. The academic world gave secondary importance to projective methods, the growth of experimental psychology and the behavioral perspectives influenced many psychologists in Turkey. In addition, other assessment methods rather than the Rorschach are receiving greater academic acceptance, such as cognitive scales and attitude measurements.

Why was the Rorschach rejected in the beginning? Diagnosis and assessment matter – still an important issue in this domain – were controversially discussed in those days. For Turkey, as Bruce Smith pointed out, I believe there are two meanings of the term "diagnostic": One is classification and the other is analyzing the cause or nature of a situation, condition, or problem (Smith, 2009). So, for many years psychologists wanted simply to diagnose the patients according to the needs of psychiatrists and tried to match the Rorschach with categories from the Diagnostic and Statistical Manual of Mental Disorders (DSM). The result was not satisfactory, and they were considered unsuccessful; tests were just seen as instruments – not as therapeutic procedures or tools for understanding the inner world of human beings.

Clinicians trained by Anastasiadis were accepted to work in laboratories, and the traditional Rorschach applications were utilized. They presented their articles at national congresses. Their works included the following areas: "Drug and Alcohol Abuse Detected by Rorschach," "Psychosomatic Illnesses and the Rorschach Test," "Neurotic Disorders and the Specific Responses in Rorschach," "Psychoses and Family Interaction by Rorschach," "Comparison of Borderline Patients and the Normal Population with Rorschach." These studies were done through the medium of the translated Rorschach. No one had ever tried to standardize or validate this test. No Turkish books were published until 2000. Psychologists had ready-made "cookbook"-type interpretations of Rorschach protocols and tried to classify patients according to medical diagnoses. Moreover, they were forced by psychiatrists to use the Rorschach several times a day just to make sure that their own diagnoses were correct. From 1937 to 1996 many research articles on the Rorschach were published (Tunaboylu-İkiz, 2001). The results seemed very promising until it was realized that most of these articles were written by Yani Anastasiadis himself. The main difficulty is also derived from the assumption that a psychologist is only a tester. In the beginning university programs did not include projective training; psychologists did not have a very large spectrum of Rorschach training programs. Because Anastasiadis was the pioneer and tried to transmit his knowledge to his students, he founded the Turkish Psychological Association but unfortunately had no successor for a long time to provide training in the field. The Turkish Psychological Association prepared several training programs for professionals, but the major interest remained in the WISC-R and the MMPI scales and not in the Rorschach Test. There was an ambivalent position in the demand of psychologists: The tendency was more toward cognitive psychology so psychologists got cognitive psychology courses, but they did not complement their studies with Exner's Comprehensive System, which was available for their training programs. Now the situation has changed, there is a handbook for the Rorschach Comprehensive System written by a Turkish Psychologist, Dr. Abdülkadir Özer (1999).

Another Important Figure in Rorschach History: Neriman Samurçay

Another academic, this time from Ankara University, a professor named Neriman Samurçay, became interested in the Rorschach Test. She received her training in psychoanalytical psychotherapy in France from Daniel Lagache. She worked with Professor Zazzo at the Henri Rouselle Hospital and learned the interpretation of the Rorschach test in the style of Didier Anzieu, French School. Professor Samurçay was interested in Freud's writings on art, so she applied this test to Turkish painters and other artists.(Samurçay, 2002). Samurçay, who taught the Rorschach test to psychologists from different parts of Turkey, was interested in psychoanalysis. These different approaches developed separately, and no common work took place. One approach is completely numerical and statistical and the other remained outside the clinical fields. Samurçay believed that the reasons for the lack of transmission of Rorschach to the next generations lay in the lack of institutions, the "devalued position of psychologists in relation to psychiatrists in hospitals and the diagnostic oriented Rorschach reports" (Samurçay, 2009).

The Current Situation of the Rorschach Test

Dr. Emine Tevfika İkiz became interested in the Rorschach during her doctoral studies in psychoanalysis. In 1992, she was given the opportunity to follow a 2-year program on projective tests at the University of Paris-Descartes V. This allowed her to learn and use the psychoanalytically oriented French system. There is a difference between Anastasiadis's work, stemming from Beck, Palem, and Bohm and her Rorschach teaching program. His efforts to implant the Rorschach among psychologists were enormous, and many psychologists at Istanbul University Psychiatry Department's Test Laboratory continue to work with Anastasiadis's method. Anastasiadis wrote several articles, and his personal courses notes on the Rorschach are still used by psychologists in that laboratory – a place that still promotes Anastasiadis's way of coding and interpreting Rorschach.

The Exner Comprehensive System was introduced in Turkey by Professor Abdülkadir Özer. He wrote a two-volume book on Exner's System (Özer, 1999). Özer has given Rorschach training privately since 1997 and has taught the Rorschach Comprehensive System to his students in Master degree programs. Doğuş University Psychology Department is based on cognitive psychology, and the Comprehensive System approach is based on more experimental principles shared by experimental psychology.

The Transmission of Rorschach and Psychoanalysis: An Important Crossroad

Transmission is a very crucial issue in Turkey. The Ottoman Empire dominated this land until 1923. When the Turkish Republic was found-

79

ed, the language was cut off from its origins. The people no longer used the Ottoman alphabet, and for generations it was impossible to access the ancient texts. This disrupted the means of interpretation. For the interpretation of a piece of knowledge we need a language. A language cut off from its origins would no longer be comprehensible (Tunaboylu-İkiz, 1996).

The Rorschach Test had the same problem: If it is not interpreted via institutions and societies, it will not reach others. As Dr. Emine Tevfika İkiz's Rorschach certificate programs continued, she began her own personal analysis and PhD programs on psychoanalysis. Eventually she began to give Rorschach courses based on psychoanalytical theories and the French scoring system. This program lasts 2 years; the first year deals with the coding system, the second year with psychopathologies and their evaluation on the Rorschach. In addition, participants are introduced to Freudian psychoanalysis. If the Rorschach practitioners do not have any theoretical background, they cannot use this test effectively. Thus, developing psychoanalysis concurrently with the Rorschach test helps them in both respects.

The Development of Psychoanalysis in Turkey

Psychoanalysis and use of the Rorschach developed in Turkey at the same time. The psychoanalytical movement began in 1994. A small group of psychoanalysts, including the author of this article (French-speaking psychologists and psychiatrists), had completed their training in France and returned to Istanbul. This small group, supported by the French Psychoanalytic Association, was transformed into the Istanbul Psychoanalytical Society in 2004. The French Psychoanalytical Society (SPP) gave support to the Turkish group, and the group regularly invites French-training psychoanalysts and members of the Paris Psychoanalytical Society to Istanbul to enable the theoretical training of the members of the group and to give conferences for other colleagues interested in psychoanalysis. Moreover, conferences given by these colleagues were very successful and played a very important role in the expansion of psychoanalysis in Turkey. After these activities, many colleagues, both psychiatrists and psychologists alike, decided to start their own personal analysis. They were analyzed by the members of the first psychoanalyst generation of Turkey. It was the first time in Turkey that a psychoanalytical group was founded with the aim of associating with the International Psychoanalytical Association (IPA).

Rorschach Test Activities

The first Turkish-French Rorschach days were organized by Prof. Marianne Baudin from Paris 7 University and Professor İkiz in 2001. The first year's subject was "Neurosis" and "Psychosomatic Disorders and Their Translation into Rorschach" the following year. These conferences continued with subjects such as "Psychosis," etc. At the same time, Prof. Michèle Emmanuelli from Paris 5 University, France, participated in conferences in order to promote the study of Adolescence with the Rorschach. The psychoanalytically oriented Rorschach book was written by Dr. Emine Tevfika İkiz "The Rorschach and its Psychoanalytical Interpretation; Scoring and Application" (Tunaboylu-İkiz, 2001). The second volume of this book was published in 2002: "The Rorschach and its Psychoanalytical Interpretation; The Investigation of Adult Psychopathology" (Tunaboylu-İkiz, 2002). Since last year the author of this article has been directing several Master's and Doctoral theses dealing with the Rorschach test. Thus, great interest has arisen among clinical psychologists to work with projective methods in order to gain insight into psychopathologies.

The First Rorschach and Projective Tests Society

The Turkish Society of Rorschach and Projective Tests was founded in May 2003 and was accepted as a member of the ISR in 2004. It currently consists of 75 members who are all clinical psychologists, trained in the psychoanalytic interpretation of the Rorschach. The objectives of the society are to organize training programs on the Rorschach and other projective tests, and to enable psychologists from all over the country to learn and to readily apply these tests. Among the activities of the society are a 2-year program in the administration and psychoanalytic interpretation of the Rorschach. "Rorschach Nights" are planned once a month where a member of the society brings a case and study. An Annual Conference, the "Turkish-French Rorschach Days," organized by the members for the last 3 years, will continue to be held every December. The event focuses on the issues of psychoanalytic psychopathology and Rorschach. The society's annual journal publication is called "Yansıtma" (Projection)-Psychopathology and Projective Tests' published since 2004 (the first volume was on the subject of neuroses).

The society's activities are not restricted to the Rorschach Test. There are also the Fairy Tale Test (developed by Carina Coulacoglou and recently translated) and the Child Drawings Tests training programs for psychologists. Currently, two books have been published on the standardization of the Rorschach: Adolescent Form Responses (Tunaboylu-İkiz et al., 2007) and on Adult Form Responses (Tunaboylu-İkiz et al., 2009).

The First National Congress of Rorschach and Projective Tests

Among these developments, the first national congress was held in September 2009 at Istanbul University. This was an important event considering that, 60 years ago, the work of Anastasiadis on the Rorschach was rejected and considered not scientific enough. A total of 41 papers were presented, three panel sessions were held as well as 1-day workshop programs with 125 participants. Other topics were presented such as drawing tests, the Fairy Tale Test, and the TAT. The aim of the congress was primarily to gather psychologists in order to gauge the level of interest in this field.

Finally, it is hoped that more training programs in projective techniques will be offered by various Turkish universities in the future and that more research will be carried out using the Rorschach. Moreover, the Turkish Society aims to promote the use of projective methods in clinical psychology. The Rorschach and projective techniques in general have much to offer to Turkish psychologists.

References

Anastasiadis, Y. (1948). *Rorschach'nın şizofrenik ve paranoid kişiliklere uygulanması.* YayınlanmamışYüksek Lisans Tezi, İ. Ü., Psikoloji Bölümü, İstanbul [The application of Rorschach Test to schizophrenic and paranoid personalities. Unpublished masters thesis, Istanbul University, Psychology Department, Istanbul, Turkey].

Anastasiadis, Y. (1954). *100 hastada Rorschach-Bernreuter Testlerinin kar ı laştırılması.* İ.Ü., Psikoloji Bölümü, Doktora Tezi, İstanbul [The comparison of Rorschach-Bernreuter Test of 100 patients. Istanbul University, Psychology Department, Doctorate Thesis, Istanbul, Turkey].

Arkonaç, S. (1995). İstanbul üniversitesi psikoloji bölümü 80.yıl [Istanbul University, Psychology Department's 80th anniversary, Turkish Psychological Bulletin]. *Türk Psikoloji Bülteni*, 2, 91-95.

Bakır, R. (1984). *Ergenlik dönemine ilişkin Rorschach bulgularının klinik açıdan değerlendirilmesi,* Yayınlanmamış Yüksek Lisans Tezi, Ankara Üniversitesi, Sosyal Bilimler Enstitüsü, Ankara [The clinical assessment of Rorschach's findings in adolescence period, Unpublished masters thesis, Ankara University, Institue of Social Sciences, Ankara)].

Bolak Boratav, H. (2004). Psychology at the cross-roads: The view from Turkey. In M.J. Steven & D. Wedding (Eds.), *The handbook of international psychology.* New York: Brunner-Routledge.

Ebadi, G.H. (1988). *Psikososyal faktörlerin konversiyon reaksiyon üzerinde etkileri,* Yayınlanmamış Doktora Tezi, İ.Ü.Sağlık Bilimleri Enstitüsü, İstanbul [The effects of psychosocial factors on conversion reaction. Unpublished doctorate thesis, Istanbul University, Institute of Medical Sciences, Istanbul, Turkey].

Erden, G., Özaydın, Ş, Kireççi, Y., & Taneli, S. (1987). *Peptik ülserli hastaların MMPI, Rorschach ve Ev-Ağaç-İnsan Çizme Testleri ile incelenmesi.* XXIII. Ulusal Psikiyatri ve Nörolojik Bilimler Kongre Kitabı, 198-203 [The evaluation of MMPI, Rorschach and Draw a House-Tree-Person Tests' of peptic ulcer patients. Book of XXIII. National Psychiatry and Neurological Sciences Convention, 198-203].

Erdener, G.E. (2002). *Kurumda yaşayan korunmaya muhtaç çocuklarda Rorschach testinin kendilik algısı, duygulanım ve fikir yürütme boyutlarının incelenmesi.* Yayınlanmamış Yüksek Lisans Tezi, İ.Ü.Sosyal Bilimler Enstitüsü. İstanbul [The evaluation of Rorschach test's self-image, affection and reasoning dimensions among the children need to be protected and living in the institution. Unpublished masters thesis, Istanbul University, Institute of Social Sciences, Istanbul, Turkey].

Gücer, Z. (1992). *Bazı psikosomatik hasta gruplarının aleksitimi açışından araştırılması.* Yayınlanmamış Yüksek Lisans Tezi, Selçuk Üniversitesi Sosyal Bilimler Enstitüsü, Konya [The assessment of some psychosomatic patient groups in terms of alexithymia. Unpublished Master thesis, Selçuk University, Institute of Social Sciences, Konya, Turkey].

Gürel, Y. (1985). *Depresyon tanışı konan hastalarda Rorschach testi ile Hamilton ve Zung ölçeklerinin karşılaştırılması.* Doktora Tezi, İ.Ü.Sağlık Bilimleri Enstitüsü, İstanbul [The comparison of Rorschach Test verses Hamilton and Zung measurements among Depression patients. Doctorate thesis, I. U. Institute of Medical Sciences, Istanbul, Turkey]

Inceer, B. (1982). Obsesif Kompulsif bozukluk ve nevrotik depresyondaki Rorschach Psikodiagnostik test beklentileri [The expectation of Rorschach Psychodiagnostical Test for obsessive-compulsive disorder a and neurotic depression]. *Psikoloji Dergisi, 4*(16), 36–38.

Oğuzkaya, N. (1991). *Girişkenliği ortalamanın altında ve üstünde olan üniversite öğrencilerinde Rorschach Testi bulgularının karşılaştırılması.* Yayınlanmamış Yüksek Lisans Tezi, Erciyes Üniversitesi Sağlık Bilimleri Enstitüsü, Kayseri [The comparison of Rorschach Test findings among university students whose assertiveness level above the average and under the average. Unpublished masters thesis, Erciyes University, Institute of Medical Sciences, Kayseri, Turkey].

Oran, S. (1986). *31 Behçet Hastalığı olgusunda psikosomatik yönden yapılan tetkiklerin değerlendirilmesi.* Tıpta Uzmanlık Tezi, Sağlık Bakanlığı, İstanbul Şşli Etfal Eğitim ve Araştırma Hastanesi, İstanbul [The evaluation of psychosomatic examinations among 31 Behçet Patients, Medical Proficiency Thesis, Health Ministry, Istanbul Şişli Etfal Education and Research Hospital, Istanbul, Turkey].

Öner, N. (1994). *Türkiye'de kullanılan Psikolojik Testler: Bir başvuru kaynağı,* Boğaziçi Üniversitesi Yayınları, İstanbul [The psychological tests used in Turkey: A reference book. Edition Boğaziçi University, İstanbul].

Özer, K. (1999). *Rorschach: Bütünleyici (Exner) Sistemi.* Boğaziçi Üniversitesi Politika, Tarih, Psikoloji, Toplum Bilim Dizisi [Rorschach: The Comprehensive (Exner) System. Boğaziçi University, Politics, History, Psychology and Society Science Series].

Samurçay, N. (2002). Nadide Akdeniz'in resminde Adem ile Havva [In the picture of Nadide Akdeniz: Adam and Eve. Hurriyet Entertainment]. *Hürriyet Gösteri, Sanat Edebiyat Dergisi,* 234.

Samurçay, N. (2009) Geçmişten Günümüze Rorschach Testi ve Klinik Uygulamaları, 1.Ulusal Rorschach ve Projektif Testler kongresi, İstanbul [From past to now Rorschach Test and its clinical applications, I. National Rorschach and Projective Tests Congress, Istanbul, Turkey].

Smith, B (2009). *The Rorschach psychodiagnostic test: Diagnosing what?* I. Ulusal Rorschach ve Projektif Testler Kongresi, İstanbul [I. National Rorschach and Projective Tests Congress, Istanbul, Turkey].

Toğrol, B. (1972). Türk Psikoloji Tarihi. *Tecrübi Psikoloji Çalışmaları,* 15.

Torun, C.K. (1994). *Sakatlık geçiren bireysel mücadele sporcularında depresyon faktörünün araştır ılması.* Yayınlanmamış Doktora Tezi, Marmara Üniversitesi Sağlık Bilimleri Enstitüsü, İstanbul [The investigation of the depression factor among individual competing athletes who became crippled. Unpublished doctorate thesis, Marmara University, Institue of Medical Sciences, Istanbul, Turkey].

Tunaboylu-İkiz, T. (1996). *L'humor et la naissance de la psychanalyse en Turquie* [Humor and the birth of psychoanalysis in Turkey]. These du Doctorat, Université Paris 13, France.

Tunaboylu-İkiz, T. (2001). *Psikanalitik Yönelimli Rorschach Test: I, Kodlama ve Uygulamalar* [Psychoanalytically oriented Rorschach Test: 1, Coding and applications]. İstanbul: Bağlam.

Tunaboylu-İkiz, T. (2002, September). *Le fonctionnement psychique de patients atteints de psoriasis* [The mental functioning of patients with psoriasis]. XVII International convention of Rorschach and Projective Methods, Rome, Italy.

Tunaboylu-İkiz, T., Pirim Düşgör, B., Yavuz, E., & Ertem-Vehid, H. (2008). The application of fairy tale test in Turkey. In C. Conlacoglou (Ed.), *Exploring the child's personality: Developmental, clinical and cross-cultural applications of the Fairy Tale Test.* Springfield, IL, USA: Charles C Thomas.

Tunaboylu-İkiz, T., Pirim-Düşgör, B., Zabcı, N., Yavuz, A. E., Erdem-Atak, İ., Ataç, S., Alsancak-Sönmez, B., & Akkapulu, F. (2007). *Rorschach Kodlama Kitabı: Ergen Normları* [Rorschach coding book: Adolescents' norms]. Istanbul: Bağlam Yayınları.

Tunaboylu-İkiz, T., Erdem-Atak, İ., Pirim-Düşgör, B., & Zabcı, N., (2009). *Rorschach Kodlama Kitabı 2: Yetişkin Normları* [Rorschach coding book: Adults' norms]. Istanbul: Bağlam Yayınları.

Üge, B. (1993). *Agresivite ve empulsivite faktörlerinin suçluların şahsiyeti yapışındaki etkileri.* Yayınlanmamış Doktora Tezi, İ.Ü.Sağlık Bilimleri Enstitüsü, İstanbul [The effects of aggressiveness and impulsiveness in criminals' personality structure, Unpublished doctorate thesis, Istanbul University, Institute of Medical Sciences, Istanbul, Turkey].

Yücel, B., Turgay, M., Gürel, Y., Demir, K., Yılmazer, N., & Özkan, S. (1998). Irritable Barsak Sendromu ve Diabetes Mellitusta Aleksitiminin Değerlendirilmesi [The assessment of alexithymia in irritable bowel syndrome and diabetes mellitus]. *Istanbul Tıp Fakültesi Mecmuası, 61,* 1.

Tevfika İkiz
Psychology Department
Istanbul University
Ordu caddesi laleli
Istanbul
Turkey
Tel. +90 532 257-1940
E-mail tevfikai@yahoo.com

Summary

This paper presents the development in Turkey of the Rorschach test – one of the most important projective tests worldwide. The historical development of Turkey, the history of Turkish psychology, and the development of psychoanalysis are taken into consideration. After introducing Hermann Rorschach's *Psychodiagnostics* to Turkey, Yani Anastasiadis, one of the most prominent figures using the tests, translated the test, introducing and training psychologists in its use. The Rorschach Test has had a long and difficult journey within the Turkish psychology. It is essential to emphasize that, in the last period of the Ottoman Empire, movement toward modernization in all areas was supposed to have originated from the East instead of West, and this was seen in the area of psychology also. During the process that started with the establishment of an experimental psychology laboratory at Istanbul University in 1915, positivistic thought dominated in all areas. The growth of experimental psychology and behavioral perspectives influenced psychologists in Turkey, whereas the test was not approved enough at the university; because of the efforts of Yani Anastasisadis, administrators at the psychology laboratories in hospitals became the seeds of its development. In due course, awareness of psychoanalytically oriented Rorschach test in Turkey through efforts of the author of this paper and the introduction of the Exner method are considered as the significant points to its spread. Correspondingly, we take into account the development of psychoanalysis in Turkey. The rise of the psychoanalytic movement is connected to the French school. The pioneering efforts of the author in both the development of psychoanalysis and the administration of psychoanalytically oriented Rorschach Test in Turkey trace the formation of its transmission. The regular meetings and seminars organized by the administrators of the French Rorschach School after 2001 consolidated the transmission of the Rorschach Test that Yani Anastasiadis had started to administer and to teach since the 1940s. Today, the Rorschach has its own society and has achieved even greater acceptance with the first national conference held in September 2009 in Istanbul. With the standardization of the Rorschach test and the generation of Turkish norms, it is believed that this positive advancement of the test will gain more respect and it will be more extensively used.

Özet

Bu çalışmanın amacı dünyada kullanılan projektif testlerin en önemlilerinden biri olan Rorschach testinin Türkiye'deki gelişimini sunmaktır. Bunu yaparken Türkiye'nin tarihsel gelişimi, Türk psikoloji tarihi ve psikanalizin gelişimide dikkate alınmıştır. Ülkemizde Hermann Rorschach'nın *Psikodiagnostik* kitabından kısa bir süre sonra ilk Türk test uygulayıcılarından olan Yani Anastasiadis tarafından tanıtılan, tercüme edilen ve psikologlara öğretilen Rorschach testinin psikoloji dünyası içerisinde geçirdiği zorlu yolculuktan bahsedebiliriz. Burada öncelikle Osmanlı İmparatorluğunun son döneminde bilimsel bilgiyi almanın doğudan değil batıdan olacağına olan inançla her alandaki modernizasyon hareketinin psikoloji alanında da kendisini gösterdiğini belirtmek gerekir. 1915'de deneysel psikoloji labaratuarının İstanbul Üniversitesinde kurulmasıyla başlayan süreçte positivistik düşüncenin tüm alanlardaki hakimiyeti söz konusudur. Üniversitede fazla kabul görmeyen bu testin Anastasiadis'in çabalarıyla hastanelerin psikoloji labaratuarlarındaki uygulamaları ve çabaları günümüzdeki gelişimin ilk tohumlarıdır. Zaman içerisinde makalenin yazarı tarafından psikanalitik yönelimli Rorschach testinin Türkiye'ye girişi, yanı sıra Exner metodunun öğretilmeye başlaması Rorschach testinin gelişiminde önemli noktalar olmuştur. Bu gelişmelerle paralal olarak Türkiye'de psikanalizin gelişimini de dikkate almalıyız. Fransız ekolüne bağlı bir psikanaliz akımının yerleşmesi makale yazarının da hem psikanalizin gelişmesinde hemde psikanalitik yönelimli Rorschach testinin Türkiye'de uygulanmasında önayak olması iletimin oluşumu hakkında bilgi vermektedir. Fransız Rorschach Okulunun uygulayıcıların ın 2001 yılından itibaren düzenli toplantılar ve seminerler düzenlemeye başlamaları Yani Anastasiadis'in 1940'lardan itibaren Türkiye'de uygulamaya ve öğretmeye başladığı Rorschach testinin devamlılığı için iletinin oluşmasına neden olmuşlardır. Günümüzde dernekleşme noktasına gelen bu gelişme yakın tarihte yapılan ilk ulusal kongre ile daha kabul edilir, önem kazanan bir çerçeveye oturmuştur. Rorschach testinin standardize edilmesi, Türk normlarının oluşturulması ile bu olumlu gelişimin testin saygınlığının artmasına ve daha çok kullanılmasına neden olacağı düşünülmektedir.

Résumé

L'objectif de cette étude est de présenter l'évolution en Turquie du test de Rorschach qui est considéré dans le monde comme l'un des plus importants tests projectiles. De même, nous tracerons les grandes lignes du développement historique en Turquie en tenant compte de l'histoire de la psychologie turque et l'évolution de la psychanalyse. Nous traiterons du voyage périlleux que le test de Rorschach a réalisé dans le monde psychologique après que l'œuvre de Hermann Rorschach intitulé *Psychodiagnostique* ait été traduite, présentée et enseignée aux psychologues turcs par Yani Anastasiadis, l'un des premiers ayant appliqué le test en Turquie. Nous devons tout d'abord préciser que dans la dernière période de l'Empire ottoman, on pensait que la connaissance scientifique devait être empruntée de l'ouest et non de l'est, et cette conviction qui se faisait sentir dans tous les domaines de la modernization avait sa place également dans le mouvement de la psychologie. Suite au processus de mise en place d'un laboratoire de psychologie expérimentale à l'Université d'Istanbul en 1915, il nous était possible de parler de l'existence d'une domination de la pensée positiviste dans tous les domaines. La croissance de la psychologie expérimentale a eu une grande influence sur les psychologues turcs. Ce test qui à l'époque n'est pas admis dans les universités, grâce aux efforts d'Anastasiadis, est appliqué dans les laboratoires psychologiques des cliniques et ainsi a pu se développer jusqu'à nos jours. Avec le temps, l'introduction en Turquie du test de Rorschach à caractère psychanalytique par l'auteur de cet article et l'enseignement de la méthode Exner ont nettement contribué à l'évolution du test de Rorschach. En parallèle à cette évolution, nous devons porter attention au développement de la psychanalyse en Turquie. Ce courant de psychanalyse appartenant à l'école française qui s'est instauré en Turquie, a non seulement contribué au développement de la psychanalyse mais aussi a permis à l'auteur de cet article d'appliquer le test de Rorschach. L'organization régulière depuis 2001 de réunions et de séminaires par les praticiens de l'école française du test de Rorschach, a permis la continuité et la transmission des travaux d'Anastasiadis qui, déjà en 1940 appliquait et enseignait le test de Rorschach en Turquie. Suite à cette évolution qui a permise d'égaler les travaux effectués dans ce domaine avec ceux en Europe, et grâce au congrès qui a été réalisé dernièrement, l'importance de ce test est désormais reconnue. Cependant avec la standardization du test et l'élaboration des normes turques, cette évolution concernant le test du Rorschach augmentera la notoriété du test et multipliera l'application de celui-ci en Turquie.

Resumen

El objetivo de este trabajo es presentar el desarollo de la prueba de Rorschach en Turquia, la cual es una de las pruebas proyectivas de mayor uso en el mundo. En este trabajo hemos tenido en cuenta la evolucion historica del pais, igual que la historia de la psicologia y la del psicoanalisis. Después de la publicacion del libro *Psicodiagnostico* de Hermann Rorschach, Yani Anastasiadis, una de las figuras prominentes en el uso de la prueba, lo tradujo en turco y lo introdujo en la practica de los psicologos. Aqui hay que senalar que en el ultimo periodo del imperio otoman predominaba la creencia en el poder del occidente en tanto autoridad y fuente principal del conocimiento cientifico. Esta creencia fue valida también para el campo de la psicologia, en donde se manifesto el movimiento de modernizacion. A partir de 1915, fecha de creacion del laboratorio de psicologia experimental en la Universidad de Istanbul, el pensamiento positivista ejercio su influencia en todas las esferas del conocimiento. El desarrollo de la psicologia experimental y las perspectivas behavioristas marcaron los psicologos en Turquia. La prueba de Rorschach, que no habia sido aceptada en la Universidad, fue practicada en los laboratorios de los hospitales, gracias a los esfuerzos de Anastasiadis. Asi éste pudo echar las semillas de su actual desarrollo. Junto al uso por parte de la autora del articulo, de la prueba de Rorschach desde la perspectiva psicoanalitica, la ensenanza del método Exner fue importante en el desarrollo de la prueba. Igualmente habria que tomar en consideracion el desarrollo del psicoanalisis en Turquia. El hecho de que un movimiento psicoanalitico asociado con la escuela frances de psicoanalisis fuera establecido, permitio a la autora de jugar un papel de avanguardia en el desarrollo del psicoanalisis y en la aplicacion de la prueba de Rorschach con orientacion psicoanalitica, lo cual demuestra a su vez la fuerza de transmision. El hecho de que a partir de 2001 las personas aplicando el método de la Escuela Francesa de Rorschach fueran presentando con cierta regularidad seminaries y reuniones, constituyo el eslabon que permitio la continuidad de su uso desde los anos '40, en que Yani Anastasiadis la practicaba y la ensenaba. La prueba de Rorschach ha atravesado un largo y dificil viaje en Turquia. Pero actualmente cuenta con una asociacion y ha tenido aun mayor aceptacion en el primer congreso nacional, celebrado en septiembre 2009 en Istanbul. Por medio de la adaptacion de la prueba a las normas en Turquia, creemos que esteadelanto positivo recibira mayor acceptacion y extension.

本論文の目的は世界的に用いられている最も重要な投映法のひとつであるロールシャッハ・テストのトルコにおける発展を示すことにある。トルコにおける歴史的な発展に関しては、トルコの心理学の歴史や精神分析の発展を考慮に入れることができる。Hermann Rorschach の"心理診断法"の紹介ののち、この検査を利用していた最も重要な人物の一人である Yani Anastasiadies がこの検査法を翻訳して、心理学者に紹介し、彼らの訓練を行った。ロールシャッハ・テストはトルコ心理学において長い苦難の旅をしてきたと言える；ここではオスマン帝国の最後の時期にあたり、あらゆる領域における近代化が支持されて東洋から西洋への変化が始まっており、これは心理学の領域でも見られたということを強調することが重要である。1915 年にイスタンブール大学に実験心理学研究室が設立されたのを始まりとする経過の中で、あらゆる領域において実証主義の考え方が有力であった。実験心理学と行動主義の考え方はトルコの心理学者に影響を与えた、一方、検査は大学では十分に認められず、Yani Anastasiadies の尽力により病院の心理学研究室の検査施行者たちがこの発展の起源となった。やがて、本論文の著者による、精神分析的な志向性を持ったロールシャッハ・テストがトルコに接近してきたことと、Exner の方法の紹介が、この検査法の進歩おいて重要なポイントであったと考えられている。同様に、我々はトルコにおける精神分析の発展も考慮しておく必要がある。精神分析の進展の始まりはフランスの学派と関連している。そこでは、トルコにおける精神分析の発展と精神分析的な方向性をもったロールシャッハの施行の両方においての著者の開拓する努力は伝道することを定式化すための情報を提供した。2001 年以降フレンチロールシャッハスクールの施行者によって組織化された定例の会合とセミナーは 1940 年代に Yani Anastasiadies が施行し始め、教え始めたロールシャッハ・テストの進化を伝道することのできる体制の設立につながった。今日、ロールシャッハはその学会を有しており、国内の最初の学会大会を 2009 年 9 月にイスタンブールでの開催を受け入れることを達成した。ロールシャッハ・テストの標準化とトルコの基準の生成することに関して、この検査法の実証的な進化がより敬意を獲得し、この検査が幅広くもちいられるであろうことが確信されている。

Rorschachiana 32, 91–116
© 2011 Hogrefe Publishing

DOI: 10.1027/1192-5604/a000017

Case Study

Rorschach Assessment of Parenting Capacity
A Case Study

Kari S. Carstairs

Carstairs Psychological Associates Ltd., Bromley, Kent, UK

Abstract. A case example of a mother who neglected her children is presented using two administrations of the Rorschach following the Comprehensive system, one before and one after treatment. Before treatment, the mother presented with limited coping skills as measured by the Coping Deficit Index and a very strong tendency to avoid complexity and deny ambiguity as measured by the Rorschach variable, Lambda. The case example raises some questions about the significance of these two Rorschach variables in parents who neglect their children. Preliminary findings for 52 such parents from the author's case files are given.

Keywords: Rorschach, parenting, child neglect

The assessment of parenting capacity in cases in which there are child protection concerns requires a full investigation of a wide range of factors.

Although the Rorschach does not assess parenting per se, many of the personality variables that it covers have implications for parenting, such as the level of adjustment, frustration tolerance, and impulsivity (Barton Evans & Schutz, 2008; Erard, 2005; Weiner, 2005). Some research also links Rorschach findings with various aspects of parenting (Johnston, Walters, & Olesen, 2005). These authors rightly advise that we cannot *predict* parenting behavior from Rorschach data on its own, though the data do provide a rich source of information that can help to confirm the clinical picture.

Furthermore, the Rorschach offers a window into the parent's personality functioning which is not dependent on self-report. It is therefore a useful complement to self-report measures.

In this article, I present a case study of one mother whom I assessed twice, once before treatment and then afterward. I then offer some preliminary data on a group 52 parents whom I have assessed for the courts in cases where there was evidence of child neglect. In all cases, the Rorschach was administered according to the Comprehensive system (Exner, 2003).

Caveat:

This case contains clinical data. In order to preserve confidentiality, I have changed several details and omitted many others but I have tried to ensure that key themes remain.

Background of the First Protocol

The patient is a mother of two boys aged 5 years and 9 years. She was referred to me in the context of child protection concerns after she had had a psychiatric assessment. The psychiatrist considered that she presented with a personality disorder and requested psychometric assessment of her personality functioning to provide further information in relation to treatment planning.

When I first saw her, she was aged 36 years. She was an unemployed single mother, the father of the children having left the family home when the youngest boy was still an infant. Their relationship was stormy but there was no domestic violence as such. The father had drifted apart from his boys and did not maintain contact, having established a new family with another partner.

The child-protection concerns concerned the presentation of the boys, who would often arrive at school in dirty clothes, smelling unwashed, and sometimes they were hungry. Attendance at school was also poor. Social services became involved when the mother went into hospital without making adequate arrangements for the children. Her own mother then stepped in to care for the boys.

When the social worker interviewed the mother, the latter spoke in a disjointed way, avoiding eye contact, shifting from one topic to another. The mother said that she had insomnia and was taking medication for this. Sometimes she overslept so the boys missed school. There was no psychiatric history and no previous psychotherapy.

During the first interview with me, she was quite agitated, angry, and upset, and I had to work hard to get her to focus on the issues because she tended to digress. The children had remained with her mother, and she was very critical of her mother's care. She was also very angry with social services.

We completed a range of psychometric tests, including the Rorschach. Her intellectual functioning was in the average range, and she recalled enjoying school, obtaining two "A" levels though she did not go onto further education because she preferred to start earning an income. She had worked in a local department store. She did not report any history of traumatic events in childhood.

I asked her about psychotherapy, and she was annoyed by the question, saying that the only reason the children were placed with her mother was because of the operation. She had gone to have elective cosmetic surgery because she wanted to feel better about herself. The operation had improved her appearance and she did not consider that she had any psychological problems.

The Rorschach protocols are given in Appendix A and Appendix B. Both protocols were scored by a second psychologist experienced in the Comprehensive system; the following percentage agreements were found: For Location, Developmental Quality, Form Quality, and Contents there was 100% agreement; for Determinants, there was 94% agreement, and for Special Scores there was 87% agreement.

Interpretation of the First Protocol

She has limited coping resources (CDI = 4, EA = 2.0), but she is probably in a stable state (D = 0, AdjD = 0) because she keeps stressful experiences to a minimum (Lambda = 5.0). She has a very strong tendency to avoid complexity and deny the presence of ambiguity.

Given her avoidant style, she is about as willing as other adults (Afr = 0.50) to process emotional stimulation. Her only color response is CF, which suggests that, when she does express her feelings, she may do so in a more intense manner than most adults.

She probably has low self-esteem ($3r + (2)/R = 0.06$) and may compare herself unfavorably to others. Her self-awareness may be limited (no FD or Vista), which may then result in adjustment problems. She is unusually preoccupied with and/or concerned about her body and bodily functions (An + Xy = 4). In this regard, it is noteworthy that one of these responses (no. 6) is a form quality minus and includes a DVd, one (no. 8) is form quality unusual, and one (no. 16) includes a DR and a FAB-

93

COM1. This is consistent with the history where she chose to go to hospital for elective cosmetic surgery, leaving the children without adequate care.

Response no. 11 is also relevant as it contains a MOR and the content is of a monster without a body, thereby drawing attention to the body by its absence. Her other MOR response is no. 18, which is also form quality minus and a FABCOM1 indicating the presence of some projection. This butterfly with bits missing wearing little pixie shoes makes me think of how she wanted to look "pretty" and went about this in a way that neglected the reality demands of her children's needs.

Her social skills are limited, and she may present as helpless or inept, with some insensitivity to the needs of others (CDI = 4). She may be conservative in close relationships, she may be cautious about getting close to others, and she may be concerned about having her own personal space (T = 0). She appears to have some interest in other people, but she probably does not understand them very well (Human content = 4, Pure H = 0). Her interpersonal behavior may be ineffective (GHR:PHR 2:2), and she does not anticipate positive interactions with others, probably feeling uncomfortable in interpersonal situations (COP = 0, AG = 0).

It is interesting to see that response no. 4 is a mask. This may relate to a tendency to present a façade in social situations, keeping her true feelings to herself, and/or it may connect with her self-image and her decision to have cosmetic surgery. Response no. 5 is a part human response. The sharp stiletto heel suggests both an interest in being fashionable and also possibly some aggression toward others that is expressed indirectly. Responses no. 7 and 11 are both monsters, one with a missing body (see above).

Her cognitive mediation is generally good (XA% = 0.78, WDA% = 0.75 – referring to the international norms). There are times when her perceptual accuracy falters, but this does not occur more often than is found in the average adult (X-% = 0.22 – referring again to the international norms of an average X-% of 0.19 with an sd of 0.11). The form quality minus responses occur in relation to Xy (see above) and in relation to her only M response, suggesting the possibility of flawed thinking and logic (see below). In straight forward situations, she is aware of the socially expected, conventional response (P = 5).

Her thinking is seriously disturbed (R = 18 and WSUM6 = 24). She is likely to make some very poor judgments and show some disorganized, inconsistent trains of thought leading to ineffective behavior in her daily life.

Other Test Data

In addition to the Rorschach, I administered two self-report measures of personality traits. The first one was the Millon Clinical Multiaxial Inventory-III (MCMI-III). Since this test was devised for clinical populations, some (e.g., Halon, 2001) have argued that it should not be used in custody cases because it may overpathologize parents. McCann (2002) discusses whether the MCMI-III overpathologizes child custody examinees and concludes that it does not with the exception of Scales 4 (Histrionic) and 7 (Compulsive) for females, adding that the standardization sample included some forensic cases.

Parents involved in a custody dispute are a different group than those parents whose parenting capacity is in question. Blood (2008) studied the use of the test in this group and found somewhat greater pathology in these parents as compared to parents in a custody dispute. In this case, I was specifically asked to provide information relating to the nature of any personality problems, so my view was that this test was appropriate.

Looking at her profile (see Appendix A), we find no evidence of any unusual test-taking attitude that would distort the MCMI-III results. We also notice that none of the clinical scales is elevated above the baserate score of 85, which is the range in which we would consider the possibility of a prominent personality disorder. Baserate scores of 75 and above indicate clinically significant personality traits. However, baserates scores above 65 can also be interpreted in relation to personality traits. Here we see that the two scales that are elevated in this range are the schizoid and the depressive scales. This would be consistent with low self-esteem, mistrust of others, and a tendency to withdraw from others or get into self-destructive relationships where she may submit to what others want and allow herself to be manipulated. The slightly elevated thought disorder and delusional disorder scales are consistent with Rorschach data pointing toward some mildly disturbed thinking.

I also used the International Personality Disorder Examination – Screening questionnaire (ICD-10 module) (IPDE screening). This is a self-report measure consisting of 59 items designed to screen for the presence of traits indicative of a personality disorder. Scores of 3 or more on any scale are considered to be suggestive of the presence of the corresponding personality disorder. This mother obtained a score of 4 on the scales that assess paranoid personality disorder and anxious (avoidant) personality disorder.

Putting these results together with the Rorschach, we can consider that her high Lambda is more likely to be reflective of her personality style rather than of situational defensiveness because she did not present as defensive on the MCMI-III. I had also administered some measures relating to parenting, and none of these yielded any sign of defensiveness either.

Overall, the test results indicate some interpersonal difficulties including a tendency to mistrust others, low self-esteem, and a vulnerability to becoming detached or withdrawn under stress. Table 1 gives some comparisons between key Rorschach variables in the case and the self-report data.

Table 1. Comparisons between the main Rorschach variables and the self-report data

Main Rorschach findings	Rorschach variable for finding	Self-report data (MCMI-III and IPDE)
Limited coping resources	CDI = 4	There is no clear parallel in the self-report data although the MCMI-III findings are not highly elevated, suggesting a more mild level of dysfunction
Cautious about interpersonal intimacy	T = 0	Some paranoid traits on IPDE and schizoid traits on MCMI-III
Ineffective interpersonal skills	CDI = 4, Pure H = 0, GHR:PHR 2:2 and COP = 0, AG = 0	Schizoid & depressive elevated together points to being withdrawn, poor social skills and a tendency to get into self-destructive relationships
Avoids complexity and/or situationally defensive	Lambda = 5.0	No situational defensiveness (MCMI-III scale Y), some avoidant traits (IPDE), but these are conceptualized differently from the sort of simplistic thinking captured by high Lambda
Low self-esteem	3r + (2)/R = 0.06	Scale 2B on MCMI-III elevated, consistent with low self-esteem
Preoccupied with her body	An + Xy = 4	Not found in the data
Reality testing intact	XA% = 0.78, WDA% = 0.75, X-% = 0.22 and P = 5	Given only mild elevations on the MCMI-III, it is unlikely that she is experiencing a psychotic disorder that would disrupt reality testing
Poor judgment, disorganized thinking	WSum6 = 24	Scales SS & PP slightly elevated on MCMI-III

Discussion

Weiner (2004) outlined four Rorschach characteristics that can present obstacles in treatment. These characteristics are rigid attitudes (a:p), self-satisfaction (D > = 0), a lack of introspection (FD = 0), and interpersonal distancing (T = 0). The Rorschach from this administration yielded evidence of three of these characteristics, with the data being insufficient in relation to a:p.

Nygren (2004) researched the question of predicting who would respond well to psychotherapy and concluded that EA, blends, Mo, Zf, FD, and AG are positive indicators, and that F% is a negative indicator.

Therefore, according to her Rorschach results, this mother is not presenting as a promising candidate. When this is combined with her negative attitude toward the question of psychotherapy in the interview, I was pessimistic about the likelihood of her engaging in and benefiting from psychotherapy.

I was therefore pleasantly surprised to receive the second referral for a reassessment following a significant period of treatment.

Background for the Second Referral

She had had 2 years of psychodynamic group psychotherapy three times weekly, which had recently come to an end. She had also stopped taking the medication. The children remained with her mother during this period, and she had regular unsupervised contact. She was now applying to have the children returned to her fulltime care. I was asked to reassess her and determine whether she had made any progress in the treatment.

The psychotherapist reported that the mother had been committed to the group work and had attended consistently. She had reportedly developed some capacity to think about her relationships and her contribution to what had happened with her children. At first, she tended to get into bitter arguments with group members and she would form relatively simple but fixed opinions very quickly, being unable to tolerate any uncertainty. Gradually, however, the arguments subsided, she became more open to others' ideas, and her insight into her feelings increased.

The mother told me that she had benefitted from the group. She said that she had read my first report, spoken with the psychiatrist, and decided that she had nothing to lose by giving psychotherapy a chance. She went doubting that it would be worthwhile and then found that it was. She took some responsibility for having stirred up trouble in the group. She thought that she used to be impulsive and think of everything in "black and white" terms but now she realized "there is something in the middle."

I did not meet her children as the area of her interactions with her boys was assessed by others. Their reports of contact between her and her children showed that she had become more sensitive to their thoughts, feelings, and needs. Previously, she tended to complain to the boys about their behavior without being able to enforce limits, and she questioned them about her mother's care of them, seeking to get them to reassure her of their loyalty and love. Now she was able to manage any behavioral issues more effectively and had learned not to place pressure on the boys to prove their love.

I readministered the Rorschach (among other measures) to obtain some test data. I was able to address the question of any change by comparing the current results to the results I had obtained three years earlier.

Interpretation of the Second Protocol

The CDI is no longer positive but there is one M– in the record so we begin this time with ideation.

Lambda is no longer elevated, and she is now presenting as an ambitent (EB 4:4.0). Her problem-solving style is not consistent: Sometimes, she will think things through, and at other times she will make decisions more intuitively.

There is no sign of ideational inflexibility (a:p = 3:3). With R = 20 and WSUM6 = 10, there may be some cognitive slippage and faulty judgment at times but this is markedly less than was seen in the first protocol.

Her perceptual accuracy remains reasonably good (XA% = 0.75, WDA% = 0.76 and X-% = 0.25), and in this area her functioning has not changed.

She has now developed an overincorporative style (Zd = +4.0, compared with the Zd of –1.5 in the first record). She is investing considerable effort in scanning the features of a situation. This is interesting in relation to the very marked reduction in Lambda.

Her EA at 8.0 is markedly higher than on the first protocol. She may not have developed a consistent problem-solving style given that she is an ambitent, but she has made significant gains in her psychological coping resources; this improvement should be evident in her capacity to manage the stresses of daily life (D = +1 and AdjD = +1). However, with a somewhat lower Adj es = 4, the possibility of overestimating her capacity for control and stress tolerance is raised. Given C' = 2, it would seem that she is holding onto feelings that she would prefer to express, leading to some tension or apprehension. This may relate to her application to regain custody of the children.

She gives more color responses compared to the first protocol. Being an ambitent, there is the potential for becoming confused by her feelings at times and some inconsistency in how she shows her feelings. There is an increase in her responsiveness to emotional stimulation (Afr = 0.67), but this is in the expected range for an ambitent.

She denies the presence of irritating or unpleasant feelings and substituting inappropriate positive emotion (CP = 1). This defensive tactic is prone to fail when challenged, making her vulnerable to mood swings. When she expresses her feelings, she can become quite intense and even inappropriate at times (FC:CF + C = 1:3 and Pure C = 1). The Pure C response is her last one, and it relates to the baby "lying on a bit of green." The content of the response suggests the presence of some passivity and immaturity.

Her self-esteem remains very low (3r + (2)/R = 0.10), and her personal identity may not be clearly established (H:(H) + Hd + (Hd) = 2:4), but she has developed some capacity for introspection (FD = 1). Her concern about her body remains above average, though now lower than it was previously (An + Xy = 2).

She remains cautious and conservative about interpersonal intimacy (T = 0), but she is interested in other people (Sum H = 6, Pure H = 2). The increase in Pure H is a positive sign, but nonetheless her interpersonal behavior may still be ineffective (GHR:PHR 3:3), and she does not anticipate positive interactions with others, probably feeling uncomfortable in interpersonal situations (COP = 0, AG = 0).

Discussion

Overall, the main changes are that CDI is no longer positive, Lambda is much lower, the WSUM6 is lower, and An + Xy is also lower. The presence of one CP is interesting. Combined with the evidence that her low self-esteem and her problems in interpersonal relationships remain, this suggests that further therapy could be beneficial. However, she has clearly made significant progress.

Most parents who are being assessed for the courts are understandably very defensive, something often reflected in the Rorschach data. This raises a question about the distinction between an elevation in Lambda that results from situational defensiveness and one which stems from an avoidant style. Exner (2000) advised that "there is no perfect guideline for distinguishing high Lambda values that are situationally related from those that represent a more trait-like avoidant response style" (p. 31) He outlined how high Lambda, low R, and low EA combined are usually the result of situational defensiveness.

Campo (2009), in her follow-up study of 30 adult patients after a year of treatment, found that Lambda tended to be resistant to change. One argument about the marked reduction in Lambda in this case that could be made is that, in the first administration, the mother was exhibiting a high level of situational defensiveness, whereas in the second administration, after meeting me for the second time, she may have been more open. However, other test data did not confirm the presence of situational defensiveness, and there was a very close parallel between the decrease in Lambda, the patient's own description of the sort of changes she had made, and the report from the therapist. It would therefore seem clear that the elevated Lambda was not just due to situational defensiveness, and that she had had an avoidant style that was successfully ameliorated in treatment.

In general, when Lambda on the Rorschach is elevated, distinguishing between situational defensiveness and the avoidant personality style is probably best achieved by turning to other measures. Some tests, such as the MCMI-III, which was used in this case, contain scales that assess this. There are also measures that specifically focus on defensiveness such as the Paulhus Deception Scales, which can assist.

I was interested to see that therapy had enabled this mother to increase her coping resources. Exner (2003) reported that the social deficits captured by a positive result on the CDI can be addressed "rather easily by well planned treatment" (p. 313) as long as the treatment is not very brief (defined as lasting only 2 to 3 months) and lasts at least 8 to 14 months, which was the case here.

My clinical experience suggests that parents who neglect their children may often present with elevated Lambda and/or a positive CDI. As a starting point for looking at this question, prompted by this case, I

Table 2. Data for CDI and Lambda for parents in cases of child neglect compared to the international norms and to parents in custody cases

CDI	My data	International norms	Custody cases
0	1 = 2%		
1	2 = 4%		
2	9 = 17%		
3	12 = 23%		
4	19 = 37%	25%	28%
5	9 = 17%	11%	10%
Lambda: average	1.37	0.83	1.06
Lambda: *SD*	1.32	0.86	1.31

abstracted some data from my files on a group of 52 parents whom I have assessed for the Courts over the past 5 years where there was evidence of child neglect.

My group of 52 parents consists of 35 mothers and 17 fathers. There are 35 white British parents in the group, 9 black British parents, 5 British parents with Pakistani backgrounds, and 3 parents from other ethnic/racial groups. The number of children ranged from one to seven. The age range of the parents is from 16 years to 52 years, with an average of 31.77. There are no data about interscorer reliability for this sample as the Rorschach protocols were not obtained as part of a research study.

I compared my data with the data for the international normative sample (Meyer, Erdberg, & Shaffer, 2007) and for child custody litigants from Singer, Hoppe, Lee, Olesen, and Walters (2008) (see Table 2). Child custody litigants are not the same as parents who are being assessed because of concerns about child neglect; it seems reasonable to assume that the latter group may be even more defensive and possibly also be less able to cope.

My sample is too small to reach any firm conclusions, and further investigation is needed. Nevertheless, the comparison of my sample with these other two samples suggests the following

1) Some situational defensiveness and/or an avoidant personality style is evident for parents in cases of child neglect at a level that may exceed that found in child custody cases.

2) The likelihood of obtaining a positive result on the CDI may be higher for parents in cases of child neglect compared with parents in child custody cases.

In my sample of 52 parents, there were 13 who presented like the mother in this case study, with both a Lambda greater than 0.99 and a CDI of 4 or 5. Conversely, there were 13 parents for whom Lambda was ≤ 0.99 and the CDI was < 4. That means that 75% of my sample of parents was positive on one or both of these variables. The combination of an elevated Lambda and a positive CDI would intuitively make sense in cases of child neglect, as it is easy to see how limited coping skills and the tendency to ignore subtle or ambiguous aspects of situations could lead to overlooking children's needs and the warning signs that they were not being cared for adequately.

As noted above, my sample provides only a starting point for a full research study. Such research should compare parents who neglect their children with those who do not. The samples would need to be matched for key variables such as number of children, gender, marital status, and age. The Rorschach should ideally be administered by examiners who are blind to which group (neglectful or not) the parents came from. The protocols should also be scored blindly as well by at least two scorers so that interscorer reliability could be investigated before conducting a statistical comparison of the Rorschach variables.

However, the present case study provides an example of how – even when the Rorschach signs are negative – positive change can occur!

Acknowledgment

Thanks to Justine McCarthy Woods for reviewing the scoring for the case example.

References

Barton Evans, F., & Schutz, B. (2008). The Rorschach in child custody and parenting plan evaluations: A new conceptualization. In C. B. Gacono & F. Barton Evans (Eds.), *The handbook of Forensic Rorschach Assessment* (pp. 233–254). New York, NY: Erlbaum.

Blood, L. (2008). The use of the MCMI-III in completing parenting capacity assessments. *Journal of Forensic Psychology Practice, 8*, 24–38.

Campo, V. (2009). Variations of Rorschach variables in therapeutic follow-up. *Rorschachiana, 30*, 101–128.

Erard, R. E. (2005). What the Rorschach can contribute to child custody and parenting time evaluations. *Journal of Child Custody, 2,* 119–142.

Exner, J. E. (2000). *A primer for Rorschach interpretation.* Asheville, NC: Rorschach Workshops.

Exner, J. E. (2003). *The Rorschach: A comprehensive system. Volume 1: Basic foundations and principles of interpretation.* Hoboken, NJ: Wiley.

Halon, R. (2001). The Millon Clinical Multiaxial Inventory-III: The normal quartet in child custody cases. *American Journal of Forensic Psychology, 19,* 57–75.

Johnston, J. R., Walters, M. G., & Olesen, N. W. (2005). Clinical ratings of parenting capacity and Rorschach protocols of custody-disputing parents: An exploratory study. *Journal of Child Custody, 2,* 159–178.

McCann, J. T. (2002). Guidelines for forensic application of the MCMI-III. *Journal of Forensic Psychology Practice, 2,* 55–69.

Meyer, G. J., Erdberg, P. & Shaffer, T. (2007). Toward international reference data for the Comprehensive system. *Journal of Personality Assessment, 89,* S201–S216.

Nygren, M. (2004). Differences in Comprehensive System Rorschach variables between groups differing in therapy suitability. *Rorschachiana, 26,* 110–146.

Singer, J., Hoppe, C., Lee, S. M., Olesen, N. & Walters, M. (2008). Child custody litigants: Rorschach data from a large sample. In C. B. Gacono & F. Barton Evans (Eds.), *The handbook of forensic Rorschach assessment* (pp. 445–464). New York, NY: Erlbaum.

Weiner, I. B. (2004). Rorschach inkblot method. In M. E. Maruish (Ed.), *The use of psychological testing for treatment planning and outcomes assessment* (pp. 553–588). New York, NY: Erlbaum.

Weiner, I. B. (2005). Rorschach assessment in Child Custody cases. *Journal of Child Custody, 2,* 99–119.

Kari S. Carstairs
Carstairs Psychological Associates Ltd.
7 Mayfield Road
Bromley, Kent
BR1 2HB
UK
Tel./Fax +44 20 8-325-1697
E-mail kari@carstairspsych.co.uk

Appendix A

Rorschach Data for the First Administration

CARD I

1) It could be some type of bug.

That bit (D4). It has little intinnias [that is how she pronounced it, instead of antennas or antennae] that's the whole shape of the body, the middle part.

2) Or it could be a bat.

These wingy-type of things, if they were more prominent. That could be part of it too (D4), so it's all of it.

Can you turn it? [that's up to you]
[So she then turns the card and says:]

3) I suppose, if you're not too good a drawer, it's a butterfly gone wrong.

Well, because of the wings, the shape, that's the body (D4). [you said it's gone wrong?] Well, it's not a very good picture – whoever did it was not a good drawer.

CARD II

4) It could be like the eye and the mask you put over your face, the eyes and the mask.

The eyes are there, the mouth, nose, that's the part of the mask that goes round the cheeks (indicates use of the whole blot, with D2 as eyes, DS5 as mouth).

CARD III

5) That would be legs and that looks like a stiletto heel but it's not.

They would be the legs and that could be a stiletto shoe with the sharp points there and there (D5 as legs, Dd33 as shoes).

6) And maybe a skeleton or something like an X-ray too.

When you see X-rays, you see the parts inside – that part (D7) – it's like part of the rib-cage and body [how do you see the rib-cage?] That line and the little bits there – sort of ribby like.

CARD IV

They're all the same!

Arm, head, with the eyes there, big legs, tail, dark markings there (using the whole blot).

7) I suppose, well, that could be a head, arms, legs, it could be a monster.

8) Or it could be an x-ray again – I can't really make out what it looks like.

This bit in here – it looks like the body – it could be the rib-cage or something like that – just the way it's shaped there (D3 with an extra bit coming down into D5 but not all of D5).

CARD V

9) It looks like a bat – legs, ears, wings and that – it resembles a bat – that's what my head would tell me to say – it looks like a bat.

The wings come out here and here, those are the little legs, the ear, the whole look of it.

CARD VI

10) Well, I suppose it could be like a leaf that way [after turning the card around].

It's a leaf – that way [upside down]I the wide bit up there is like one of the leaves from a tree, that is the stem there (using the whole blot).

CARD VII

I can't really say . . .
It's just shapes . . . I can't make head or tail of it.

11) It could a little monster dancing without a body in the middle – that's the legs and the arms.

That's the face – it's got a big, wide face, little arms, little feet, and there 's a big gap in the middle for the body, where the body should be (whole blot with DS10 as the missing body).

12) Someone put a bit of paint on the page and smudged it.

Yeah, as if someone maybe got 2 paint brushes and went like that [shows] with a gap in the middle between the smudges (whole blot again).

CARD VIII

It's just colors. Different shapes and colors.

13) It could be a flower, I suppose.

The prettiness of all the colors makes it look like a flower – the pinks, oranges, the shape too, like petals and it comes up to a peak at the top (whole).

14) That could be a spine going down there.

That bit, the whole length of it and the little pieces here and here – curvy spiny sort of sticking out bits (Dd21 with the extra side bits of D3).

15) It could be some type of squirrel or something, if it had a bushier tail – face, feet, like a beaver or something like that.

Those 2 could be beavers – that's the face, the feet and that's another foot (D1).

CARD IX

I have no idea [take your time].
16) Well, I'm seeing a spine, if you're thinking about the body.

All down there (D5). [what about it looks like a spine?] The length of it all, going into a uterus or something, the insides of a woman.

17) Maybe an insect

Very vaguely, the whole of it – sort of insecty – those bits at the top (D3 as part of insect with insect as whole blot).

CARD X

18) It looks more like a butterfly that way (upside down) with bits missing – the white parts should be filled in to make wings and things.

The whole shape of it, that should be filled in and that could be a pair of legs and little shoes, like pixie shoes (D8) – a butterfly with shoes.

Sequence of Scores

Card	Resp. No.	Location and DQ	Loc. No.	Determinant(s) and Form Quality	(2)	Content(s)	Pop	ZScore	Special Scores
I	1	Do	4	Fo		A			DV
	2	Wo	1	Fo		A	P	1.0	DV
	3	Wo	1	Fo		A	P	1.0	DR
II	4	WSo	1	Fu		(Hd)		4.5	GHR
III	5	D+	5	Fo		Hd, Cg		3.0	PHR
	6	Do	7	F–		Xy			DV
IV	7	Wo	1	FYo		(H)	P	2.0	GHR
	8	Ddo	99	Fu		Xy			
V	9	Wo	1	Fo		A	P	1.0	DR2
VI	10	Wo	1	Fu		Bt		2.5	
VII	11	Wo	1	Ma–		(H)		2.5	MOR, PHR
	12	Wv	1	Fu		Art			
VIII	13	Wo	1	CFo		Bt		4.5	
	14	Ddo	99	Fo		An			
	15	Do	1	Fo	2	A	P		
IX	16	Do	5	Fo		An			DR, FAB
	17	Wo	1	F–		A		5.5	DV
X	18	W+	1	F–		A, Cg		5.5	FAB, MOR

Summary of Approach

I:	D.W.W		VI:	W
II:	WS		VII:	W.W
III:	D.D		VIII:	W.Dd.D
IV:	W.Dd		IX:	D.W
V:	W		X:	W

Structural Summary

Location Features		
Zf	=	11
ZSum	=	33.0
ZEst	=	34.5
W	=	11
(Wv	=	1)
D	=	5
W+D	=	16
Dd	=	2
S	=	1

DQ		(FQ-)
+	= 2	(1)
o	= 15	(3)
v/+	= 0	(0)
v	= 1	(0)

Form Quality			
	FQx	MQual	W+D
+	= 0	0	0
o	= 10	0	9
u	= 4	0	3
-	= 4	1	4
none	= 0	0	0

Determinants		Contents	
Blends	**Single**	H = 0	
	M = 1	(H) = 2	
	FM = 0	Hd = 1	
	m = 0	(Hd) = 1	
	FC = 0	Hx = 0	
	CF = 1	A = 7	
	C = 0	(A) = 0	
	Cn = 0	Ad = 0	
	FC' = 0	(Ad) = 0	
	C'F = 0	An = 2	
	C' = 0	Art = 1	
	FT = 0	Ay = 0	
	TF = 0	Bl = 0	
	T = 0	Bt = 2	
	FV = 0	Cg = 2	
	VF = 0	Cl = 0	
	V = 0	Ex = 0	
	FY = 1	Fd = 0	
	YF = 0	Fi = 0	
	Y = 0	Ge = 0	
	Fr = 0	Hh = 0	
	rF = 0	Ls = 0	
	FD = 0	Na = 0	
	F = 15	Sc = 0	
		Sx = 0	
	(2) = 1	Xy = 2	
		Idio = 0	

S-Constellation

☐	FV+VF+V+FD > 2	
☐	Col-Shd Blends > 0	
☑	Ego < .31 or > .44	
☐	MOR > 3	
☐	Zd > ±3.5	
☐	es > EA	
☑	CF + C > FC	
☑	X+% < .70	
☐	S > 3	
☐	P < 3 or > 8	
☑	Pure H < 2	
☐	R < 17	
4	Total	

Special Scores		
	Lvl-1	Lvl-2
DV =	4 x1	0 x2
INC =	0 x2	0 x4
DR =	2 x3	1 x6
FAB =	2 x4	0 x7
ALOG =	0 x5	
CON =	0 x7	
Raw Sum6 =	9	
Wgtd Sum6 =	24	
AB = 0	GHR = 2	
AG = 0	PHR = 2	
COP = 0	MOR = 2	
CP = 0	PER = 0	
	PSV = 0	

RATIOS, PERCENTAGES, AND DERIVATIONS

R = 18	L = 5.00

EB	= 1 : 1.0	EA = 2.0	EBPer = N/A
eb	= 0 : 1	es = 1	D = 0
		Adj es = 1	Adj D = 0

FM = 0	SumC' = 0	SumT = 0
m = 0	SumV = 0	SumY = 1

AFFECT

FC:CF+C	= 0 : 1
Pure C	= 0
SumC' : WSumC	= 0 : 1.0
Afr	= 0.50
S	= 1
Blends:R	= 0 : 18
CP	= 0

INTERPERSONAL

COP = 0	AG = 0	
GHR:PHR	= 2 : 2	
a:p	= 1 : 0	
Food	= 0	
SumT	= 0	
Human Content	= 4	
Pure H	= 0	
PER	= 0	
Isolation Index	= 0.11	

IDEATION

a:p	= 1 : 0	Sum6	= 9
Ma:Mp	= 1 : 0	Lvl-2	= 1
2AB+(Art+Ay)	= 1	WSum6	= 24
MOR	= 2	M-	= 1
		M none	= 0

MEDIATION

XA%	= 0.78
WDA%	= 0.75
X-%	= 0.22
S-	= 0
P	= 5
X+%	= 0.56
Xu%	= 0.22

PROCESSING

Zf	= 11
W:D:Dd	= 11:5:2
W : M	= 11 : 1
Zd	= -1.5
PSV	= 0
DQ+	= 2
DQv	= 1

SELF-PERCEPTION

3r+(2)/R	= 0.06
Fr+rF	= 0
SumV	= 0
FD	= 0
An+Xy	= 4
MOR	= 2
H:(H)+Hd+(Hd)	= 0 : 4

PTI = 1	☐ DEPI = 4	☑ CDI = 4	☐ S-CON = 4	☐ HVI = No	☐ OBS = No

MCMI-III data

Category	Scale	BR score
Modifying index	Disclosure	50
	Desirability	59
	Debasement	64
Clinical Personality Patterns	Schizoid	69
	Avoidant	26
	Depressive	69
	Dependent	27
	Histrionic	55
	Narcissistic	60
	Antisocial	60
	Sadistic	48
	Compulsive	52
	Negativistic	27
	Masochistic	60
Severe personality patterns	Schizotypal	60
	Borderline	38
	Paranoid	63
Clinical syndromes	Anxiety	60
	Somatoform	9
	Bipolar: manic	64
	Dysthymia	60
	Alcohol dependence	63
	Drug dependence	60
	Post-traumatic stress	50
Severe clinical syndromes	Thought disorder	66
	Major depression	52
	Delusional disorder	68

Appendix B

Rorschach Data for the Second Administration

CARD I

1) To me it looks like a butterfly.

The whole shape, obviously, the wings there, little antennas (yes, this time she said this correctly!) up here, and the way it's made.

Or – are we just saying what the shape resembles or what it means? [just tell me what it looks like to you, what it might be.]

2) Some type of bug.

Antennas again, the body – it's a long beetle type of bug – the whole appearance (D4) – it could be a bug.

CARD II

3) It could be a fat man with a black cloak on.

Nose (D4), eyes (D2), mouth (DdS29), cloak (Dd21)– it's black [you said a fat man?] yes, the whole way it comes out (gestures to how D6 comes out) – can you see it? [that's fine, thank you].

4) It could be a butterfly again too.

That (D6) – the wings are there, that is top part and that bit at the bottom (D3) is like a pretty little red wing on the end.

CARD III

5) (turns card upside down). A monster with his arms up in the air.

Yes, that's the head (D7) and those are his arms (D5) – he's holding them up in the air like this (shows me the posture).

6) (right way up) Or some type of face – the eyes, the mouth.

The eyes are there (Dd31) and that is the mouth (D8) – that's an arm (D5) – it's crawling – it's an alien with the body type thing (points to Dd34).

CARD IV

7) A big monster! And that looks like a pair of high heels (points to D2).

There's the head (D3) and it's the whole of this, with the big body and the legs – one, two. [what in the blot makes it look big?] It's the way the head is, the shape, it's smaller as if it's above you and the big high heels that could be on his feet.

CARD V

8) That looks more like a bat – legs, ears, wings – yeah, that's more like a bat.

Those are the ears (Dd31), the head, it has big wings spread out, with the legs hanging down (D9).

CARD VI

9) It could be a leaf.

This whole part – it's a nice green leaf and the bottom bit too – that's the stem.

10) It could be some type of insect with those little things coming out – that's the head, so those are like little whiskers.

It's that bit (Dd23) with those bits (Dd26) – it's like an insect – I don't know if you can see it – my eyesight is going but can you see a face in there (in Dd23) with a little eye and a mouth? It just looks buggish – you know, insects have those little things coming out – the shape of those (Dd26).

11) All the spine.

That (D5) looks like a spine [what makes it look like a spine?] I think spines look like that – or perhaps I'm wrong?

CARD VII

12) (upside down) Just looks like someone dancing in the middle, that's part of their body – and – it could be like a shadow dancing – with the body missed out – that being the hands and that being the feet and that body where the body is left out.

That's a hand (Dd21) little arms, little legs, dancing like this (shows how the hands are held out) – but it's totally blank in the middle, so the body is missing. [you said it's like a shadow?] Yes, it's gray and it's just like a dark shadow – and it's not got a face that you can see.

CARD VIII

13) A pretty butterfly again.

All of it – it's got a pretty body, wings, it's a pretty color – butterflies can be pretty colors and the shape of it.

14) With the spine coming down.

Looking at that bit (Dd21). [what makes it look like a spine?] I've assumed that a spine is straight – I've seen it on TV and it looks like that.

15) Oh and if you look closely, that could be a little mole – see the head and the feet – do you see what I mean? Looking that way (turns the card sideways to show me) – there's a little creature on each side.

See – a little mole there (D1) and there's one there too – that's the head and those are the legs.

CARD IX

16) Well, it's a butterfly again, I'd say.

Yeah, it's the whole of it, it's got pretty wings – all the colors make it look pretty. It's got wings there(D3) and there (D1) and there (D4).

CARD X

17) They could be little creatures –these 2 there (points to D7) they're coming out there on the side.

They have little legs, and oval-shaped bodies and they're coming out.

18) That could be a little creature (points to D1).

It could be a little octopus with all the legs.

19) That could be a little tadpole (D2) – there.

It's like a tadpole, it's got a fish face, those could be little wings, they've got little bodies.

20) And I suppose, that could be a baby's head, the feet and the arms, it's lying on a bit of green.

Yes, that's the head and the legs (points to D5 for the baby) and the green there – if that was all filled in – it's lying on the green bit.

Sequence of Scores

Card	Resp. No.	Location and DQ	Loc. No.	Determinant(s) and Form Quality	(2)	Content(s)	Pop	ZScore	Special Scores
I	1	Wo	1	Fo		A	P	1.0	
	2	Do	4	Fo		A			
II	3	WS+	1	FC'-		H, Cg		4.5	PHR
	4	Ddo	99	FCu		A			
III	5	Do	1	Mpu		(H)			GHR
	6	Do	1	Mau		(H)			GHR
IV	7	W+	1	FDo		(H), Cg	P	4.0	FAB, PHR
V	8	Wo	1	FMpo		A	P	1.0	
VI	9	Wo	1	Fu		Bt		2.5	CP
	10	Ddo	23	F-		A			DV
	11	Do	5	Fo		An			
VII	12	WSo	1	Ma.FC'-		(H)		4.0	MOR, PHR
VIII	13	Wo	1	CF-		A		4.5	
	14	Ddo	21	Fo		An			PER
	15	Do	1	Fo	2	A	P		
IX	16	Wo	1	CF-		A		5.5	
X	17	Do	7	FMau	2	A			
	18	Do	1	Fo		A			
	19	Do	2	Fu		A			INC
	20	D+	10	Mp.Co		H, Id		4.5	GHR

Summary of Approach

I:	W.D		VI:	W.Dd.D
II:	WS.Dd		VII:	WS
III:	D.D		VIII:	W.Dd.D
IV:	W		IX:	W
V:	W		X:	D.D.D.D

Structural Summary

Location Features

Zf	=	9
ZSum	=	31.5
ZEst	=	27.5
W	=	8
(Wv	=	0)
D	=	9
W+D	=	17
Dd	=	3
S	=	2

DQ

		(FQ-)
+	= 3	(1)
o	= 17	(4)
v/+	= 0	(0)
v	= 0	(0)

Form Quality

	FQx	MQual	W+D
+	= 0	0	0
o	= 9	1	8
u	= 6	2	5
-	= 5	1	4
none	= 0	0	0

Determinants

Blends
M.FC'
M.C

Single

M	=	2
FM	=	2
m	=	0
FC	=	1
CF	=	2
C	=	0
Cn	=	0
FC'	=	1
C'F	=	0
C'	=	0
FT	=	0
TF	=	0
T	=	0
FV	=	0
VF	=	0
V	=	0
FY	=	0
YF	=	0
Y	=	0
Fr	=	0
rF	=	0
FD	=	1
F	=	9
(2)	=	2

Contents

H	= 2
(H)	= 4
Hd	= 0
(Hd)	= 0
Hx	= 0
A	= 11
(A)	= 0
Ad	= 0
(Ad)	= 0
An	= 2
Art	= 0
Ay	= 0
Bl	= 0
Bt	= 1
Cg	= 2
Cl	= 0
Ex	= 0
Fd	= 0
Fi	= 0
Ge	= 0
Hh	= 0
Ls	= 0
Na	= 0
Sc	= 0
Sx	= 0
Xy	= 0
Idio	= 1

S-Constellation

☐	FV+VF+V+FD > 2
☐	Col-Shd Blends > 0
☑	Ego < .31 or > .44
☐	MOR > 3
☑	Zd > ±3.5
☐	es > EA
☑	CF + C > FC
☑	X+% < .70
☐	S > 3
☐	P < 3 or > 8
☐	Pure H < 2
☐	R < 17
4	Total

Special Scores

		Lvl-1	Lvl-2
DV	=	1 x1	0 x2
INC	=	1 x2	0 x4
DR	=	0 x3	0 x6
FAB	=	1 x4	0 x7
ALOG	=	0 x5	
CON	=	0 x7	

Raw Sum6	=	3
Wgtd Sum6	=	7

AB	= 0		GHR	= 3
AG	= 0		PHR	= 3
COP	= 0		MOR	= 1
CP	= 1		PER	= 1
			PSV	= 0

RATIOS, PERCENTAGES, AND DERIVATIONS

R = 20		L = 0.82

EB	=	4 : 4.0	EA	= 8.0	EBPer =	N/A
eb	=	2 : 2	es	= 4	D =	+1
			Adj es	= 4	Adj D =	+1

FM	=	2	SumC' = 2	SumT =	0
m	=	0	SumV = 0	SumY =	0

AFFECT

FC:CF+C	= 1 : 3
Pure C	= 1
SumC' : WSumC	= 2 : 4.0
Afr	= 0.67
S	= 2
Blends:R	= 2 : 20
CP	= 1

INTERPERSONAL

COP = 0		AG =	0
GHR:PHR		=	3 : 3
a:p		=	3 : 3
Food		=	0
SumT		=	0
Human Content		=	6
Pure H		=	2
PER		=	1
Isolation Index		=	0.05

IDEATION

a:p	= 3 : 3	Sum6	= 3
Ma:Mp	= 2 : 2	Lvl-2	= 0
2AB+(Art+Ay)	= 0	WSum6	= 7
MOR	= 1	M-	= 1
		M none	= 0

MEDIATION

XA%	= 0.75
WDA%	= 0.76
X-%	= 0.25
S-	= 2
P	= 4
X+%	= 0.45
Xu%	= 0.30

PROCESSING

Zf	= 9
W:D:Dd	= 8:9:3
W : M	= 8 : 4
Zd	= +4.0
PSV	= 0
DQ+	= 3
DQv	= 0

SELF-PERCEPTION

3r+(2)/R	= 0.10
Fr-rF	= 0
SumV	= 0
FD	= 1
An+Xy	= 2
MOR	= 1
H:(H)+Hd+(Hd)	= 2 : 4

PTI = 0	☐ DEPI = 3	☐ CDI = 1	☐ S-CON = 4	☐ HVI = No	☐ OBS = No

Summary

The assessment of parenting capacity in cases in which there are child protection concerns requires a full investigation of a wide range of factors. The Rorschach does not assess parenting per se, but it does provide a rich source of information that can help to confirm the clinical picture, and it is a useful complement to self-report measures.

This case study offers Rorschach data for two protocols from a mother who had neglected her children. The first protocol was obtained prior to treatment. The mother had a positive Coping Deficit Index and a very high Lambda (at 5.0). A high level of somatic concern (with $Xy + An = 4$) was consistent with the history of her having sought cosmetic surgery. She was dismissive about the prospect of psychotherapy. Her children were in the care of her mother.

The second administration was carried out 3 years later, after she had had psychodynamic group psychotherapy three times weekly. She was applying to regain the custody of her children, and the purpose of the second evaluation was to determine whether she had made progress. Although evidence of low self-esteem and some interpersonal problems remained, there was also evidence of significant progress, notably a marked decrease in Lambda (now at 0.82) and in the Coping Deficit Index, which was no longer positive. Feedback from the therapist confirmed that her previous tendency to very quickly form simple, fixed opinions had gradually given way to more tolerance for ambiguity. The mother herself described the change as moving from thinking in "black and white" terms to realizing that "there is something in the middle."

Some data for Lambda and the Coping Deficit Index from 52 other parents who were assessed in relation to concerns about child neglect are presented and compared to the international norms and to a sample of child custody litigants. The data suggest that parents who neglect their children may have high levels of situational defensiveness and/or an avoidant personality style and limited coping skills.

Résumé

L'évaluation de la capacité éducative des parents, dans les cas où la protection de l'enfance est en jeu, nécessite l'investigation d'un large éventail de facteurs. Le Rorschach n'offre pas une mesure des capacités éducatives parentales en soi, mais permet de fournir une riche source d'informations qui peuvent confirmer le tableau clinique en complément de l'information obtenue grâce aux questionnaires d'auto-évaluation.

Cette étude de cas présente les données de deux protocoles du Rorschach concernantune mère ayant négligé ses enfants. Le premier protocole fut réalisé avant toute intervention thérapeutique. La mère obtint un score positif au "Coping Deficit Index" ainsi qu' un score Lambda très élevé à 0,50. Son niveau élevé de préoccupation somatique (Xy + An = 4) est cohérent avec sa volonté de se soumettre à une intervention de chirurgie esthétique. Elle était méprisante à l'idée d'entreprendre une psychothérapie. Sa mère avait la garde de ses enfants.

La seconde passation se déroula trois ans plus tard, après qu'elle a participé à une psychothérapie psychodynamique de groupe trois fois par semaine. Elle avait fait une demande pour récupérer la garde de ses enfants et l'évaluation devait déterminer si elle avait fait des progrès. Bien que son estime de soi demeurait toujours faible et que certains problèmes interpersonnels résiduels étaient toujours non résolus, le test mit également à jour des signes de progrès significatifs. Son score Lambda avait diminué à 0.82 et son "Coping Deficit Index" n'était plus positif. Les remarques de son thérapeute confirmèrent une diminution graduelle de sa tendance à former des opinions simples et rigides très rapidement, parallèlement à une augmentation de sa tolérance à l'ambigüité. Elle même décrivit ce changement comme la capacité à ne plus penser seulement en «_noir et blanc » mais à accepter qu'il puisse y avoir «_quelque chose au milieu ».

Des données du "Coping Deficit Index" et du score Lambda de 52 parents, évalués dans le cadre d'enquêtes sur la maltraitance envers des enfants, sont présentées et comparées aux normes internationales et à un échantillon de demandes légales de gardes d'enfant. Les données suggèrent que les parents d'enfants négligés peuvent présenter un niveau élevé de comportements défensifs et/ou une personnalité schizoïde avec une capacité à faire face aux problèmes limitée.

Resumen

La evaluación de la capacidad para la función parental en casos en los que preocupa la protección del niño requiere la investigación completa de una amplia gama de factores. El Rorschach no evalúa la capacidad parental *per se*, pero supone una valiosa fuente informativa que ayuda a confirmar el cuadro clínico y complementa los registros y autoinformes.

A través del estudio de un caso se ofrecen los datos Rorschach de dos protocolos de una madre que había sido muy negligente con sus hijos. El primer protocolo se administró antes del tratamiento. La madre mostró un +ndice *de Inhabilidad Social* (*CDI*) *positivo* y un *Lambda muy elevado* (= 5.0). También aparecían muchas preocupaciones somáticas (con *Xy* + *An* = 4), confirmadas por una historia de operaciones quirúrgicas por motivos estéticos. Ella era muy reticente a la psicoterapia y sus hijos estaban al cuidado de su propia madre.

El segundo Rorschach se aplicó tres años más tarde, tras haber asistido a un grupo de psicoterapia de orientación dinámica tres veces por semana. Ella quería recuperar la custodia de sus hijos y esta segunda evaluación se hizo para determinar si había habido mejorías en su funcionamiento. Aunque continuaba presentando baja autoestima y ciertos problemas interpersonales, también se observaron progresos significativos, entre ellos un marcado descenso del *Lambda* (= 0.82) y un *CDI negativo*. La información de su terapeuta confirmó que su tendencia previa a elaborar opiniones de forma precipitada, simple y rígida había mejorado, dando lugar gradualmente a una mayor tolerancia a la ambigüedad. Ella misma describía los cambios que se habían producido, señalando que había pasado de un pensamiento "en blanco y negro" a entender que "había posiciones intermedias."

Se presentan también los datos sobre *Lambda* y *CDI* de otros 52 padres evaluados por negligencia con sus hijos y se comparan con las normas internacionales y con una muestra de padres en litigio por la custodia de sus hijos. Los datos sugieren que los padres negligentes presentan mayor grado de defensividad situacional y/o estilos de personalidad evitativos con limitados recursos de afrontamiento.

　チャイルド・プロテクションの関与のある親のケースにおいて子どもを育てる能力のアセスメントには広い範囲の要因を十分に精査する必要がある。ロールシャッハは子どもを育てるそれ自体はアセスメントしないが、臨床像を確かなものにするのに役に立つ豊かな情報を有する資源を提供し、自己報告式の測定を有効に補うものである。この事例研究では子ども達をネグレクトしていた母親の2つのプロトコルが提供された。最初のプロトコルはいかなる治療の前に得られたものである。母親は対処不全指標が該当しており、ラムダが非常に高かった。身体への関心が非常に高かった（Xy+An は4であった）ことは彼女の美容整形手術を求め続けた臨床歴とも一貫する。彼女の心理療法の可能性に関しては否定的であった。彼女の子ども達は彼女が世話をしていた。

2回目の施行は3年後におこなわれ、彼女は週3回の力動的な集団心理療法を続けていた。彼女は彼女の子ども達の後見を再獲得することを申請しており、この 2 回目の評価の目的は彼女が進歩しているかどうかを決めることであった。低い自己評価の証拠やいくらかの対人関係の問題は残されていたものの、一方で重要な進展の証拠もあった、ラムダ（現在は 0.82）と対処不全指標はあきらかに目立って減少しており、対処不全指標にはもはや該当しなくなっていた。心理療法担当者からのフィードバックによれば彼女の以前の単純に固定した考えを素早く形成してしまう傾向は、徐々にあいまいさにより耐えることができるようになっていた。母親自身が自らの変化を、"白か黒か"の言葉で考えることから"中途に何かある"と理解することへの動きと説明していた。

子どもをネグレクトしたことについての事案に関連してアセスメントを受けた52名の親から得られたラムダと対処不全指標が提示され、国際的な標準と子どもの後見について係争中の標本と比較された。データによれば、自分の子どもをネグレクトする親は高い状況的な防衛を有しているかもしれず、かつあるいはまた、回避的なパーソナリティであり、対処スキルが限定されているかもしれない。

Rorschachiana 32, 117–120
© 2011 Hogrefe Publishing

DOI: 10.1027/1192-5604/a000018

Editorial

Special Section:
Studies with Children and Adolescents

Latife Yazigi

*Department of Psychiatry, Escola Paulista de Medicina,
Universidade Federal de São Paulo, Brazil*

Performing psychological assessment with children and adolescents is always a challenge. Both objective and projective tests have to deal with difficulties arising from the fact that verbal communication is not yet completely developed, which demands an ingenious management and an extra effort in the approach to children and adolescents.

Psychological tests seek to capture the subject's mental processing either through more specific and precise tasks or through more flexible and free expression ones. Consequently, both objective and projective tests search to unravel the processing underlying mental functioning, whether affective, motor, or cognitive. The challenge is to uncover the transposition of all the inner aspects of the personality and the inner mental processes into an external performance – and afterward to decode them in a comprehensive and contextualized frame of reference.

As for the Rorschach test, professionals interested in working with children and adolescents soon realize its rich potential as a unique instrument not only to reach the subject's internal world, but also to provide important information on psychological development.

Among the pioneers were Beck and his paper on the Rorschach in problem children in 1930; Kerr, who in 1934 wrote on the application of the Rorschach in children; Hertz and her Rorschach norms for adolescents in 1935 as well as her articles on personality patterns in adolescence in 1941; Piotrowski and his papers on child psychopathology in 1937 and 1945; Dworetzki and her study on the evolution of the perception in children in 1939; Klopfer with his studies on Rorschach reactions in early childhood in 1939 (Klopfer, Margulies, Murphy, & Stone, 1941)

117

and on personality diagnosis in childhood in 1945 (Klopfer, 1945); Swift's study with preschool children in 1944 (Swift, 1944a,b); Ford and her book *The Application of the Rorschach Text to Young Children* in 1946; Loosli-Usteri and *Le diagnostic Individuel chez L'Enfant au Moyen du Test de Rorschach* [The Child through the Rorschach Test], in 1948; Schachtel and Levy on the Rorschach with nursery-age children in 1945; Ames, Métraux, Rodell, and Walker in their 1974 article *Child Rorschach: Developmental trends from two to ten years* with some 72 references of English literature on the Rorschach with children.

This special issue on studies with children includes an attractive variety of papers from different countries and cultures, systems, and methodological approaches.

Belmont, from Peru, presents a remarkable study in which he compares 30 Rorschach protocols of Peruvian Andean Quechua-speaking children educated in Spanish with 30 protocols of Spanish-speaking children from the Peruvian coast. The selected variables, besides R and Lambda, were those related to self-perception. The results showed intriguing data that was extremely high in the Andean group, though the other variables in a certain way showed better results in this Andean group, perhaps because of the high Lambda. The author discusses his data, warning that educational and clinical issues should be taken into consideration when we deal with a diversity of cultures in psychological assessment. Besides, there is a lack of studies oriented toward small cultural groups lying at the margin of a society. This study is an excellent example of crosscultural research in which the Rorschach proved to be of great value.

Appel, from Israel, provides us with a very appealing qualitative-clinical analysis of two outpatient adolescents with the same psychosomatic complaint of abdominal pains. Her frame of reference is psychoanalytic and includes concepts of Winnicott's transitional space, Ogden's collapse of potential or transitional space between reality and fantasy, McDougall's notion of difficulty for symbolization, and Sifneos' alexithymia. As for the Rorschach she uses Tibon, Handelzalts, and Weinberger's Reality-Fantasy Scale (2005), based on a series of variables. Both cases are presented separately and illustrated with the full protocols and structural summaries. Thus, the reader will be able to evaluate the quality of the patient's images stimulated by the cards. It is a good example of an idiographic study, and the author's discussion is a testimony of the richness of the Rorschach for unraveling the underlying aspects of the psychosomatic dynamic.

Silva, from Portugal, offers a stimulating theoretical/conceptual discussion supported by his own research on Rorschach color responses in Portuguese children. He analyzes the subjacent processes involved in the production of color responses on the Rorschach and the peculiarities of this process in children. He reminds us of the phenomenological approach, which emphasizes the passive behavior of the subject facing color as well as the perceptive-cognitive activity involved in a color response. He develops a critical discussion on the role of color responses at the Rorschach based on a comparison between children and adults protocols.

Raspantini, Fernandes, and Pasian, from Brazil, offer an extensive review of the literature on Rorschach and children in different systems and countries. The authors discuss the issue of validity of psychological tests and stress the imperative for the need for normative parameters relating to a certain country or culture. Their review of the literature strongly supports their position. Their study compiled the normative data on the Rorschach French approach, mainly by Rausch de Traubenberg, of a normative study with Brazilian sample of 140 children 10, 11, and 12 years of age. The purpose was to update the normative tables for Brazilian children for this specific Rorschach system. Comparisons with findings from other studies using the same Rorschach system are also presented. This is a well-designed nomothetic study.

Roman, from Switzerland, give us the opportunity to discover a new assessment instrument to be used with children from 6 months to 4 years – the Projective Kit for Early Childhood (P. K. E. C.). The P. K. E. C. is a projective play test in the tradition of the Sceno Test, capable of assessing affective dynamics in children. The author describes how the test is administrated and how observations derived from the session are analyzed. He illustrates its possibilities presenting findings from an interesting study on West syndrome, a form of epilepsy that may lead to an autistic disorder. The study involved a sample of 20 children assessed initially at between 15 and 18 months and reevaluated once a year. Both quantitative and qualitative analyses were conducted, and the author presents a thorough discussion of each feature of the test. The author illustrates with three cases his exposition and stresses the importance of the clinical phenomenon of transference-countertransference in the relationship between the examiner and the infant in an observational situation.

Latife Yazigi

References

Ames, L. B., Métraux, R. W., Rodell, J. L., & Walker, R. N. (1974). *Child Rorschach responses: Developmental trends from 2 to 10 years*. New York: Brunner/Mazel.

Beck, S. (1930). The Rorschach test in problem children. *American Journal of Orthopsychiatry, I*, 501–509.

Dworetzki, G. (1939). Le test de Rorschach et l'évolution de la perception [The development of perception in the Rorschach]. *Archives of Psychology, 27*, 107–108, 233–396.

Ford, M. (1946). *The application of the Rorschach test in young children*. Minneapolis, MN: University of Minnesota Press.

Hertz, M. R. (1935). Rorschach norms for an adolescent age group. *Child Development, 6*, 69–75.

Hertz, M. R. (1941). Evaluation of the Rorschach method and its application to normal childhood and adolescence. *Character and Personality, 10*, 151–162.

Kerr, M. (1934). The Rorschach test applied to children. *British Journal of Psychology, 25*, 170–185.

Klopfer, B. (1939). Personality diagnosis in early childhood. *Psychological Bulletin, 36*, 662.

Klopfer, B., Margulies, H., Murphy, L. B., & Stone, L. J. (1941). Rorschach reactions in early childhood. *Rorschach Research Exchange, 5*, 1–23.

Loosli-Usteri, M. (1948). *Le Diagnostic Individuel Chez L'Enfant au Moyen du Test de Rorschach* [The child through the Rorschach test]. Paris: Hermann & Cie.

Piotrowski, Z. (1937). A comparison of congenitally defective children with schizophrenic children in regard to personality structure and intelligence type. *Proceedings of the American Association on Mental Deficiency, 61*, 78–90.

Piotrowski, Z. (1945). Rorschach records of children with a tic syndrome. *The Nervous Child, 24*, 342–352.

Schachtel, A. H., & Levy, M. B. (1945). Character structure of day nursery children. *American Journal of Orthopsychiatry, 15*, 213–222.

Swift, J. W. (1944a). Reliability of Rorschach scoring categories with preschool children. *Child Development, 15*, 207–216.

Swift, J. W. (1944b). Rorschach responses of eighty-two preschool children. *Rorschach Research Exchange, 9*, 74–84.

Tibon, S., Handelzalts, J. E., & Weinberger, Y. (2005). Using the Rorschach for exploring the concept of transitional space within the political context of the Middle East. *International Journal of Applied Psychoanalytic Studies, 2*, 40–57.

Latife Yazigi
Department of Psychiatry, Escola Paulista de Medicina
Universidade Federal de São Paulo
Brazil
E-mail lyazigi@aclnet.com.br

Rorschachiana 32, 121–150
© 2011 Hogrefe Publishing

DOI: 10.1027/1192-5604/a000019

Original Article

Self-Perception in Andean Quechua-Speaking Children Entering School Using the Rorschach Method

Alejandro Rafael Belmont

Pontificia Universidad Católica del Perú (PUCP), Lima, Peru

Abstract. Using the Rorschach Psychodiagnostic Test, this study examines self-perception in Andean Quechua-speaking children beginning their education in Spanish. A comparative analysis was made between 30 Quechua-speaking children from a community in the Peruvian Andes and 30 Spanish-speaking children from the Lima, Peru, all 6 and 7 years old. Student's *t*-test and Z-test statistical analyses were used to compare data. Results show significant differences in self-concept (self-perception) for morbid content (MOR) between groups as well as for structural variables included in the Rorschach analysis. Quantitative data also illustrate the disparity between both groups and age-related norms published by Exner. Different aspects of validity for the Rorschach test are discussed as well as educational issues, considering this culturally heterogeneous population that has rarely been studied or made itself accessible to evaluation.

Keywords: Andean culture, education, language, Rorschach in children, self-perception

Introduction

Research on the psychological characteristics of Andean children is still incipient in Peru (Jara, 2000; Panez, 2004; Vargas, 2003), despite a growing interest. In this regard, for example, the emotional and cognitive impact on the Andean child upon first encounter with diverging Western standards, something that inevitably occurs when the child begins school, is unknown. The home-to-school transition is complex because

121

it involves changing from a Quechua-speaking environment with Andean customs (adult tasks demanded of children, collective parenting norms, etc.) to a school based on Western norms and education in Spanish.

In that respect, one of the main aspects of the child's personality that is influenced by entering school is self-perception (Raffo, 1993, 1995), because in this context the necessary conditions for its expression and development are created based on a more intense integration of cognitive, affective, and social aspects.

Given that self-concept is formed on the basis of a series of cognitive perceptions of oneself (Hattie, 1992) which are associated with the person's cognitive and social conditions and resources, entering a new sociocultural context such as the Spanish-speaking school, can affect the Andean child's perception of self, even more when this change of environment involves denigrating the native language and culture.

The child's first space of cultural influence is the family, where sociocultural rules and norms are established. There the child also introjects and develops the concept of self. However, upon entering school, contact with new peers and teachers will also include a new source of information to define themselves and others and how others will define them. In this case, because Quechua is substituted with Spanish within the Western school system, Andean children must adapt to and adopt Western characteristics associated with their education as students and members of a society that, according to Callirgos (1993), in fact denigrates the Andean. Likewise, the difficulties of performing academically in a new language, in this case Spanish, can affect the child's global achievement, especially compared to peers who come from Spanish-speaking households, giving them greater ease in learning and performing in this language. According to Harter (1999), ideas associated with academic achievement, as well as other ideas regarding daily life, will be the first materials for building their self-image, which will then be integrated in adolescence and continue to be strengthened through social interaction.

Self-Perception in the Andean Quechua-Speaking Child

In the Rorschach test, using the Comprehensive System, Exner (2000) defines the "self-perception" construct as the combination of attributes, attitudes, and concepts individuals builds about themselves in order to form self-worth and self-knowledge in accordance with reality. Exner also considers that the concept to include three fundamental aspects: self-image, self-esteem, and self-centeredness (Sendín, 2007). In the case of younger children, this internal vocabulary starts off quite concretely and is related to specific activities that are not yet grouped into larger categories due to the level of cognitive development (Harter, 1999). That is, a child can say he is good at playing with marbles or he is bad at playing poker, but he cannot yet refer to himself as a "good player." Likewise, the contrast between oneself and others becomes more important with age, as the individual begins to have a more marked vision of the external world and thus, greater possibilities of referencing information for self-evaluation (Harter, 1999). More specifically, Harter refers to certain typical characteristics of children between early childhood and middle childhood (5 and 7 years of age), including a fairly positive vision of oneself, with an overestimation of one's capacities. However, because their thinking is structured in one dimensional, the assigned attributes can become either all positive or all negative.

At the same time, social intervention affects the content of self-perception (Harter, 1999). On the one hand, the child's socializing environment (family members, peers, teachers, etc.) are going to influence the content and evaluative aspects of self-perception, that is, how the child considers himself to be competent or not, or worthy of affection or esteem. Likewise, the ecological or nonhuman environment is going to have a cognitive and affective impact on the child as part of the construction of the concept of self (Heerwagen & Orians, 2002; Kahn, 2002; Kellert, 2002).

When considering the Andean child, what characteristics should be taken into account in the formation of self-perception? First, it is essential to consider the environment as a source of both collectivist and individual values, beliefs, and attitudes that make up a way of seeing the world and functioning within it, that is, a cultural foundation. As shown by Hart and Fegley (1997), self-perception in people raised in individualistic cultures can be differentiated from those raised in collectivist cultures, due to the more social orientation of the latter.

On the one hand, social interaction, especially with the family, is the first experience that influences and internalizes the child's cultural background, from the structure of daily life to the transmission of the concept of the person (Hart & Fegley, 1997). In the case of Andean children, due to poverty, limitations to the possibilities for protection and stimulation are evident and harm their cognitive development, and they also cause a sense of frustration passed from father to son, reducing the children's confidence in their environment and self and generating a poor sense of their own efficacy (Raffo, 1995; Tessier, 1994; Thorne, Moreno, & López, 1996). In addition, in the socialization process, in some cases one encounters a distant and unexpressive communication between parents and children, which does not provide the necessary companionship and emotional security (Ortiz, 1994), but instead imposes a disciplinary severity in work (including physical punishment) with no significant reward (Panez, 2004).

Families in the Andes are found to be closer than families in urban areas, and they allow other family members to participate in raising children (Jara, 2000, 2008), in addition to providing constant stimulation and challenges, especially as models for the relationship patterns that prevail in the community (Anderson, 1994; Ortiz, 1993). In this case, the identification of the child with the father or mother also influences what the child attributes to himself and others, and it is dependent on how parents model those attributes in their actions and the roles they perform in the culture (Hart & Fegley, 1997).

One specific characteristic of the Andean culture is the role of providing care and affection, which is often passed on to the older children. They become the main sources of protection and affection for their younger siblings, in the absence of affection from their parents and faced with the lack of confidence caused by their environment (Panez, 2004). As caregivers, they must fulfill a complex task that demands their dealing with the children at different times and satisfy their needs. These tasks may be a defining source for the formation of a more complex and developmentally advanced self-concept than is expected of a Western child of the same age, whose behavior does not imply this level of responsibility, probably already integrated into the Andean child's self.

Faced with these demands, there are a series of cognitive and emotional needs, including the incorporation of new elements within the perception of oneself, expressed in what Panez (2004) calls "work-play." Here, the Andean child incorporates play into work activities assigned by their parents, such as tending cattle, pasturing, cooking, or gathering firewood, which allow contact with natural refuges. These spaces provide more opportunities to handle objects and a greater sense of enclosure than in refuges built in man-made parks, for example, leading to more imaginative and theatrical play (Kellert, 2002). In this case, by exploring their surroundings, children develop a broad sense of orientation with a large variety of cognitive stimuli (distant objects and spatial relationships between objects) at their disposal (Jara, 2000; Heerwagen & Orians, 2002), and generally learn diverse abilities and skills according to their age and gender.

The Impact of Entering the School Environment

Andean children, raised mainly within a certain idiosyncrasy and language, enter the Westernized, Spanish-speaking world (represented and reified in the school environment), which is not only culturally and socially different than their own, but also involves discrimination, paternalism, superiority, and domination with respect to the "other Peru" (Matos Mar, 2004). As Jara suggested (2000), this condition leads to the transmission or realization of the rejection of one's own cultural characteristics (such as language and dress) and the resulting sense of disadvantage in comparison with Western culture. Evidently, this is unfavorable for the construction of an integrated and true perception of themselves and, moreover, leads to negativity about their own characteristics, which in turn requires restructuring in order to acquire the desired cultural values (Hattie, 1992). Studies like those by Craven and Marsh (2005) show that low socioeconomic levels, racism, and marginalization can produce lower self-perception levels in indigenous populations than in nonindigenous populations.

Coupled with the cultural component, the school environment has other aspects that influence Andean schoolchildren. The self-concept that children acquire plays a central role in their interest and satisfaction in school, actively participating in academic achievements and future aspirations (Craven & Marsh, 2005). Papalia (2005) considers self-perception in schoolchildren to be developed and structured significantly between 6 and 12 years of age, as they respond to different demands, responsibilities, and responses to the needs of others and voluntary actions in the school environment. This context allows them to see themselves as part of society and put their self at stake through competition, comparison, appreciation, evaluation, affirmation, realization, and reputation (Benlliure, 2006; Raffo, 1995).

Upon entering school, Andean children already have diverse knowledge developed through cultural practices and by their responsibilities within the family, such as tending cattle and caring for younger siblings, which exceed those expected of a Western child and participate in the

125

development of self-perception (Markus, Mullally, & Kitayama, 1997). From this perspective, the child's entering school involves a socialization process that interrupts his or her own socialization to start another process that imposes forms of behavior and learning that may in fact deconstruct the child's way of thinking, seeing the world, and affectivity (Dunlop & Fabian, 2007; Griebel & Niesel, 2000). The parent's perspective is in favor of the adoption of Spanish and involves activities outside of the community that are more urban and more valuable; the children in turn learn to idealize school in an early desire for self-improvement (Panez, 2004).

Objectives

There are two major justifications for this study on self-perception in Andean children: (1) Children who been brought up with cultural norms, idiosyncrasies, and a language different from the school system they are submitted to may generate dissimilar characteristics than children who have not experienced this cultural clash, or who have developed differently because of their own cultural setting. (2) Personality tests such as the Rorschach have not been sufficiently probed in other cultural backgrounds such as the Andean, where social, economic, and cultural conditions differ greatly from Western standards. Thus, this paper explore the psychological impact of an aculturally relevant transition, in this case entering school, in the perception of one's self through the use of a Western-normed instrument. We intended to verify (1) whether Andean children have different characteristics of self-perception than children from the city, and (2) the soundness of the Rorschach Test for measuring self-perception and additional associated variables in Andean culture.

Method

Participants

Participants in this study were 30 children of both sexes, from 6 to 7 years of age, from the South-Andean department of Cuzco, Peru. The sample composition was based on the following inclusion criteria:

1) Age: 6 and 7 years
2) Native language: Quechua
3) Place of birth and upbringing: born and raised in the Andes
4) School level: the first year of school
5) Socioeconomic level: levels D and E (Apoyo, 2003)
6) Parents' origin: born and living in the Andes.

A comparison group was also established, composed of 30 children from the coastal district of Lima, Peru, in the same age range and socioeconomic level, but with differences in their native language (Spanish), place of birth and upbringing (Lima), and parents' origin (born and lived their whole lives in Lima). Table 1 describes the sociodemographic characteristics of the study and comparison groups.

Table 1. Sociodemographic characteristics of the study and comparison groups

Variables	Study group		Comparison group		Total	
	n	%	*n*	%	*n*	%
Sex						
Male	17	56.7	13	43.3	30	50
Female	13	43.3	17	56.7	30	50
Age						
Six	13	39.4	20	60.6	30	50
Seven	17	63	10	37	30	50
Place of origin						
Lima	0	0	30	100	30	50
Cuzco	30	100	0	0	30	50

This study considered self-perception cluster indicators, which refer to the set of descriptive and valuation elements subjects develop with regard to themselves (Exner & Sendín, 1998).
   The following indicators were included in the analysis:
1) *Egocentricity Index (3r + (2)/R) and Reflexes (Fr + rF)*, which indicate the person's level of self-centeredness;
2) *FD (Form-Dimension)* and *V (Shading-Vista)*, both related to the self-examination process, although FD is more associated with a positive sign of introspection and V is a cause of mainly negative emotions;
3) *An (anatomical content)* + *Xy (x-ray content)*, both related to an increased preoccupation with the body;

4) *MOR Quantity and Content*, which indicates a self-image with more negative, dysphoric, and damaged characteristics than usual;
5) *GHR:PHR*, which provide information on the subject's perception of himself and others.

Procedure

Education authorities at a school in the community authorized the application of the Rorschach Psychodiagnostic Test to 30 Quechua-speaking Andean children during their first year of school. A Quechua-speaking anthropologist interpreted the conversations with some authorities, as well as the instructions and children's responses in the evaluation process.

A drawing activity was carried out before the Rorschach test was applied and consisted of games in which each child went to a board and drew an object while the rest of the children tried to guess what the object was. This helped build rapport and generate answers in the actual evaluation. The test was performed during school hours and required three visits to complete. The comparison group was studied later in a school in a rural area of Lima, part of the same school organization. The Rorschach test was given to 30 children during school hours, using the same process as the study group and also requiring three visits to complete.

In both groups, databases were obtained for the children covering most of the required information. Missing data were provided by teachers (for both groups) and by the school's nursing staff (for the study group).

Once the test application process had been completed for the 60 children – and having considered protocols with at least 14 responses (there were no protocols with less than 14 responses) (Exner & Sendín, 1998) – 10 randomly chosen protocols of each group were passed on to two judges for the coding reliability analysis process (Hernández et al., 2006). The interrater reliability coefficient obtained was .89. Following the reliability analysis, complete coding of the protocols was performed, ensuring that the rating criteria were homogeneous according to the coding rules of Exner (1994). After the coding was accepted, protocols were scored. Statistical analyses were conducted by groups (mean, standard deviation), as well as *t*-tests for independent groups to compare means and Z-tests for proportions. No adjustments for multiple significance tests were made.

Results

Following the study's objectives, the presentation has been divided into two parts: (1) analysis of the structural variables of the Rorschach Psychodiagnostic test; (2) comparison for the variables associated with and included in the self-perception cluster.

Rorschach Structural and Associated Indicators

Because of the proximity of the values for all of the variables presented both in the sample and in Exner's normative standards (2001), the age groups (6 and 7) were combined with only one adjusted range for each variable. The differences between the study group, the comparison group, and the reference standards established by Exner were made by independent and one-sample t-tests. These are provided in Table 2.

Table 2. Descriptive statistics and t-test scores for the study group, comparison group and the Exner sample

Variables	Study group	Compari- son group	Total	Exner sample	Statistics	
	Mean (SD)	Mean (SD)	Mean (SD)	Mean (SD)	p^1	p^2
R	16.00(3.14)	19.30(6.20)	17.65(5.15)	19.42(1.25)	0.012*	0.01*
Lambda	3.95(4.56)	2.75(3.27)	3.35(3.98)	0.79(0.16)	0.246	<0.001*
Zf	4.13(2.83)	7.70(2.73)	5.92(3.29)	10.83(1.46)	<0.001*	<0.001*
P	1.07(0.98)	1.73(1.46)	1.40(1.28)	4.89(1.43)	0.042*	<0.001*
3r(2)/R	0.20(0.15)	0.22(0.16)	0.21(0.15)	0.66(0.15)	0.72	<0.001*
Fr + rF	0.00(0.00)	0.00(0.00)	0.00(0.00)	0.29(0.40)	1	N/A
MOR	0.07(0.25)	0.67(0.96)	0.37(0.76)	0.86(0.58)	0.002*	<0.001*
FD	0.07(0.25)	0.07(0.25)	0.07(0.25)	0.31(0.70)	1	<0.001*
V	0.00(0.00)	0.00(0.00)	0.00(0.00)	0.00(0.00)	1	N/A
An + Xy	0.43(0.86)	0.67(0.99)	0.55(0.93)	0.19(0.48)	0.335	0.004*

Notes. P^1 = Study group mean vs. comparison group mean. t-test significance (*$p \leq$ .05). P^2 = total group mean vs. Exner sample mean t-test significance (*$p \leq$ .05).

With respect to the differences in the study and comparison groups, within the variables of main section we find a significant difference ($p =$ .012) between the study and comparison groups with respect to the number of responses (R). Likewise, the Exner sample (2001) shows a significant difference ($p = .01$) with respect to the total group mean. This difference is a result of the low R mean from the study group. Similar significant differences ($p < .001$) between the total group mean and the Exner sample are also found with Lambda, Zf, and Popular (P). In the case of Lambda, both groups present higher values than the Exner sample, but in the range of other country samples extending from 1.3 (US Mexican American) to 8.47 (Japanese) (Shaffer, Erdberg, & Meyer, 2007). For Zf and P, we find significant differences between the study and comparison groups, with lower values than those expected for these age groups.

Self-Perception Cluster Indicators

In the self-perception cluster, we started with the egocentricity index and reflex responses. No significant differences between the study group and the comparison group were found, though the total mean of the both groups did contrast significantly from Exner's sample ($p < .001$). Nonetheless, compared to international samples for the same age groups such as Portugal (mean = 0.24) and Italy (mean = 0.23) (Shaffer et al., 2007), we find very similar values.

In the case of Form-Dimension (FD) and Vista (V) indicators, although its presence is not expected in children, in the case of FD it is a positive indicator provided that its frequency is not overly elevated, that is, FD ≤ 2 (Exner, 2001). On the other hand, Vista responses are associated with a more negative self-examination. Significant differences between the groups are not found in either variable. In the case of FD, we find a significant difference ($p < .001$) between the total group mean and Exner's normative sample.

For the responses with anatomical and x-ray content (An + Xy), when the sum of both is ≥ 2, it is considered an excessive preoccupation with the body. The results obtained do not show significant differences between the study group and the comparison group. Yet, again, we do find a significant difference ($p = .004$) between the total group mean and Exner's data.

The results of the sum of MOR responses indicate a self-image with

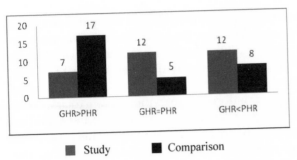

Figure 1. Proportion of GHR:PHR responses.

N=30 per group

negative characteristics or with a sense of imperfection, if the score obtained equals to MOR > 1. In this case, the results show significant differences (p = .002) between the study and comparison groups. Of the total number of subjects evaluated, two from the study group and 13 from the comparison group had MOR responses. Of the total number of children, only five obtained MOR > 1 (all five subjects belong to the comparison group and have a MOR equal to 2 or 4).

As to the GHR:PHR proportion, the comparison group has a greater number of cases in which GHR exceeds PHR than in the study group (Z = –2.635; p = .008). Meanwhile, the number of cases in which PHR is equal to GHR is greater in the study group than in the comparison group (Z = 2.005; p = .045). It is expected that GHR exceed PHR in the majority of responses for children of 6 and 7 years of age (Exner, 2001). The results can be seen in Figure 1.

Discussion

In order to organize the information, the discussion is divided into four parts: (1) discussion of reference standards; (2) comparative analysis of the study and comparison groups; (3) procedural aspects; and (4) suggestions.

The reference standards established by Exner (2000) for the 6- and 7-year-old population not only correspond to the Western First World (United States of America), but also include a sample in which the majority of the children have an average or high cognitive level. These standards cannot be used to validly measure either of the groups included in this study because of significant socioeconomic and cultural differences, as reaffirmed in previous studies performed in the Peruvian context (Cornejo, 2005; Puga, 2008). In such a case, the adjusted ranges for the Andean children's sample suggest the need to create specific standards that will allow effective comparisons between the groups. Having found very marked variations between the reference samples for children in different countries throughout the world, with unstable values and frequent extremes in the variables, emphasis has been placed on reviewing sample types as well as administering and scoring difficulties that may be affecting Rorschach results (Meyer, Erdberg, & Shaffer, 2007). In this respect, coding differences have been considered to be the main factor in these variations (Mattlar, 2008).

With respect to the cultural variable, some of the variables to be considered in the Andean children's sample, in addition to the self-perception cluster, are Organization Activity (Zf), Lambda (L), and Popular responses (P). The differences in the ranges of the study group and Exner's standards (2001) are significant for these variables, which at a first glance may suggest that the Andean children's group tends to economize and avoid complexity when processing information. Following Exner, this may possibly be an intellectual limitation and/or lack of motivation; nevertheless, we are still in the process of determining standards for other populations. When considering international samples, ranges are comparable to the Andean/Peruvian sample. This may confirm cultural/social particulars.

In the case of the popular responses, the range is also lower than expected in children of the ages studied (Exner, 2001). Again, this does not define a perceptive adjustment problem, but possibly an unconventional popular response group, for they belong to an environment that is culturally and ecologically different from the Western context. As explained previously, many of the names for the objects take on a different value, both because of their meaning in the original language (Quechua), and because of the way they are represented in these children's external world. Though it is known that these differences have been based on the mean number of P by subject, or on the absence of a P in certain cards (Sendín, 2007), this does not rule out the possibility that in even more distinct contexts – and with a more pronounced contact with nature – some responses can be considered popular for one population and not for another. Thus, it is hasty to determine that the number of popular responses is a definitive measure of perceptive adaptation and conventionality. In addition, it is interesting to note that many protocols also have a high FQu, which may possibly point to specific popular responses for the Andean population. Adding to what Meyer et al. (2007) may suggest with the International Reference Samples, most if not all of those are composed of Western-influenced sectors of each country's population, where the ranges of the variables may evidence the spectrum of cultural conventions, without undermining the particular nature of each culture(s) in a single country, as is the case with multicultural Peru. For exploratory purposes, as is the case here, we can consider the Exner norms as benchmarks to consider possible factors of influence.

With respect to the variables belonging to the area of self-perception, in the case of the Egocentricity Index $((3r + (2))/R)$ the low value of both groups compared to the Exner norms may account for a lack of self-concern, which may relate to highly demanding and unsupportive environments. This finding calls into question the developmental theory according to Piaget (1964) and confirmed by Exner (1994), where this stage of development is defined by egocentricity and self-centeredness, characteristic of emotional and cognitive immaturity, as well as reduced interpersonal focus. Possible explanations for the low levels of egocentricity may relate to two study group factors: first, sociocultural characteristics related to the development of self-perception; second, Andean parental expectations regarding education and progress.

With respect to the first, the Andean group, with its lower egocentricity value, is influenced by a developmental advancement brought on by the tasks of protecting and caring for younger siblings and pasturing, in the absence of signs of affection and with a marked disciplinary severity (Ortiz, 1994; Panez, 2004). This represents a highly demanding situation, without the necessary support as compensation. Likewise, it is not just a question of demands per se, as the concern for others and a more social sense of responsibility may generate a lower level of egocentricity than expected for this age group.

Furthermore, when taking parental expectations regarding education into account, the preexisting level of demand is increased while undermining the sense of efficacy achieved through the cognitive efforts and activities during the tasks typically performed (Anderson, 1994; Ortiz, 1993). By not providing opportunities to show or increase the abilities acquired through these activities, the Andean child begins to feel less effective with regard to an education that prioritizes a language other than his or her own – and also serves to impart knowledge through actions that are incompatible with those that generated their sense of

133

efficacy in the first place. This situation is also greatly affected by the sense of frustration passed on from father to son with respect to conditions of poverty (Raffo, 1995; Tessier, 1994; Thorne et al., 1996).

From this perspective, Western education represents an important demand on the child, especially if the parents reinforce it as a requirement for progress. This may generate a gradual increase in rejection (lesser self-centeredness) of one's own cultural characteristics (language and dress), which is associated with a sense of disadvantage compared to Western culture as a synonym for progress. Likewise, on a group level, self-perception is directly related to the child's position within the group of peers in terms of belonging, identification, personal value, and status. In this case, an education that "marginalizes" the social group they belong to through the language taught may affect their own sense of belonging.

Another noteworthy aspect with respect to self-perception is the tendency toward an increased preoccupation with the body, which is evident in the comparison group. One could hypothesize that, although both groups belong to a low socioeconomic level, where inadequate health conditions can be expected and resources in the rural Andes regions are even scarcer and could cause a real increase in preoccupation with physical illness, the Andean group of children have become accustomed to these difficulties. The difficulty of working at such a young age, often outdoors and in adverse weather conditions, strengthens a level of resilience that is significant in Andean children, unlike children from the coast, who are for the most part not subjected to such great demands that are not part of their normal everyday routine in an urban environment.

These results coincide with the absence of morbid responses associated with these contents, which according to Exner (2000) are frequent in subjects with physical problems. The comparison group's results suggest the tendency to incorporate more negative and damaged characteristics than usual as part of their self-image (Exner & Sendín, 1998). If we take the previous explanation of the possible existence of threatening environments into consideration as a cause of low levels of self-centeredness, the intensification of negative and dysphoric characteristics may be related to the rejection of a demanding environment that does not support them adequately. Possibly, while in the group of Andean children this emotionally and physically threatening environment is incorporated as something "normal" in their everyday context (perhaps even as something positive under certain circumstances as mentioned above), in the comparison group life in the city and their place within the family prevent them from incorporating it as normal, which becomes represented through symbolized damage (increase in MOR responses).

From this perspective, two types of resilience can be found in the group of Andean children: One that tends to be unconcerned with bodily dysfunctions, without much cognitive-emotional elaboration (less MOR responses and poorer protocols with an absence of Animal or Human Movement responses); and second, a lack of concern over the bodily dysfunctions with cognitive-emotional elaboration (less MOR and more complex protocols with Animal, Human, and Inanimate Movement responses, in addition to greater developmental quality). This suggests that, although both groups show resilience in the face of adversity, the first kind of child has less intellectual resources to cope with adversity and is more timid and passive: resilience through inhibition. The second kind of child, with greater intellectual resources and levels of self-centeredness, shows active coping abilities and makes use of the environment and the available resources to survive adversity, showing how integrated nature is as a source of support and a space in which to develop their resources.

If we take all of the variables studied into consideration, we note significant differences between the study and comparison groups, such as R, MOR, Zf, and P, due largely to cultural distinctions. Nonetheless, a factor that raises concerns in making valid evaluations is poverty. One of the most characteristic repercussions of poverty is malnutrition, which affects children's cognitive levels (evident in the large number of protocols with high Lambdas/low Zf and R). Several studies (Gorman, 1995; Grantham-McGregor, 1995; Pollitt, 2001; Wachs, 1995) show how chronic malnutrition in children, common in several regions of Peru, can cause brain damage that affects intellectual development and academic performance. On the one hand, this limits the possibilities of evaluations with the Rorschach Psychodiagnostic Test, which requires the formulation of verbal responses that are structured and obtained using developmentally appropriate cognitive processing (excluding cases of pathology). With this, one would expect to achieve group studies or individual diagnoses with greater precision, breadth, and diversifiability.

Moreover, malnutrition prevents the educational development of children who cannot respond to the demands of the school environment because of their educability or active learning capability (Pollitt, 2001). This concept includes nutritional and physical aspects, as well socioemotional aspects regarding motivation and self-efficacy. This last aspect can be called "chronic lack of motivation," a parallel to chronic malnutrition. In other words, as children's academic responsiveness is biologically reduced by a lack of nutrients, the possibility of their using their abilities as an instrument to reach their goals and gain control over the environment is also limited by a self-perception that is charged with pessimism and fragility (Craven, Marsh, & Burnett, 2003; Harter, 1999; Pajares & Schunk, 2005). Likewise, both problems, malnutrition and a lack of motivation, mutually reinforce one another, and in many cases it is difficult to decide if the child's performance is related to either factor, especially under the current normative standards.

As suggestions for the application of the Rorschach test in this population, it is important to clarify that it was necessary to use Exner's (2000) and Jara's (2000) suggestions for application, in addition to the use of a group activity. On the one hand, in order for the child to have greater ease in the process of recovering the information given for each card and deal with attention and inhibition issues, questions were asked after each card (Exner, 2000). This allowed the child to respond to the inquiry's indications, remembering and associating the responses. Likewise, it was indispensable to use Jara's suggestions (2000) for Andean children with regard to modifications to the inquiry in order to facilitate comprehension. Before the inquiry, it was necessary to use a real object as an example (a chair for example) and ask the following: "What is this called?" and "How do you know it is a chair?" Later, during the inquiry phase, the instructions were the following: "In what way is this drawing (the blot) similar to the butterfly (or the mentioned object)?" and "How do you know this drawing is a butterfly?" (Jara, 2000).

On the other hand, the simultaneous interpretation from Quechua to Spanish was also a special condition in all of the applications for the Andean children. In order to translate effectively, the interpreter was previously informed of the objective of the test and what types of questions were allowed during the inquiry phase. In addition, it was established that the translation of the children's responses and the evaluator's questions would be absolutely literal.

Due to syntax differences and, in some cases, semantic differences between Spanish and Quechua, it was necessary to limit the interpreter's tendency to rearrange and paraphrase the children's responses or evaluator's questions to comply with either language's morpho-syntactic rules. This presented a necessary challenge in two ways: for coding responses and for the evaluated child's comprehension.

With regard to response coding, the substitution of equivalent but semantically different words when interpreting the responses from Quechua to Spanish could affect the coding precision of the developmental quality (DQ), formal quality (FQ), popular responses (P), and special codes, such as Deviated Verbalizations (DV) or Incongruent Combinations (INCOM). Thus, the exact translation of certain objects seen in the cards was essential, since many of these objects were specific to the region, and their identification also involved the recognition of cultural wealth and diversity.

One common example in the Andean children's sample appears in card V, where many saw a *pillpinto* – an insect belonging to the order *Lepidoptera*, mainly *Rhopalocera*, having suctorial mouthparts and four to six membranous wings covered with small scales. In such cases, it is important to determine whether the object possesses an exact translation or only an approximate one, which in this case would be the word "butterfly." This makes it difficult to decide on a perceptual distortion or conceptual error because the characteristics of the blot may or may not coincide with the object. If a more precise term to define the blot can be used, it would not be advisable to codify it as popular, or, in other cases, with a determined formal quality without having tracked the proper determinants. Therefore, we attempted to inquire about the object's parts, in order to later corroborate them with the definition in Quechua, rather than using an imprecise definition in Spanish. Although the extent of a child's vocabulary may be limited and may lack the necessary conceptual precision, the evaluator's inquiry capacity is crucial to deciding whether the respondent does not know another term or does not have an exact definition for the object and thus generalizes it adequately (sees it well). Clearly, this also implies the need for a clinician who is trained or assisted with regard to the vocabulary for the language in question, in order to avoid coding errors.

On the other hand, when considering the Andean child's comprehension, it was important to respect Quechua syntax in order for the child to understand the instructions and questions being translated from Spanish during the application. It was interesting to note that what was often first perceived as shyness or inhibition was actually associated with the child's lack of understanding when not changing the syntax of the sentences in Spanish into Quechua. Although they were able to identify specific objects in the blot during the response phase, during the inquiry, when they were asked to point out the parts of the object in the blot, say, in the case of an animal, they were unable to say anything at first. In some cases, after repeating the question, they began to point out the parts of the whole blot, but not those related to the object. With this, it became evident that the question had not been understood, and the phrase was tuned to the Quechua word order and phrasing. With this, the children were able to describe the object and its determinants, responding to the question "How do you know this picture is a butterfly?" with the response, "Because it is black, like a butterfly." The second part of the phrase ("like a butterfly") confirmed that it was no longer the description of the blot. Therefore, it is evident that the test instructions and questions must be translated into phrases that communicate the question in the common or everyday phrasing of the language – which is not necessarily the same as it was conceived in the former language, in this case Spanish.

Conclusions

From this study, we can observe significant differences in self-concept (self-perception) for morbid content (MOR) between groups as well as structural variables included in the Rorschach analysis (R, ZF, and P). This is largely due to cultural differences that influence children's upbringing, primarily based on family rituals. We also find a disparity between both groups and age-related norms published by Exner. Nonetheless, certain international samples do have similar ranges in egocentrism, which confirms variability relating to self-perception and development.

There are certain limitations to keep in mind for this study. For one, the size of the sample is fairly small (30 per group) in order to establish generalizations. For this reason, the study did not have this as an objective, but rather to use self-perception as a variable to test the Rorschach and its capacity to analyze personality in this culturally specific sample. Additionally, the procedure used for the Rorschach, even if operational, does not guarantee complete validity when dealing with the creation of an international sample, or making clinical assertions. This would require more testing and evaluation of results, with the standardization of specific conditions (e.g., translation between languages during testing).

As to improvements, effective research to promote the development of low-income schoolchildren needs to address intervening factors like malnutrition (coupled with the above-mentioned normative aspects). In this way, evaluations could be conducted to obtain valid and accurate data of the child's personality. Previous normative studies (Yazigi, Ribeiro, & Semer, 2008) have already considered the need to apply screening tests such as Raven's Progressive Matrices in order to ensure that the sample children can respond successfully to the test, excluding cases with borderline intelligence or mental retardation. Furthermore, considering that tests like the Rorschach are essentially evaluations based on language, one may also consider the need for screening. No longer obscured by the impact of limited resources, the way in which these children enter school with their previously acquired cultural norms and experiences would be clearer, and the effects of the transition from home to school on self-perception could thus be redefined. As Crain (1996) says, it is essential first to understand how the constituent characteristics and their corresponding interaction relate to self-perception in order to study the associated aspects. In addition to proving their validity and reliability in different cultures, significant interpretations of data obtained through psychometric tests should also detect culturally significant content (Byrne, 2003; Harter, 1999). This is particularly true in the case of self-report or other types of self-perception tests made up of items that underlie specific operational definitions of the construct, which are influenced by response patterns and have perspectives that vary from culture to culture (Byrne, 2003). For example, the Chinese and Japanese cultures do not coincide with the same areas of self-perception in self-report tests as the Anglo-Saxon culture, because of their individualist/collectivist dichotomy (Meredith, Wang, & Zheng, 1993).

Finally, we want to stress that our study focused on approaching a group of persons who has rarely been studied in the field of psychology. This approach involved dealing with methodological, theoretical, and practical issues necessary for generating further research. In order to define the effects of entering the school environment on the self-perception of Andean Quechua-speaking children, it is necessary to conduct research based on psychometric precision and standards, with a sample fit for testing – or rather a test that fits the sample. If unfavorable conditions, such as chronic malnutrition, prevent the tests from detecting the possible differences between human groups subject to the same poverty levels, the extent to which culture, education, and socialization processes influence self-perception and other areas of the personality cannot be determined.

A. R. Belmont

Acknowledgments

My sincere appreciation to Mrs. Lupe Jara for her contribution to this study. Also to Centro Bartolomé de Las Casas for interpretation services, and to the Fe y Alegría schools, where the research was conducted.

References

Anderson, J. (1994). *La socialización infantil en comunidades andinas y de migrantes urbanos en el Perú* [Infant socialization in Andean and urban migrant communities in Peru]. Lima: Fundación Bernard Van Leer.

Apoyo (2003). *Niveles socioeconómicos Perú* [Socioeconomic levels Peru]. Lima: Opinion y Mercado.

Benlliure, V. (2006). Desarrollo de la personalidad [Personality development]. In A. I. Córdoba, A. Descals, & M. D. Gil (Eds.), *Psicología del desarrollo en la edad escolar* (pp. 181–196). Madrid: Ediciones Pirámide.

Byrne, B. (2003). Testing for equivalent self-concept measurement across culture. In H. Marsh, R. Craven, & D. McInerney (Eds.), *International advances in self research* (Vol. 1, pp. 291–313). Greenwich, CT: Information Age Publishing.

Callirgos, J. (1993). *El racismo. La cuestión del otro (y del uno)* [Racism. The question of the other (and of one)]. Lima: DESCO.

Cornejo, M. (2005). *Características de personalidad en niños talentosos limeños que viven en condiciones de pobreza, a través del psicodiagnóstico de Rorschach* [Personality characteristics in talented children from Lima that live in conditions of poverty using the Rorschach Test]. (Thesis for obtaining the Licensure in Educational Psychology). Pontificia Universidad Católica del Perú, Lima, Peru.

Crain, R. M. (1996). The influences of age, race, and gender on child and adolescent multidimensional self-concept. In B. A. Bracken (Ed.), *Handbook of self-concept* (pp. 395–420). New York: Wiley.

Craven, R., & Marsh, H. W. (2005). Dreaming Futures: An empirical analysis of indigenous Australian students' aspirations, self-concepts, and realities. In H. Marsh, R. Craven, & D. McInerney (Eds.), *International advances in self research* (Vol. 2, pp. 195–210). Greenwich, CT: Information Age Publishing.

Craven, R. G., Marsh, H. W., & Burnett, P. (2003). Cracking the self-concept enhancement conundrum: A call and blueprint for the next generation of self-concept enhancement research. In H. W. Marsh, R. G. Craven, & D. McInerney (Eds.), *International advances in self research* (Vol. 1, pp. 91–126). Greenwich, CT: Information Age Press.

Dunlop, A.-M., & Fabian, H. (2007). *Outcomes for good practice in transition processes for children entering primary school.* La Haya: Bernard Van Leer Foundation.

Exner, J. (1994). *El Rorschach. Un sistema comprehensivo* [The Rorschach. A Comprehensive System]. Volumen 1: Fundamentos Básicos. Madrid: Psimática.

Exner, J. (2000). *Principios de Interpretación del Rorschach: Manual para el Sistema Comprehensivo* [Interpretation principles of the Rorschach: Manual for the Comprehensive System]. Madrid: Psimática.

Exner, J. (2001). *Manual de Codificación del Rorschach: Para el Sistema Comprehensivo* [Codification manual for the Rorschach's Comprehensive System]. Madrid: Psimática.

Exner, J., & Sendín, C. (1998). *Manual de interpretación del Rorschach* [Interpretation manual for the Rorschach]. Madrid: Psimática.

Gorman, K. S. (1995). Malnutrition and cognition development: Evidence from experimental/quasiexperimental studies among the mild-to-moderately malnourished. *Journal of Nutrition, 25,* 2239-2244.

Grantham-McGregor, S. (1995). A review of studies of the effect of severe malnutrition on mental development. *Journal of Nutrition, 25,* 2233-2238.

Griebel, W., & Niesel, R. (2000, August). *The children's voice in the complex transition into Kindergarten and school.* Paper presented at the 10th European Conference on Quality in Early Childhood Education, London.

Hart, D., & Fegley, S. (1997). The development of self-awareness and self-understanding in cultural context. In U. Neisser & D. Jopling (Eds.), *Culture, experience, and the conceptual self* (pp. 128-153). New York: Cambridge University Press.

Harter, S. (1999). *The construction of the self.* New York: Guilford.

Hattie, J. (1992). *Self-concept.* New Jersey: Erlbaum.

Heerwagen, J. H., & Orians, G. H. (2002). The ecological world of children. In P. H. Kahn, Jr., & S. R. Kellert (Eds.), *Children and nature: Psychological, sociocultural, and evolutionary investigations.* Cambridge, MA: MIT.

Hernández, F. & Baptista, P. (2006). *Metodología de la investigación* [Research Methodology]. México, D. F.: McGraw-Hill Interamericana.

Jara, L. (2000). Conociendo a los niños andinos a través de sus dibujos y sus sueños [Learning about Andean children through their drawings and their dreams]. In R. Panez, G. Silva, & M. Silva (Eds.), *Resiliencia en el Ande: un modelo para promoverla en los niños* (pp. 249-284). Lima: Panez & Silva Ediciones.

Jara, L. (2008). *Representaciones sobre el maltrato infantil en niños limeños y andinos a través de sus dibujos* [Representations on child abuse through drawings in children from Lima and the Andes]. (Thesis for obtaining the title of Master in Psychology). Pontificia Universidad Católica del Perú, Lima, Peru.

Kahn, P. H., Jr. (2002). Children's affiliations with nature: Structure, development, and the problem of environmental generational amnesia. In P. H. Kahn, Jr., & S. R. Kellert (Eds.), *Children and nature: Psychological, sociocultural, and evolutionary investigations* (pp. 93-116). Cambridge, MA: MIT.

Kellert, S. R. (2002). Experiencing nature: Affective, cognitive, and evaluative development in children. In P. H. Kahn, Jr., & S. R. Kellert (Eds.), *Children and nature: Psychological, sociocultural, and evolutionary investigations* (pp. 117-151). Cambridge, MA: MIT.

Markus, H. R., Mullally, P., & Kitayama, S. (1997). Selfways: Diversity in modes of cultural participation. In U. Neisser & D. Jopling (Eds.), *The conceptual self in context: Culture, experience, self-understanding* (pp. 13–61). Cambridge: Cambridge University Press.

Matos Mar, J. (2004). *Desborde popular y crisis de Estado. Veinte años después* [Popular overflow and state crisis. Twenty years later]. Lima: Fondo Editorial del Congreso del Perú.

Mattlar, C. (2008, July). *Gathering nonpatient children reference data.* Paper presented at the XIXth IRS Congress of Rorschach and Projective Methods, Leuven, Belgium.

Meredith, W. H., Wang, A., & Zheng, F. M. (1993). Determining constructs of self-perception for children in Chinese cultures. *School Psychology International, 14,* 371–380.

Meyer, G., Erdberg, P., & Shaffer, T. (2007). Toward international normative reference data for the comprehensive system. *Journal of Personality Assessment, 89,* 201–216.

Ortiz, A. (1993). *La pareja y el mito. Estudio sobre las concepciones de la persona y de la pareja en los Andes* [Couple and myth. A study on the concept of person and couple of the Andes]. Lima: Fondo Editorial de la Pontificia Universidad Católica del Perú.

Ortiz, A. (1994). *Un estudio sobre los grupos autónomos de niños a partir de un trabajo de campo en Champaccocha, Andahuaylas. Proyecto de invocacionespedagógicas no formales* [A study on autonomous groups of children based on empirical work in Champaccocha, Andahuaylas. A project on nonformal pedagogical invocations]. Lima: Ministerio de Educación – Fundación Bernard Van Leer.

Pajares, F., & Schunk, D. (2005). Self-efficacy and self-concept beliefs: Jointly contributing to the quality of human life. In H. W. Marsh, R. G. Craven, & D. McInerney (Eds.), *International advances in self research* (Vol. 2, pp. 239–266). Greenwich, CT: Information Age Publishing.

Panez, R. (2004). *El lenguaje silencioso de los niños* [The silent language of children]. Lima: Panez & Silva Ediciones.

Papalia, D. (2005). *Desarrollo humano* [Human development]. México, DF: McGraw-Hill.

Piaget, J. (1964). *The moral judgment of the child.* New York: Free Press.

Pollitt, E. (2001). The developmental and probabilistic nature of the functional consequences of iron-deficiency anemia in children. *Journal of Nutrition, 131,* 669–675.

Puga, L. (2008). *Relaciones interpersonales en un grupo de niños que reciben castigo físico y emocional* [Interpersonal relationship in a group of children that receive emotional and physical punishment]. (Thesis for obtaining the title of Licensure in Clinical Psychology). Pontificia Universidad Católica del Perú, Lima, Peru.

Raffo, L. (1993). *El autoconcepto en el niño escolar* [Self-concept in the school-aged child]. Lima: PEA Asesores.

Raffo, L. (1995). *Autoconcepto del niño escolar: fundamentos y estrategias* [Self-concept in the school-aged child: Foundations and strategies]. Lima: San Marcos.

Sendín, C. (2007). *Manual de Interpretación del Rorschach para el Sistema Comprehensivo* [Interpretation manual for the Rorschach Comprehensive System]. Madrid: Psimática.

Shaffer, T. W., Erdberg, P., & Meyer, G. J. (2007). Toward international normative reference data for the Comprehensive System. *Journal of Personality Assessment, 89*(1), 201–216.

Tessier, R. (1994). Dimensiones ecológicas de la familia: la situación social de los niños [Ecological dimensions of the family: The social situations of children]. *Revista de Psicología de la PUCP, 1,* 3–32.

Thorne, C., Moreno, M., & López, E. (1996). El niño eje del cambio social para una educación de calidad [The child as the axis of social change for quality education]. *Cuadernos de la facultad de Letras y Ciencias Humanas de la PUCP, No. 17,* 13–24.

Vargas, V. (2003). *Características psicológicas de niños y niñas que trabajan en dos centros mineros artesanales de Perú* [Psychological characteristics of boys and girls who work in two artisans mining centers of Peru]. (Thesis for obtaining the title of Licensure in Educational Psychology). University of Lima, Lima, Peru.

Wachs, T. (1995). Relation of mild-to-moderate malnutrition to human development: Correlational studies. *Journal of Clinical Nutrition, 42,* 2245–2254.

Yazigi, L., Ribeiro, R., & Semer, N. L. (2008, July). *Normative study of the Rorschach Comprehensive System in Brazilian children.* Paper presented at the XIXth IRS Congress of Rorschach and Projective Methods, Leuven, Belgium.

Alejandro Rafael Belmont
Coronel Portillo 230 apt#12 San Isidro
Lima27
Lima, Peru
E-mail arb281@mail.harvard.edu
Currently affiliated with Harvard University

Summary

This study analyzes the characteristics of self-perception in a group of Andean Quechua-speaking children entering school using the Rorschach method.Self-perception is shaped in part by family interactions, and also through schooling. In Andean culture, several patterns of child-rearing and day-to-day rituals that are associated with collective societies have an impact on a child's development of self-perception. Moreover, the transition into a school setting introduces principles and values that contrast Andean culture and impact the way self-perception develops. As this is one of the only studies with this population, we explore and not define or generalize the differences that originate from living in an Andean society that is culturally different from the West.

At the same time, the Rorschach method has not been utilized enough in populations that are not essentially Western, resulting in a lack of normative data to assess personality in other cultures and consider the validity of any kind of psychological claim. That is why this study focuses on presenting issues related to assessment and, more specifically, coding.

The sample used for this study included 30 Quechua-speaking children of both sexes, from 6 to 7 years of age, from the South-Andean district of Cuzco, Peru. To contrast the Andean children, another group of 30 children from the coastal department of Lima, Peru, were included, all of the same age range and socioeconomic level, but with differences in their native language (Spanish), place of birth and upbringing (Lima), and parents' origin (born and living permanently in Lima).

The two groups were compared considering 5 variables from the self-perception cluster: Egocentricity Index (EGO) and Reflexes (rF/Fr), related to self-esteem and self-perception; Form-Dimension (FD) and Vista (V), related to self-examination; Anatomical content (An) and x-ray content (Xy), related to an increased preoccupation with the body; MOR responses, indicating a self-image with more negative, dysphoric and damaged characteristics than usual; and GHR:PHR (Good Human Response: Poor Human Response), for information on the subject's perception of himself and others. Additionally, structural variables such as Zf, R, Lambda and P. All of the mentioned variables were also contrasted with Exner's sample (2001).

The results show significant differences between the study and the comparison group for the following variables: R ($p = .012$), MOR ($p = .002$), Zf ($p < .001$), P (0.042),y GHR exceeding PHR ($p = .008$), with higher values for the comparison group. There were also significant differences between the total means values of both groups and Exner's sample for all variables used in the study (p values ranging from .004 to $< .001$).From this data, it is important to mention that low values such as the Egocentricity Index may be a consequence of culturally-specific forms of interaction with high collective demands with low sense of efficacy, which are also intensified by poverty. Following Exner, structural variables with low values such as Zf, R and Lambda are signs of an intellectual limitation and/or lack of motivation. Nevertheless, when considering international samples, ranges are comparable to the Andean/Peruvian sample. This may confirm cultural/social particulars,

144

which include linguistic differences as critical for coding purposes, and in that sense, for the validity and precision of any interpretation. At the same time, a homogenization of groups with lower-end values may be due to repercussions of poverty such as malnutrition that affect overall test taking capacities in children. These issues are central for developing international samples and establishing crosscultural comparisons.

Resumen

El objetivo de este estudio es analizar las características de autopercepción en un grupo de niños andinos quechuahablantes que ingresan al ámbito escolar usando el Psicodiagnóstico de Rorschach. En estas edades, el desarrollo de la autopercepción se da a través de la influencia de la familia y el colegio. En la cultura andina, existen patrones de cuidado materno y rituales familiares típicos de sociedades colectivistas que afectan la autopercepción de manera específica. Siendo este uno de los únicos estudios con esta población en particular, exploramos las diferencias que se originan en la sociedad Andina al compararla con el Occidente. Asimismo, ubicarnos en la transición del hogar quechuahablante a la escuela hispanohablante significa la introducción a principios y valores contrastantes que afectan el desarrollo de la autopercepción. Sin embargo, no pretendemos generalizar o definir las características de los niños andinos.

Además, el Rorschach no ha sido utilizado lo suficiente en poblaciones diferentes a la occidental, por lo que carecen normas para una evaluación válida de la personalidad en otras culturas. Por esta razón, el estudio está principalmente enfocado en presentar y analizar cuestiones relacionadas al proceso de evaluación y, más específicamente, a la codificación de las respuestas.

La muestra de este estudio incluye 30 niños quechuahablantes de ambos sexos, de seis y ocho años de edad, del departamento sur andino de Cuzco, Perú. Para el grupo de comparación, se incluyeron otros 30 niños del departamento de Lima, Perú, todos del mismo rango de edad y nivel socioeconómico, salvo diferencias en el idioma (español), lugar de nacimiento (Lima), y el origen de sus padres (haber nacido y vivido permanentemente en Lima).

Se comparó ambos grupos en base a 5 variables del cluster de autopercepción: Índice de Egocentrismo (EGO) y reflejos (rF/Fr), relacionados al autoestima y la autopercepción; Forma-Dimensión (FD) y

Vista (V), relacionados al autoexamen; Contenidos Anatómicos (An) y Contenidos de Rayos-X, relacionados a una preocupación por el cuerpo mayor a la usual; y GHR:PHR, para información sobre la percepción de uno mismo y de otros. Además, variables estructurales tales como Zf, R, Lambda y P. Todas las variables mencionadas también fueron contrastadas con la muestra de Exner (2001).

Los resultados muestran diferencias significativas entre el grupo de estudio y el de comparación para las siguientes variables: R ($p = .012$), MOR ($p = .002$), Zf ($p < .001$), P (0.042), y GHR mayor a PHR ($p = .008$), todas con valores superiores en el grupo de comparación. Igualmente, hubieron diferencias significativas entre los valores totales de los grupos combinados y la muestras de Exner para todas las variables estudiadas (valores p entre .004 hasta $< .001$). Más allá de las diferencias específicas entre grupos, es importante resaltar que valores bajos como el índice de egocentrismo podrían ser consecuencia de formas de interacción culturalmente específicas, donde existen altas demandas para un pobre sentimiento de autoeficacia, ambos intensificados por el factor pobreza. Si seguimos a Exner, niveles bajos en las variables estructurales como el Zf, el R y el Lambda son señales de una limitación intelectual y/o una motivación pobre, con mucha mayor resonancia en el grupo de estudio. Sin embargo, al considerar las muestras internacionales vemos que los rangos son semejantes a la nuestra. Esto sin duda es señal de particularidades culturales/sociales, incluyendo diferencias lingüísticas que serían críticas para los procesos de codificación, y por ende para la validez y la precisión de las interpretaciones. Al mismo tiempo, la homogenización de grupos en torno a valores bajos podría estar asociada a las repercusiones de la pobreza tales como la malnutrición, la cual afecta las capacidades para responder a la prueba. Estos asuntos son centrales para el desarrollo de muestras internacionales representativas que puedan permitir comparaciones entre culturas, sociedades y grupos humanos.

Résumé

Cette étude porte sur l'analyse, à l'aide du test du Rorschach, des caractéristiques de la perception de soi chez des enfants originaires des Andes parlant le quechua et débutant leur scolarité. La perception de soi est en partie façonnée par nos interactions familiales ainsi que par notre expérience éducative. Dans la culture andine, la manière d'élever les enfants et les divers rituels journaliers, présents dans ces sociétés collectives, ont un impact sur le développement de la perception de soi chez l'enfant. De plus, la transition vers un milieu scolaire introduit des principes et des valeurs qui contrastent avec celles de la culture andine d'origine et ont un impact sur le développement de la perception de soi chez l'enfant. Cette étude étant parmi les premières portant sur des enfants originaires des Andes, nous souhaitons explorer les différences entre le modèle social andin et ceux des pays occidentaux, sans chercher à les catégoriser et en évitant toute généralisation.

En outre, la méthode du Rorschach a été principalement validée dans les pays occidentaux et nous ne disposons pas de normes applicables qui nous permettent de procéder à l'évaluation de la personnalité dans d'autres cultures ou à la validation de toutes donnée psychologique pour ces cultures. C'est pourquoi cette étude porte principalement sur les questions d'évaluation et de cotations.

La population de cette étude est composée de trente enfants des deux sexes parlant le quechua, âgés de six à sept ans, et originaires du département de Cuzco au Pérou. Les auteurs ont inclus un groupe de comparaison de trente enfants andins venant d'un département côtier de Lima, du même âge et de même niveau socioéconomique, mais dont la langue (l'espagnol), le lieu de naissance, l'éducation et l'origine des parents (nés et vivant à Lima) sont différents du premier groupe .

Les deux groupes ont été comparés sur 5 variables en lien avec la perception de soi: L'index d'égocentricité (EGO); les réflexions (rF/Fr), traduisant l'estime de soi; la forme-dimension (FD) et les Vistas (V), portant sur l'introspection; les réponses anatomie et rayon X permettant d'analyser une préoccupation croissante à l'égard de la perception de son corps; les réponses morbides (MOR) permettant d'identifier une image de soi plus négative, dysphorique et endommagée que de coutume; et GHR:PHR (bonne/mauvaise représentation humaine) qui nous informe sur la perception de soi et des autres. De plus, les auteurs ont ajouté les variables structurelles Zf, R, Lambda et P. Toutes les variables ont été comparées à l'échantillon d'Exner (2001).

Des différences significatives intergroupes peuvent être observées pour les variables suivantes: R (p = .012); MOR (p = .002); Zf (p < .001); P (p = .042); et GHR plus élevé que PHR (p = .008) pour le groupe de comparaison. Des différences significatives peuvent également être observées entre la valeur totale des moyennes des deux groupes de cette étude et l'échantillon d'Exner (valeurs p entre .004 et < .001). Il est important de mentionner, au vue de ces résultats, que les valeurs inférieures observées, comme pour l'index d'égocentricité, sont la conséquence de formes d'interaction spécifiquement culturelles, marquées par des demandes collectives, non gratifiantes, et rendues plus prégnantes par le niveau de pauvreté. Selon Exner, des valeurs inférieures aux variables Zf R et Lambda sont le signe d'un retard mental et/ou d'un manque de motivation. Toutefois, lorsque l'on prend en compte d'autres échantillons internationaux, les variations sont similaires à celles observées dans l'échantillon andin. Cela semble confirmer la présence de spécificités socioculturelles, dont les différences linguistiques, qui sont un élément crucial pour l'établissement d'une cotation et donc pour la validité et la précision de toute interprétation. Parallèlement, l'homogénéisation constatée des groupes de valeurs inférieures peut être due à la pauvreté et ses conséquences dont la malnutrition, qui affecte les performances des enfants lors des tests. Ces questions sont centrales pour le développement de normes internationales et afin de pouvoir procéder à des comparaisons interculturelles.

アンデスの小学校に入学するケチュア語を話す子どものロールシャッハを用いた自己知覚

　本研究の目的はロールシャッハ法を用いて、アンデスの小学校に入学するケチュア語を話す子どもたちの自己知覚の特徴を分析することである。自己知覚はある程度は家族の相互関係により形成されるが、また学校教育を通しても形成される。アンデスの文化においては、幾種類かの子どもを育てる様式と、集団主義社会と関連している日常の儀式が子どもの自己知覚の発達に衝撃を与えている。さらに、学校という設定に入ってゆくという過渡がアンデス文化とは対比をなす原則や価値観を導入することになり、自己知覚の発達の様相に衝撃を与える。この研究はこの集団における唯一の研究であるので、われわれは探求するが、西洋とは文化的に異なっているアンデス社会の生活から生起する差異が明らかであると決めつけたり、その差異を一般化したりしない。

　同時に、本質的に西洋ではない集団にはロールシャッハ法は十分には用いてこられておらず、他の文化におけるパーソナリティをアセスメントするための、そしていかなる種類の心理学的な要求の妥当性を考慮するための、標準データが欠けるという結果となっている。これが、この研究がアセスメント、よりとりわけコーディングに関係した問題を提示することに焦点を当てている理由である。

　本研究にもちいられているサンプルにはクスコの南アンデスの領域から30名の両方の性別の、6〜7歳のケチュア語を話す子どもが含まれている。アンデスの子どもたちと対比するために、ペルーのリマの沿岸部から同じ年令の範囲で同じ社会経済的レベルの30名の子どものグループが含まれたが、母語（スペイン語）と出生し育った場所（リマ）と両親の出身地（リマで生まれ、ずっと住んでいる）は異なっていた。

　2つのグループは自己知覚のクラスターの5つの変数が検討のために比較された：自己評価と自己知覚に関連している自己中心性指標（EGO）と反射反応（r F/Fr）；自己検閲と関連している形態立体反応（FD）と濃淡立体（V）；身体へのとらわれの増大と関連している解剖（An）とエックス線写真（Xy）；通常よりネガティブで不快で、ダメージを負った特徴をともなった自己イメージを示しているMOR；被験者の自身や他者の知覚に関する情報を示しているGHR:PHR（良質人間反応：貧質人間反応）：さらに、ZfやR、ラムダ、Pといった構造の変数。上述したすべての変数がExner（2001）のサンプルと対比された。

　結果は以下の変数において、本研究のグループと比較グループにおいて有意差が示された：R(p=0.012)、MOR(p=0.002)、Zf(p＜001)、P(0.042)、GHRがPHRを上回る(p=0.008)、比較グループの方が値が高かった。本研究でもちいられたすべての変数について両方のグループをあわせた平均とExnerのサンプルの比較においても有意差が認められた（pは0.004からP<0.001）。このデータから、自己中心性指標のような指標の低い値は、低い効能感をもたらす高い集団主義の要求、そしてそれは貧困によってまた増大させられるので

A. R. Belmont

あるが、をともなった文化に特徴的な相互作用の形式の結果であるかもしれないと述べることは重要なことであろう。Exner によれば、構造的変数の低い値、例えば Zf や R、ラムダは知能の限界や動機付けの欠如のサインかもしれない。にもかかわらず、国際的なサンプルを考慮した場合、範囲はアンデス／ペルーのサンプルとして比較可能なものである。これは文化的／社会的特色を裏づけているかも知れないし、そこにはコーディングのためには重要な問題であり、いかなる解釈においても妥当性と正確さにとっても重要な問題となってくる、言語の相違という問題を含んでいる。同時に、値が低いほうのグループの同質性は、子どもの検査を受ける能力に全般的に影響を与える栄養失調といった貧困の影響によるものかも知れない。こういった問題は国際的なサンプルを発展させたり、異文化間の比較を達成したりする際には中心的な問題になる。

Rorschachiana 32, 151–182
© 2011 Hogrefe Publishing

DOI: 10.1027/1192-5604/a000020

Original Article

The Collapse of Potential Space in Adolescents with Psychosomatic Disorders

A Rorschach Illustration of Two Case Studies

Liat Appel

Department of Psychology, Bar-Ilan University, Ramat-Gan, Israel

Abstract. The study applies Winnicott's (1971) conceptualization of potential space to explore psychosomatic phenomena as manifested in Rorschach protocols of two adolescent outpatients. This approach for understanding psychosomatic disorders is based on Ogden's (1986) model for defining different forms of collapse of potential or transitional space between reality and fantasy. Following Smith (1990), who applies this conceptualization to Rorschach work, the study compares data related to cognitive functioning derived from the Rorschach Comprehensive System (CS; Exner, 2003) from protocols of two adolescents with psychosomatic symptoms. The study also compares the results of a Rorschach index, the Reality-Fantasy Scale (RFS; Tibon, Handelzalts, & Weinberger, 2005), to detect different types of psychopathological manifestations conceptualized as forms of collapse of potential space. The results point toward substantial differences between the two protocols that are interpreted in terms of forms of collapse of potential space, demonstrating reality collapse into fantasy being revealed by one protocol and fantasy collapse into reality by the other. In conclusion, because similar psychosomatic pictures in adolescents might represent different, often apparently opposite, psychopathological states, using the Rorschach in adolescents with psychosomatic symptoms seem particularly important for revealing these states. Implications for treatment are discussed.

Keywords: potential space, psychosomatics, Rorschach Reality-Fantasy Scale

Introduction

Functional somatic symptoms (FSS) or psychosomatic phenomena are defined as physical symptoms of unknown source and affect 10%–30% of children and adolescents (Beck, 2008). Since empirical research shows considerable heterogeneity in the clinical presentation, course, and outcome of FSS in adolescents, many perspectives for studying FSS in adolescence have been suggested to explore these phenomena; most of them focus on the affective dimension of the psychosomatic symptoms. In contrast, this study explores the *cognitive* dimension, by applying Winnicott's (1971) construct of potential or transitional space between reality and fantasy to the body-mind matrix.

The construct of potential space describes the intermediate place between inner and outer experiences. This is where creative personal meaning is obtained. It is the intermediate area of experience, the area between inner psychic reality and actual or external reality, between me and not-me. Ogden (1986) suggests understanding the ability to preserve potential space as a mental state based on a series of dialectical processes between reality and fantasy, in which each pole creates and negates the other. Accordingly, when the dialectical processes between the two poles of the reality-fantasy continuum are impaired and the poles fail to create, inform, preserve, and negate one another, phenomena related to a *psychopathology of symbolization* might occur.

The term *psychopathology of symbolization* has been used to describe both psychotic and psychosomatic symptoms. McDougall (1989) describes patients with psychosomatics as having emotional and fantasy experiences that are not contained in normal-neurotic structures. These patients demonstrate anxiety states and depressive episodes that are attached to the feeling of being unable to cope with normal life situations. McDougall (1991) further proposes that psychosomatics and psychosis reveal similar psychic structures: In both states one can observe collapse of reality into fantasy. On the other hand, psychosomatic patients also show a collapse of the fantasy pole into the reality pole. In these states the capacity to imagine is impaired, and experience is robbed of its vitality. This state can be observed in severe obsessional states or in psychosomatic patients, who are frequently being characterized by alexithymia. Alexithymia is a multifacet phenomenon that includes difficulties identifying and communicating feelings, trouble distinguishing between feelings and somatic sensations of emotional arousal, an impoverished and restricted imaginative life as well as a concrete and reality-oriented thinking style (Taylor, Bagby, & Parker, 1991, 1997, 2003). The lack of manifested neurotic or psychotic symptoms in these patients led McDougall (1980) to name them *normopaths*.

The present study suggests differentiating between two types of adolescents with psychosomatic symptoms, by locating them at two opposite poles of the reality-fantasy continuum. One type is characterized by alexithymia, showing a collapse to the reality pole; the other is dominated by psychotic thought processes, showing a collapse to the fantasy pole. Indeed, Winnicott (1971) refers to some of the psychosomatic cases as having psychosis as their core disturbance. In these cases the patient has enough psychoneurotic organization to be able to present a psychosomatic disturbance whenever the central psychotic anxiety threatens to burst out in its raw form.

Smith (1990) suggests applying Winnicott's (1971) and Ogden's (1986) conceptions of the transitional space and its collapse to the Rorschach. He views the response process to the Rorschach cards as occurring in the potential space between reality and fantasy. The cards, like a transitional object, exist in reality, but the attribution of meaning from the subject's inner reality into the card reflects the creative play between reality and fantasy – and gives the percept its special quality, with which the subject creates a unique relationship. Accordingly, subjects who show collapse to the fantasy pole may experience difficulty differentiating between their inner world and the real world, while subjects who show collapse toward the reality pole may experience great difficulty with the Rorschach assignment, finding it almost impossible to inject their inner world into the blot.

Which of the Rorschach Comprehensive System (CS; Exner, 2003) variables do we expect to find with psychosomatic subjects? An intuitive answer to that question, and therefore one with a high face value, will be variables that relate to the body as articulating physical concern: anatomical and radiographic contents (An + Xy). However, empirical studies show that, while some psychosomatic patients may have elevated An + Xy, others don't (Ihanus, 1984; Porcelli & Meyer, 2002; Porcelli & Mihura, 2010). Bash (1986) attributes this diversity to inadequate conceptualization and categorization of psychosomatic disease, and suggests that psychosomatic symptoms may represent different types of dynamics. Indeed, when alexithymic psychosomatic patients are considered as a distinguished group within the psychosomatics population, some common Rorschach variables are found (Acklin & Alexander, 1988; Porcelli & Meyer, 2002; Pizza, Spitaleri, & d'Amato, 2001), most of which are associated with constricted affective and cognitive expression, including low human movement (M), low ability to modulate affect (FC), low available resource (EA), low complexity (Blends), and low willingness being open to experience (high Lambda).

A question might be raised as to identifying nonalexithymic psychosomatics using the Rorschach. The Reality-Fantasy Scale (RFS; Tibon, Handelzalts, & Weinberger, 2005) that operationalizes the concept of transitional space is apparently suitable for this purpose. The RFS was designed to detect different types of psychopathological manifestations conceptualized as forms of collapse of potential space. The scale is an 11-point scale ranging from –5 (reality collapse into fantasy) to +5 (fantasy collapse into reality). A score of –5 represents the most extreme case of reliance on fantasy, with minimum contact with external reality; a score of +5 represents a strong reliance on the real features of the blot, with minimal input of fantasy. Previous research in both patient and nonpatient samples showed that the RFS mean score of a protocol lies around zero in normative healthy samples, but was significantly lower within the negative range of the scale in patients with psychotic proneness – and significantly higher within the positive range of the scale in alexithymic-psychosomatic patients (Tibon, Handelzalts, & Weinberger, 2005; Tibon, Weinberger, Handelzalts, & Porcelli, 2005).

In order to examine the perspective of dialectical relationship between reality and fantasy and its application to psychosomatics in adolescents, I present two case studies.

Method

Participants

Both patients were part of a sample composed from adolescents referred to consultation at the Department of Gastroenterology, Schneider Children's Medical Center of Israel (SCMCI), due to complaints of abdominal pain. Biochemical, ultrasonographic, and endoscopic examinations revealed no evidence of any structural organic disease. They were classified as meeting the criteria of Childhood Functional Abdominal Pain (Rome III; Drossman, 2006): At least once per week for at least 2 months bouts of continuous or episodic abdominal pain unrelated to eating, defecation or menses, and insufficient criteria for other functional gastrointestinal disorders that would explain the pain. The study was approved by Schneider's Helsinki Committee. All subjects and their parents received a detailed explanation of the study, and the parents gave written informed consents.

The two patients were selected because they clearly demonstrate the role of the Rorschach in determining different types of collapse of potential space as representing different psychopathological states.

Measures

20-Item Toronto Alexithymia Scale (TAS-20)

The Toronto Alexithymia Scale (TAS20; Bagby, Parker, & Taylor, 1994a, 1994b; Parker, Taylor, & Bagby, 2003) is a well-established, empirically validated self-report measure of alexithymia (Taylor et al., 1991). The scale, which is the most widely used alexithymia assessment instrument, has demonstrated significantly strong reliability and validity (Taylor et al., 1997, 2003). In the present study I used a Hebrew translation of the TAS-20 developed by using backtranslation and then crossvalidated in a large heterogeneous sample collected in Israel (Appel, 2011). By using established TAS-20 cutoff scores (Taylor et al., 1997) patients were divided into those with alexithymia (TAS-20 score > 60); those for whom alexithymia was indeterminate (TAS-20 score between 51 and 60), and those without alexithymia (TAS-20 score < 50).

Rorschach

The Rorschach is a performance-based method to assess personality. Responses to the Rorschach make up the end product of a complex, cognitive-perceptual problem-solving process. Administration and scoring of the Rorschach protocols were done according to Exner's CS guidelines (2003). The protocols were processed by the *RIAP5* scoring program (Exner & Weiner, 2004). Protocols were reviewed by two clinical psychologists with proper training in the CS (including the author) to ensure coding accuracy. Disagreements were resolved through discussions. Interpretation was made based on Rorschach data for adolescents (Meyer, Erdberg, & Shaffer, 2007), taking their problematic nature into consideration.

The Rorschach Reality-Fantasy Scale (RFS)

The Rorschach Reality-Fantasy Scale (RFS; Tibon, Handelzalts et al., 2005) includes a group of Rorschach variables or combinations of variables interpreted as indicating various levels of reality contact and the capacity to make use of fantasy. Apart from a new variable of RC, all the variables are based on Exner's (2003) CS. The RC score is given to responses in which the subject is observed reacting or is presumably reacting as if the blot is the thing itself ("I can smell it"). As stated above, the 11-point scale ranges from –5 (*reality collapse into fantasy*) to +5 (*fantasy collapse into reality*). The scoring of a Rorschach protocol on the RFS is done for each response separately according to specific steps. Following the scoring of each response on the RFS, the mean (RFS-P) and the standard deviation (RFS-S) of a given protocol is computed. The present results focus only on the RFS-P. An RFS-P score of zero represents a balanced combination between reality and fantasy, whereas a significantly lower or higher RFS-P represents collapse of potential space toward fantasy or reality, respectively. Computations were made using the RFS software (Tibon & Suchowski, 2005).

Procedure

The assessment took place in the participants' homes, in two sessions of 2.5 h each. The author administered all tests. The first session included self-report inventories (Somatic Complaints List; SCL, Jellesma, Rieffe, & Terwogt, 2007), the TAS-20, the Depressive Experiences Questionnaire for Adolescents, Short-form (DEQ-A; Fichman, Koestner, & Zuroff, 1994), Screen for Child Anxiety Related Emotional Disorders (SCARED-R; Birmaher et al., 1997)), the Rorschach, and a semantic judgment task for metaphor comprehension (Faust & Mashal, 2007). The second session included the Strengths and Difficulties Questionnaire (SDQ; Goodman, 1999, 2001) and the Development and Well-Being Assessment (DAWBA; Goodman, Ford, Richards, Gatward, & Meltzer, 2000), which was conducted separately on the participants and their parents. However, because of the aim of the article, only the results of TAS-20 and the Rorschach are discussed. For the case presented first, the second meeting failed to take place because of the participant's refusal to continue the meetings.

Results

The two patients and the assessment results are presented one after other. Table 1 presents the Rorschach cognitive variables for comparison.

Case 1: Maya

Maya, a 14-year-old girl, is the second of four children to parents who are both professionals in the high-tech industry. She was referred to consultation at the Department of Gastroenterology because of abdominal pain that started about a year ago. In addition, Maya complains on suffering from dizziness, fatigue, headaches, and general weakness that contribute to frequent absences from school. She also reports having attentional difficulties at school.

Behavioral Observation

The assessment meeting seemed to be very inconvenient for Maya. While answering self-report questionnaires, in which she was asked to relate to her internal feelings and thoughts, she expressed remarkable discomfort, asking a few times if the procedure was going to take a long time. Her distress became even more intense during the Rorschach task and in particular during the inquiry phase, as will be described later, after which she refused to continue our meetings, ending the assessment process prematurely.

Table 1. Selected variables for comparison

	Maya	Bar
R	29	25
Lambda	2.22	1.5
Ideation		
a:p	0:4	5:5
Ma:Mp	0:3	2:3
2AB + (Art + Ay)	1	2
MOR	0	3
Sum6	2	12
Lvl-2	0	4
WSum6	2	38
M–	0	1
M none	0	0
Mediation		
XA%	0.83	0.64
WDA%	0.94	0.86
X–%	0.14	0.36
S–	0	2
P	3	3
X +%	0.34	0.32
Xu%	0.48	0.32
Processing		
Zf	3	9
W:D:Dd	2:14:13	6:8:11
W:M	2:3	6:5
Zd	–0.5	–6.0
PSV	0	0
DQ +	1	4
DQv	2	0
RFS-P	**1.28**	**–1.4**

Assessment Results

According to the TAS-20, Maya meets the criteria for alexithymia (TAS-20 = 68). In line with these results one can expect her Rorschach protocol to show reality-bound, concrete thinking. Indeed, Maya's elevated Lambda (L = 2.22) confirms her concrete cognitive style being dominated by lack of adequate openness to experience and an overly narrow focus of attention. Moreover, her responses seem to be very strict, simple, and concrete, and the content is very poor. She repeatedly starts her responses with "I don't know," a phrase that appears 10 times in the response phase and 17 times in the inquiry. Particularly notable are the lifeless, impersonal images that she fails to animate by any embellishment (*a shoe; a fish; legs*). Overall she seems to lack fantasy. Maya's elevated RFS-P (1.28), points toward a collapse of potential space toward the reality pole.

Ideation

She shows logical and coherent thinking (Sum6 = 2, Lvl-2 = 0, WSum6 = 2) and good capacity to form realistic impressions of people (M- = 0). Nevertheless, her 0:4 active to passive movement (a:p) ratio suggests cognitive inflexibility that hinders contemplation and decision making because of a preference to hold onto long-held beliefs, making adaptation difficult. In addition, she attempts to deal with situations in her life not by thinking through what she should do about them, but rather by imagining how other people will make her decisions and solve her problem for her (Ma:Mp = 0:3), which suggests she has infantile dependency needs.

Mediation

Her Form Quality variables (XA% = .86, WDA% = .94, X +% = .34, X-% = .14) point to a realistic perception of events enabling her to correctly comprehend her own capacities, the intentions of others, and the requirements of the situations in which she finds herself. Nevertheless, and quite surprising, she shows idiosyncrasy in her preferences and view of the world (Xu% = .48; P = 3). However, this finding has to be interpreted cautiously, since it appears to characterize Israeli adolescents in general (Tibon, Rothschild, & Appel, 2011).

Processing

Despite her tendency to assign inordinate attention to unusual aspects of experience, Maya shows a good ability to establish cognitive focusing on the most relevant aspect of the stimulus field, but she appears to be insufficiently attuned to how events relate to each other (W:D:Dd = 2:14:13, Zf = 3, DQ+ = 1; DQv = 2). In addition, she is also cautious and conservative in defining her goals (W:M = 2:3), therefore keeping an adaptive balance between the amount of information she absorbs and her capacity to process this amount of information (Zd = -0.5).

In conclusion, Maya's Rorschach reveals her tendency to collapse toward the reality pole, which is manifested in constricted cognitive experience. We can conclude that Maya, in addition to her overt somatic symptoms, suffers from a *psychopathology of symbolization* (Ogden, 1986), in which fantasy collapses into reality. In this state, reality usage serves as a defense against fantasy; reality robs the fantasy's vitality, and imagination is foreclosed. This psychopathology is manifested in difficulties in describing, naming, recognizing, containing, or working through subjective feelings; problems in distinguishing between feelings and the bodily sensations of emotional arousal; and impoverished and constricted imaginative capacities. These manifestations can be identified with the alexithymia construct, which was also found by the TAS-20 to represent Maya. This tendency suggests to the clinician a possible approach, since alexithymia is associated with better outcomes with structured cognitive-behavioral treatments in comparison to those focusing on insight, emotional awareness, and a close alliance with a therapist (Lumley, Neely, & Burger, 2007).

Case 2: Bar

Bar, a 14-year-old boy, is the second of three children. He was referred to consultation at the Department of Gastroenterology because of abdominal pain that began about a year ago. His mother is a secretary, and his father works in marketing. His grandfather died a year and a half ago from intestinal cancer, and he seems worried about his own and his family's health. He reports feeling "enormous unreasonable rage" toward a child in his class whom he hates, cannot think of any reason for that feeling, but still imagines on a regular basis how he beats this child and how "other bad things" happen to him. He says he doesn't implement his imaginations out of fear of punishment. He also reports being worried about the Iranian threat, afraid of using the elevator when he is alone and of heights. In conclusion, it seems that Bar has aggressive, obsessive, intrusive thoughts.

Behavioral Observation

The assessment process was characterized by marked spontaneous fluctuations between willingness to collaborate and to reveal distressful feelings, on the one hand, and guardedness, hypervigilance, and even antagonism on the other. At times Bar seemed emotionally expressive and fluent, while at other times he became reserved and closed. His responses to the different tasks frequently changed from obedient compliance to negativistic devaluation of the tasks.

Assessment Results

According to the TAS-20, Bar does not meet the criteria for alexithymia (TAS-20 = 49). In addition, his Lambda (1.50), which is within the normative range, demonstrates his ability to alternate in approaching to experience between oversimplification to overcomplication in appropriate relation. Bar's lowered RFS-P (−1.4) points toward a collapse of potential space toward the fantasy pole.

Ideation

Bar tends to reach erroneous conclusions based only on concrete spatial relationship between the different parts of the blot (Sum6 = 12, WSum6 = 38). These highly elevated scores show both his tendency to combine objects, ideas (INCOM, FABCOM), and impressions (ALOG) in bizarre ways, and his dissociated thinking in which ideas emerge out of sequence or intrude on each other to produce strange verbalizations (DR and DV). Moreover, almost half of his special scores have Level 2 quality (Lvl-2 = 4). These severe thinking distortions reflect his tendency to impose meaning onto situations, imbuing them with meaning associated more with his own emotional/internal concerns than with objective aspects of the situation. He also shows an excessive reliance on fantasy which interferes with good adjustment (Ma:Mp = 2:3), albeit demonstrating ideational flexibility in making decisions and adapting to new situations and unfamiliar demands (a:p = 5:5).

Mediation

Alongside the ideation problems, distortions in perception (XA% = .64, X +% = .32, X−% = .36) are also apparent and even intensify when he becomes distracted by peripheral and minor details most other people ignore (WDA% = .86). In addition, he tends to translate his perception in a more personalized manner (Xu% = .32). His low number of popular answers (P = 3) further supports this finding, suggesting that even when obvious cues concerning a translation exist, he does not give the obvious response – which accentuates the reality-testing impairment demonstrated by the high X-%. Although these impairments are spread all over the protocol, it is important to note that 44% of them occurred in the last two cards, after he experienced a serious psychotic break manifested in his ALOG response to card IX. This may indicate that his reality testing is less disturbed than his thinking processes.

Processing

Bar tends to focus his attention on global or unusual aspects of experience rather than on what is ordinary, which leads him to unconventional attitudes or behavioral tendencies (W:D:Dd = 6:8:11). Furthermore, the impaired ability of establishing cognitive focusing on the most relevant aspect of the stimulus field, which usually characterizes the psychotic level of organization, is indicated by polarities between impulsivity and hypervigilance, revealed by the coexistence of opposite scanning approaches (elevated W beside elevated Dd). This polarity in attention focusing brings him to come to conclusions hastily, after only cursory attention to relevant considerations, and therefore to arrive to ill-considered conclusions and inferior products (Zf = 9, Zd = -6.0, DQ + = 3, DQv = 0). This may also contribute to his cautiousness and conservative way of defining his goals (W:M = 6:5).

In conclusion, Bar's Rorschach reveals his tendency to collapse toward the fantasy pole, manifested in severe thinking disorders accompanied with reality distortions. Thus, we can conclude that Bar, in addition to his overt somatic symptoms, suffers from *psychopathology of symbolization* (Ogden, 1986) in which reality collapses into fantasy. In this state, the fantasy becomes as tangible, powerful, dangerous, and satisfying, like the external reality from which it cannot be differentiated. This tendency suggests a different approach to the clinician than the one suggested in the former case – despite the common overt somatic symptoms. In this case supportive psychotherapy would appear to be the treatment of choice. In addition, one might consider pharmacotherapy as an adjunct to help Bar control his thinking disturbances.

Discussion

This article illustrates that similar psychosomatic symptoms in adolescents may reflect very different psychopathological states – and therefore may imply very different treatment considerations. This under-

161

standing is based on Winnicott's (1971) conceptualization as applied by Ogden (1986) to different psychopathological states, viewing these states in terms of collapse of potential or transitional space between reality and fantasy. Following Smith (1990), this conceptualization is presented by Rorschach protocols of two adolescents with psychosomatic disorders. The first case illustrates a tendency to collapse toward the reality pole – a state usually identified with alexithymia; the other illustrates a tendency to collapse toward the fantasy pole – a state usually identified with psychosis. The cases are analyzed using cognitive variables derived from the Rorschach CS (Exner, 2003) and the Reality-Fantasy scale (Tibon, Handelzalts et al., 2005), a Rorschach index that assesses adaptive use, creation, and preservation of potential space between reality and fantasy.

This approach may be helpful in understanding the complexity of the psychosomatic phenomena and its relationship to diverse personality structures. Placing the body-mind matrix inside the conceptualization of the potential space and the experience of living relates to the body-mind experience as being revealed between the boundaries of reality and fantasy. A failure to maintain this dialectic tension between reality and fantasy may result in different forms of psychopathology – albeit in similar symptoms (i.e., psychosomatics). It is suggested that this model might particularly be valuable with regard to the understanding of somatic symptoms in adolescents, since at this complex period of life, predispositions to psychosomatics established at toddler age may reappear and may therefore also be reformed.

Understanding the psychological organization and capacity that lie beneath overt symptoms and behavior may have important implications for treatment planning. As Peebles-Kleiger (2002) points out, identifying the nature of specific underlying disturbance can aid in selecting from a myriad of available treatments across the supportive-expressive spectrum. As to the current cases, with Maya, whose underlying disturbance was alexithymia, a cognitive therapy may be the treatment of choice. While alexithymia predicts poor outcomes to psychodynamic psychotherapy for functional gastrointestinal disorders (Porcelli, De Carne, & Todarello, 2004; Porcelli et al., 2003), it is associated with better outcomes for cognitive-behavioral treatments (Lumley et al., 2007). Nonetheless, for Bar, who showed severe thinking disorders, the recommended treatment should include a combination of two essential interventions – optimal dosages of antipsychotic medication, with counseling and psychotherapy aimed at helping him to understand and to deal with his situation. Furthermore, much suffering later in life can probably be avoided with treatment planning encompassing both body and mind and their dialectical relationship. Indeed, results from a recent study show that young adults who had many psychosomatic symptoms in adolescence suffered more often than other adults from somatization and anxiety symptoms in early adulthood. In addition, women had more symptoms of depression and paranoid ideation, and men had more interpersonal sensitivity and psychotic symptoms (Kinnunen, Laukkanen, & Kylma, 2010).

The evaluations presented follow the recommendation that the assessment of psychological constructs should use multiple measures, particularly via different methods, by combining the Rorschach, a performance-based method, with the TAS-20, a self-report inventory. As to Maya, the Rorschach as well as TAS-20 provided information that was consistent with the structure of alexithymia, so the information gathered from the two methods further confirmed this finding. For Bar, on the other hand, the Rorschach findings complemented the information obtained by the TAS-20 by identifying severe thinking disorders. This important information would not have been mined using the self-report questionnaire alone. Thus, by administering both objective and projective measures of a particular construct to the same patient clinicians and researchers can obtain a more complete picture of that patient's underlying and expressed strivings.

Some limitations need to be considered regarding this article. Given the problematic nature of nomothetic Rorschach data for adolescents (Meyer et al., 2007), interpretation of Rorschach data is rooted in the analysis of constellations of formal scores, content, and behavioral observation. Where nomothetic interpretations are offered, they are based predominantly on extreme scores in comparison to Meyer et al.'s (2007) synthesis of the most recent international norms. Nonetheless, in order to make full use of the tool, generating international normative CS reference values for adolescents is needed. In addition, as far as I know, this study is the first to use RFS-P with adolescents. Further research should examine RFS-P scores of adolescent samples to address the validity of the scale across different adolescent groups.

Moreover, the findings in these two cases illustrate the applicability of the transitional space and its collapse as to adolescents with functional abdominal pain and represent the results of an empirical study (Appel, 2011). However, it should also be interesting to examine this concept as to other somatic symptoms in adolescence. Since substantial differences might be revealed within this group, further studies of subjects with other psychosomatic symptoms are also needed.

L. Appel

References

Acklin, M. W., & Alexander, G. (1988). Alexithymia and somatization: A Rorschach study of four psychosomatic groups. *The Journal of Nervous and Mental Disease, 176*, 343–350.

Appel, L. (2011). *Somatic symptoms in adolescents from a psychoanalytic perspective: Alexithymia, difficulties in metaphors comprehension and production and anaclitic depression as manifestations of collapse of potential space between reality and fantasy.* (Unpublished doctoral dissertation). Bar Ilan University, Israel.

Bagby, R. M., Parker, J. D. A., & Taylor, G. J. (1994a). The 20-item Toronto Alexithymia Scale: I. Item selection and crossvalidation of the factor structure. *Journal of Psychosomatic Research, 38*, 23–32.

Bagby, R. M., Parker, J. D. A., & Taylor, G. J. (1994b). The twenty-item Toronto Alexithymia Scale: II. Convergent, discriminant, and concurrent validity. *Journal of Psychosomatic Research, 38*, 33–40.

Bash, K. W. (1986). Psychosomatic diseases and the Rorschach test. *Journal of Personality Assessment, 50*, 350–357.

Beck, J. E. (2008). A developmental perspective on functional somatic symptoms. *Journal of Pediatric Psychology, 33*, 547–562.

Birmaher, B., Khetarpal, S., Brent, D., Cully, M., Ballach, L., Kaufman, J., & Neer, S. M. (1997). The Screen for Child Anxiety Related Emotional Disorders (SCARED): Scale construction and psychometric characteristics. *Journal of the American Academy of Child and Adolescent Psychiatry, 36*, 545–553.

Drossman, D. A. (Ed.). (2006). *ROME III: The functional gastrointestinal disorders.* Boston: Little, Brown.

Exner, J. E. (2003). *The Rorschach: A comprehensive system: Vol. 1. Basic foundations and principles of interpretation* (4th ed.). Hoboken, NJ: Wiley.

Exner, J. E., & Weiner, I. B. (2004). *Rorschach Interpretation Assistance Program* (Version 5). Lutz, FL: Psychological Assessment Resources.

Faust, M., & Mashal, N. (2007). The role of the right hemisphere in processing novel metaphoric expressions taken from poetry: a divided visual field study. *Neuropsychologia, 45*, 860–870.

Fichman, L., Koestner, R., & Zuroff, D. C. (1994). Depressive styles in adolescence: Assessment, relation to social functioning and developmental trends. *Journal of Youth and Adolescence, 23*, 315–330.

Goodman, R. (1999). The extended version of the Strengths and Difficulties Questionnaire as a guide to child psychiatric caseness and consequent burden. *Journal of Child Psychology and Psychiatry, 40*, 791–799.

Goodman, R. (2001). Psychometric properties of the strengths and difficulties questionnaire. *Journal of the American Academy of Child and Adolescent Psychiatry, 40*, 1337–1345.

Goodman, R., Ford, T., Richards, H., Gatward, R., & Meltzer, H. (2000). The development and well-being assessment: Description and initial validation of an integrated assessment of child and adolescent psychopathology. *Journal of Child Psychology and Psychiatry, 41*, 645–655.

Ihanus, J. (1984). Anatomical Rorschach responses of gravely psychosomatics patients. *Perceptual and Motor Skills, 59*, 337–338.

Jellesma, F. C., Rieffe, C., & Terwogt, M. M. (2007). The somatic complaint list: Validation of a self-report questionnaire assessing somatic complaints in children. *Journal of Psychosomatic Research, 63*, 399–401.

Kinnunen, P., Laukkanen, E,., & Kylma, J. (2010). Associations between psychosomatic symptoms in adolescence and mental health symptoms in early adulthood. *International Journal of Nursing Practice, 16*, 43–50.

Lumley, M. A., Neely, L. C., & Burger, A. J. (2007). The assessment of alexithymia in medical settings: Implications for understanding and treating health problems. *Journal of Personality Assessment, 89*, 230–246.

McDougall, J. (1980). *Plea for a measure of abnormality*. New York: International Universities Press.

McDougall, J. (1989). *Theatres of the body: A psychoanalytic approach to psychosomatic illness*. London: Free Association Books.

McDougall, J. (1991). *Theaters of the mind*. New York: Brunner/Mazel.

Meyer, G. J., Erdberg, P., & Shaffer, T. W. (2007). Toward international normative reference data for the comprehensive system, international monograph supplement. *Journal of Personality Assessment, 89*, 201–220.

Ogden, T. H. (1986). *The matrix of the mind*. Northvale, NJ: Jason Aronson.

Parker, J. D. A., Taylor, G. J., & Bagby, R. M. (2003). The 20-Item Toronto Alexithymia Scale: III. Reliability and factorial validity in a community population. *Journal of Psychosomatic Research, 55*, 269–275.

Peebles-Kleiger, M. J. (2002). *Beginnings: The art and science of planning psychotherapy*. Hillsdale, NJ: Erlbaum.

Pizza, V., Spitaleri, D. L. A., & d'Amato, C. C. (2001). The personality profile and alexithymic syndrome in primary headache: A Rorschach study. *Journal of Headache and Pain, 1*, 31–37.

Porcelli, P., Bagby, R. M., Taylor, G. J., De Carne, M., Leandro, G., & Todarello, O. (2003). Alexithymia as a predictor of treatment outcome in patients with functional gastrointestinal disorders. *Psychosomatic Medicine, 65*, 911–918.

Porcelli, P., De Carne, M., & Todarello, O. (2004). Prediction of treatment outcome of patients with functional gastrointestinal disorders by the diagnostic criteria for psychosomatic research. *Psychotherapy and Psychosomatics, 73*, 166–173.

Porcelli, P., & Meyer, G. J. (2002). Construct validity of Rorschach variables of alexithymia. *Psychosomatics, 43*, 360–369.

Porcelli, P., & Mihura, J. L. (2010). Assessment of alexithymia with the Rorschach Comprehensive System: The Rorschach Alexithymia Scale (RAS). *Journal of Personality Assessment, 92*, 128–136.

Smith, B. L. (1990). Potential space and the Rorschach: An application of object relations theory. *Journal of Personality Assessment, 55*, 756–767.

Taylor, G. J., Bagby, R. M., & Parker, J. D. (1991). The alexithymia construct. A potential paradigm for psychosomatic medicine. *Psychosomatics, 32,* 153–164.

Taylor, G. J., Bagby, R. M., & Parker, J. D. A. (1997). *Disorders of affect regulation: Alexithymia in medical and psychiatric illness.* Cambridge, UK: Cambridge University Press.

Taylor, G. J., Bagby, R. M., & Parker, J. D. A. (2003). The 20-Item Toronto Alexithymia Scale. IV. Reliability and factorial validity in different languages and cultures. *Journal of Psychosomatic Research, 55,* 277–283.

Tibon, R., & Suchowski, R. (2005). The RFS software. A software for calculating the Rorschach Reality-Fantasy Scale. Retrieved from http://www.rps-rfs.com

Tibon, S., Handelzalts, J. E., & Weinberger, Y. (2005). Using the Rorschach for exploring the concept of transitional space within the political context of the Middle East. *International Journal of Applied Psychoanalytic Studies, 2,* 40–57.

Tibon, S., Rothschild, L., & Appel, L. (2011). Rorschach Comprehensive System (CS) reference data for Israeli adolescents. *Journal for Personality Assessment.* Manuscript submitted.

Tibon, S., Weinberger, Y., Handelzalts, J. E., & Porcelli, P. (2005). Construct validation of the Rorschach reality-fantasy scale in alexithymia. *Psychoanalytic Psychology, 22,* 508–523.

Winnicott, D. W. (1971). *Playing and reality.* New York: Basic Books.

Liat Appel
Department of Psychology
Bar-Ilan University
52900 Ramat-Gan
Israel
Tel. +972 52 6261626
Fax +972 77 6261624
E-mail liat_appel@yahoo.com

Appendix A

Case 1 Rorschach protocol

Card #	Resp. #	Response	Inquiry
I	1	I don't know. It looks like a man who prays, I think. (Usually . . .).	As if standing here. And as if his hands are like this. This is such a head and these are the foot.
	2 v	I don't know, it's a kind of an animal here, something, I don't know what it is, I don't know.	This is a tail and here is the eye and here is the . . . (Here is the . . .?) It's like a bottom, I don't know. (Eye?) Because there is such a thing in black and it's whiter inside. (The animal was seen in part of D2).
II	3	It looks like a tower, I think. I don't really understand in this stuff.	Here it is. (Tower?) Because it's a triangle that goes up and it's thin, and there is this thing in the middle. (Thing?) Some kind of a line, I don't know. Like a tower, it looked to me like that. Because a tower always has a line. (Explain?) Because there is this line in black.
	4	I don't know, here it looks like a light, a sparkling light. That's it really.	This, that you have these lines that go out. (Where?) Here and here.
III	5	This looks like a heart.	It is in red and also in this shape. (Draws with her finger a shape of a drawn heart).
	6	This looks like a shoe.	Because here it's sharp and then there is a hill.
	7 v	And here it's a fish.	Because he has a head in the shape of a fish, and he has this tail, fin, whatever it's called.
IV	8	Here it doesn't look like anything. (Usually . . .). I don't know, I don't understand it. This painting is not that understood. (Try . . .). I don't know, it's a snake, I don't know.	Here. (Snake?) It is thin and long.
	9	Like a big man, that's it.	Here is the head, here are his feet.
	10	Here a shoe.	Yes, here. (Shoe?) It has this shape. Also sometimes I don't know to explain what I see.
V	11	A butterfly.	Everything is the butterfly. (Butterfly?) The wings.
	12	Legs.	They are in this shape, I don't know.
	13	This thing here, an antenna, something like that.	Because this is the way antenna goes.

167

Card #	Resp. #	Response	Inquiry
	14	A bat.	This is its head and this is an antenna.
VI	15	Looks like a man standing with that thing (spreading her hands), what do I know.	These are the hands, this is the head. (that thing?) These two, I don't know what it is. (Try . . .). I don't know, nobody ever showed me this kind of paintings.
	16	Birds and that's it.	Here. I don't know why, this is what I saw. (Can you explain?) I don't know, by their nose. (You said birds?) Only the nose.
VII	17	Eyes.	I don't know, there's a hole. (Hole?) That everything is gray and suddenly there is a white hole. (The eyes were seen in part of D2)
	18	A nose.	I don't know, This is what I saw; This is how it looked to me. (Can you explain?) I don't know, I told you, sometimes I can't explain what I see. (Can you help me see?) I don't know, that it has this thing here, this shape.
	19	And wings.	Here. (Wings?) It looks, the shape.
VIII	20	Oh, how this animal is called? An animal, I don't remember how it's called.	Here it is. And on the other side, too. (Can you show me?) Hands, legs, I don't know.
	21	Hands.	Here they are, here and here. It's the shape.
	22	A fish.	I don't remember where I saw it. (You've seen once . . .). I don't know, never mind, let's go on. (I'm sure you'll find again). I don't remember where I saw it.
	23	Maybe legs, I'm not that certain.	Because it looks like ballerina legs, that they are tight above the end of the fingers.
IX	24	I don't know. (Usually . . .). I don't know. Like a body looks to me. Really un-understandable paintings.	Here are the hands, this is the head. That's it. (Head?) Here, all this. That it's round.
	25	And two fingers, this is what I saw here.	This pink here, by their shape.
X	26	Leaves.	Here they are. (Leaves?) That they are green.
	27	Eh, this thing that exists in the sea, I don't remember how it's called.	This. (What gave you the impression?) By what I saw in the sea. This is its hands and this is the body.
	28	A flower.	And this is the flower I saw. This, this blue. I don't know, it was such an imagination. (Can you help me see?) I don't know, it looks like it, I don't know to explain.
	29	A stick.	Here, it's long. And that's it.

Appendix B

Case 1: Sequence of scores

Card #	Resp. #	Location and DQ	Loc. #	Determinant(s) and Form Quality	(2)	Content(s)	Pop	Z Score	Special Scores
I	1	Do	4	Mpo		H			GHR
	2	Ddo	99	FY–		A,Sx			
II	3	Do	4	FC'o		Sc			
	4	Dv	3	Y.mpu		Id			
III	5	Ddo	29	CFu		Art			
	6	Ddo	33	Fo		Cg			
	7	Do	5	Fo		A			
IV	8	Ddo	99	Fu		A			
	9	Wo	1	Fo		H	P	2.0	GHR
	10	Do	2	Fo		Cg			
V	11	Wo	1	Fo		A	P	1.0	
	12	Do	9	Fu	2	Hd			PHR
	13	Ddo	34	Fo	2	Ad			
	14	Do	6	Fu		A			
VI	15	D+	3	Mpu		H		2.5	GHR
	16	Ddo	21	Fu	2	Ad			DV
VII	17	Ddo	99	FC'–	2	Hd			PHR
	18	Ddo	21	Fu	2	Hd			PHR
	19	Do	5	Fu	2	Ad			
VIII	20	Do	1	Fo	2	A	P		
	21	Ddo	99	Fu	2	Hd			PHR
	22	Ddo	99	F–		A			
	23	Ddo	24	Mpu	2	Hd			PHR
IX	24	Ddo	99	F–		Hd			PHR
	25	Ddo	99	Fu	2	Hd			PHR
X	26	Dv	12	C	2	Bt			
	27	Do	7	Fo	2	A			PER, DV
	28	Do	1	Fu		Bt			
	29	Do	14	Fu		Bt			

Summary of approach

I:	D.Dd	VI:	D.Dd
II:	D.D	VII:	Dd.Dd.D
III:	Dd.Dd.D	VIII:	D.Dd.Dd.Dd
IV:	Dd.W.D	IX:	Dd.Dd
V:	W.D.Dd.D	X:	D.D.D.D

Appendix C

Case 1: Rorschach structural summary

Location Features		
Zf	=	3
ZSum	=	5.5
ZEst	=	6.0
W	=	2
(Wv	=	0)
D	=	14
W+D	=	16
Dd	=	13
S	=	0

DQ		
		(FQ-)
+	= 1	(0)
o	= 26	(4)
v/+	= 0	(0)
v	= 2	(0)

Form Quality			
	FQx	MQual	W+D
+	= 0	0	0
o	= 10	1	8
u	= 14	2	7
-	= 4	0	0
none	= 1	0	1

Determinants		
Blends	Single	
Y.m	M = 3	
	FM = 0	
	m = 0	
	FC = 0	
	CF = 1	
	C = 1	
	Cn = 0	
	FC' = 2	
	C'F = 0	
	C' = 0	
	FT = 0	
	TF = 0	
	T = 0	
	FV = 0	
	VF = 0	
	V = 0	
	FY = 1	
	YF = 0	
	Y = 0	
	Fr = 0	
	rF = 0	
	FD = 0	
	F = 20	
	(2) = 12	

Contents	
H	= 3
(H)	= 0
Hd	= 7
(Hd)	= 0
Hx	= 0
A	= 8
(A)	= 0
Ad	= 3
(Ad)	= 0
An	= 0
Art	= 1
Ay	= 0
Bl	= 0
Bt	= 3
Cg	= 2
Cl	= 0
Ex	= 0
Fd	= 0
Fi	= 0
Ge	= 0
Hh	= 0
Ls	= 0
Na	= 0
Sc	= 1
Sx	= 1
Xy	= 0
Idio	= 1

S-Constellation
S-CON is not applicable for individuals less than 15 years of age.

Special Scores			
		Lvl-1	Lvl-2
DV	=	2 x1	0 x2
INC	=	0 x2	0 x4
DR	=	0 x3	0 x6
FAB	=	0 x4	0 x7
ALOG	=	0 x5	
CON	=	0 x7	
Raw Sum6	=		2
Wgtd Sum6	=		2
AB = 0	GHR = 3		
AG = 0	PHR = 7		
COP = 0	MOR = 0		
CP = 0	PER = 1		
	PSV = 0		

RATIOS, PERCENTAGES, AND DERIVATIONS

R = 29	L = 2.22	
EB = 3 : 2.5	EA = 5.5	EBPer = N/A
eb = 1 : 4	es = 5	D = 0
	Adj es = 4	Adj D = 0
FM = 0	SumC' = 2	SumT = 0
m = 1	SumV = 0	SumY = 2

AFFECT

FC:CF+C	= 0 : 2
Pure C	= 1
SumC' : WSumC	= 2 : 2.5
Afr	= 0.53
S	= 0
Blends:R	= 1 : 29
CP	= 0

INTERPERSONAL

COP = 0		AG = 0	
GHR:PHR		= 3 : 7	
a:p		= 0 : 4	
Food		= 0	
SumT		= 0	
Human Content		= 10	
Pure H		= 3	
PER		= 1	
Isolation Index		= 0.10	

IDEATION

a:p	= 0 : 4	Sum6 = 2
Ma:Mp	= 0 : 3	Lvl-2 = 0
2AB+(Art+Ay)	= 1	WSum6 = 2
MOR	= 0	M- = 0
		M none = 0

MEDIATION

XA%	= 0.83
WDA%	= 0.94
X-%	= 0.14
S-	= 0
P	= 3
X+%	= 0.34
Xu%	= 0.48

PROCESSING

Zf	= 3
W:D:Dd	= 2:14:13
W : M	= 2 : 3
Zd	= -0.5
PSV	= 0
DQ+	= 1
DQv	= 2

SELF-PERCEPTION

3r+(2)/R	= 0.41
Fr+rF	= 0
SumV	= 0
FD	= 0
An+Xy	= 0
MOR	= 0
H:(H)+Hd+(Hd)	= 3 : 7

PTI = 0	☐ DEPI = 3	☐ CDI = 3	☐ S-CON = N/A	☐ HVI = No	☐ OBS = No

Constellations table

S-Constellation (Suicide Potential)	PTI (Perceptual-Thinking Index)

S-CON is not applicable for individuals less than 15 years of age.	☐ (XA% [0.83] < 0.70) *and* (WDA% [0.94] < 0.75)
	☐ X-% [0.14] > 0.29
	☐ (Sum Level 2 Special Scores [0] > 2)
	   and (FAB2 [0] > 0)
	☐ ((R [29] < 17) *and* (WSum6 [2] > 12)) *or*
	   ((R [29] > 16) *and* (WSum6 [2] > 17))
	☐ (M- [0] > 1) *or* (X-% [0.14] > 0.40)
	0 Total

DEPI (Depression Index)	CDI (Coping Deficit Index)
☐ Positive if 5 or more conditions are true:	☐ Positive if 4 or more conditions are true:

☐ (FV + VF + V [0] > 0) *or* (FD [0] > 2)
☐ (Col-Shd Blends [0] > 0) *or* (S [0] > 2)
☐ (3r + (2)/R [0.41] > 0.54* *and* Fr + rF [0] = 0)
   or (3r + (2)/R [0.41] < 0.37*)
   (Afr [0.53] < 0.46) *or* (Blends [1] < 4)
   (SumShading [4] > FM + m [1])
   or (SumC' [2] > 2)
☐ (MOR [0] > 2) *or* (2xAB + Art + Ay [1] > 3)
   (COP [0] < 2)
   or ([Bt+2xCl+Ge+Ls+2xNa]/R [0.10] > 0.24)
3   Total
	☐ (EA [5.5] < 6) *or* (AdjD [0] < 0)
	   (COP [0] < 2) *and* (AG [0] < 2)
	☐ (Weighted Sum C [2.5] < 2.5)
	   or (Afr [0.53] < 0.46)
	   (Passive [4] > Active + 1 [1])
	   or (Pure H [3] < 2)
	☐ (Sum T [0] > 1)
	   or (Isolate/R [0.10] > 0.24)
	   or (Food [0] > 0)
	3 Total

HVI (Hypervigilance Index)	OBS (Obsessive Style Index)
☐ Positive if condition 1 is true and at least 4 of the others are true: (1) FT + TF + T [0] = 0 - ☐ (2) Zf [3] > 12 ☐ (3) Zd [-0.5] > +3.5 ☐ (4) S [0] > 3 (5) H + (H) + Hd + (Hd) [10] > 6 ☐ (6) (H) + (A) + (Hd) + (Ad) [0] > 3 (7) H + A : Hd + Ad [11:10] < 4 : 1 ☐ (8) Cg [2] > 3	☐ (1) Dd [13] > 3 ☐ (2) Zf [3] > 12 ☐ (3) Zd [-0.5] > +3.0 ☐ (4) Populars [3] > 7 ☐ (5) FQ+ [0] > 1 - ☐ Positive if one or more is true: ☐ Conditions 1 to 5 are all true ☐ Two or more of 1 to 4 are true *and* FQ+ [0] > 3 ☐ 3 or more of 1 to 5 are true *and* X+% [0.34] > 0.89 ☐ FQ+ [0] > 3 *and* X+% [0.34] > 0.89

NOTE: '*' *indicates a cutoff that has been adjusted for age norms.*

L. Appel

Appendix D

Case 2: Rorschach protocol

Card #	Resp. #	Response	Inquiry
I	1	This and this look like a head of a dog.	It has a shape of a dog's head. It has such a stretched mouth; it has ears, kind of. (Stretched mouth?) No, his face is stretched like a dog (demonstrates, means lengthwise).
	2	This and this look like wings.	This and this. That are stretched like this (demonstrates). (Note: The word "stretched" as the participant used it in Hebrew, also means tensed and nervous).
	3	These look like hands.	Yes, here. That this is like hands. As if they are two people that are standing with the side and raise hands. Here are their two heads.
	4	And this looks like kind of legs.	Legs? No, I didn't say that. (You saw it before, I'm sure you can find it again). I don't see any legs here.
	5	And I see here such a face, two eyes and a mouth. Like a demon. Like a cat, all this painting. An angry cat.	Yes. These are two eyes, this here and this like that. I have a cat; I know how it looks like. These are angry ears. (Angry?) Yes, all animal, when is angry, its ears are back. And I see here cheeks until it reaches the chin. (You said demon?) Angry demon cat, a demon cat.
II	6	Is it upside down? (You can turn it upside down if you want. Turns and returns). These two reds look to me like eyes, like a nose, like a mouth and a beard. It's a kind of face. And cheeks here.	Two eyes, this is the nose, this is the mouth and this is the beard. These are the cheeks. (Beard?) The face couldn't have just something that sticks out from the face. (Sticks out?) Also by the color, by the color.
III	7	two animals or two humans or half and half, that pull something, tear it apart.	Here are their heads, here it's the back, the hands and legs that are pulling something. (Animals or humans?) In the beginning it looks like a human. Then, when you move to the legs it's not, so it's half human half animal. (Pulling something?) Kind of rocks, joined, and it tears apart what there is in between them. (Rocks?) By their shape. (Tears apart?) There is a shape of rags here.
	8	And it also looks like a smile, a nose and eyes of a cat.	These are eyes; this is a nose and such a smile.
	9v	From here it looks like a cockroach with teeth. These are hands; these are teeth, eyes and body.	This is its body, these are its hands, these are the eyes and this is the mouth with such teeth. (Asks for a break, goes to his mother and complains that the meeting is too long).

172

Card #	Resp. #	Response	Inquiry
IV	10	This looks like a dragon head.	Yes, here. By these teeth, canine and front teeth. Here are the eyes, eyelashes and ears.
	11	And there are two giant legs here, little hands; this is like a body of a giant monster with a dragon tail and without a head.	I watch too many cartoons. These are the legs; these are the hands, small as opposed to the big legs. And anyone who has legs and hands has to have a head, and he is without a head, and this is a tail that hides behind him. (Demonstrates dimensionality. Hides behind him?) A tail cannot be in the front.
V	12	A butterfly.	These are the wings, these are his antenna and these are legs and this is the head.
	13	Like a symbol of Batman, a bat.	The same principle on the bat too. (Can you show it to me?) Also, wings, legs, antenna. In a bat it's not antenna, it's ears. I don't even know if a butterfly has an antenna. (Batman?) Yes, because Batman liked, in the beginning he didn't like, he was afraid of them until he got connected to them. When I remember a bat, I remember Batman. You have a lot to write in this job.
VI	14	I don't know what it is. (Usually . . .). It looks here like kind of a scorpion. Eyes, teeth and these that it . . . (demonstrates a vice-grip).	Yes, these are the eyes, these are the teeth and these are the ones (demonstrates a vice-grip).
	15	See here two witches' heads, laughing.	Here is the mouth, chin, tongue, big witches' nose and eyes. (Eyes?) Face has to have eyes. (Laughing?) Yes, because their mouth is open and usually witches laugh, don't know why.
VII	16 v	two heads, this is a body up to the end of the belly, two bodies up to the end of the belly.	These are the heads, with a neck, and up to the end of the belly. And with a long nose.
	17	Hair of a child with no face, just the hair. Without clothes. And these are the braids.	Yes. This is the scalp and this is what girls have here (means hair parting) and these are her braids. A kind of a wig. (Wig?) That there is no face and a wig doesn't have to be on a face, because it's a wig. (What girls have here?) Because every girl's hair has it, or men, if they have long hair.
	18	And if I turn it upside down, it looks like two girls with hands aside on a kind of swing, like this (demonstrates).	Yes. It's not like a swing; it's like a baby facility, swinging. Do you know the plastic one that little children have? And these are their faces. Also a throat, and their hand goes like this (demonstrates). You don't see their legs because they are inside. (Inside?) Not inside, one leg has to be in front and one leg in the back. But you don't see the legs because they are in the facility's color.

L. Appel

Card #	Resp. #	Response	Inquiry
VIII	19	I see here two animals, but I don't exactly know the kind. Looks like a lamb or something, something similar to a strong ox.	Here, they also have four legs and also a face, and a body of muscles, a solid body. (A body of muscles, a solid body?) By its size. Not every animal has such a body.
	20	I see half a crown.	Here. (Half a crown?) It looks like a crown. (You said half a crown?) Now it looks whole to me. (Can you explain what you saw before?) Because if it needs to be put on a head, then it interferes (means the continuation of the blot). So I thought it's a half, but now I see it's a whole.
	21	And I see here a head and horns.	Here are head and horns. It's like a skeleton and horns. (Skeleton?) As if the animal is dead, you can see only the skeleton. Like dinosaurs. Aren't there in the U.S. in the walls skeletons, you can also see it in the movies, so it looks like that. (Skeleton?) Because she doesn't have a body.
IX	22	And I see here face. Here it's like two eyes, a nose and a mouth.	These are two eyes and this is a mouth. This is a nose. (Eyes?) That they are in the center of the picture. (Mouth?) If there are eyes and nose there is also a mouth.
	23	And these look like ... I forgot how this animal is called, gerbil or something.	This. I recognize it by its head. This is how this animal is called? Gerbil? And this is its body.
X	24	I see here the neck and two lungs, all the inside of a man.	This is the throat, the gullet, don't know how it's called, and these are the lungs. As if there is here the food trachea and the breath trachea, half half, and then it goes down to the lungs. (Lungs?) Don't know, it's shape. (The inside of a man?) I see that as a human body, what exists inside the stomach. (What gave you the impression?) By the lungs.
	25	I see here two hearts.	Yes, here and here. (Hearts?) Similar. (By what?) Also the veins and also the shape of the heart. I used to think that heart is similar to the one you decorate. But then I saw in the movies how does a heart really look like.

Appendix E

Case 2: Sequence of scores

Card #	Resp. #	Location and DQ	Loc. #	Determinant(s) and Form Quality	(2)	Content(s)	Pop	Z Score	Special Scores
I	1	Ddo	28	FMp–	2	Ad			DV
	2	Ddo	34	FMau	2	Ad			DV
	3	Do	4	Mpo	2	H			GHR
	4	Ddo	31	Fu	2	Hd			PHR
	5	WSo	1	FMao		(Ad),Hx		3.5	AG, PER, DV2, PHR
II	6	WSo	1	FV–		Hd		4.5	PHR
III	7	D+	1	Ma.mpu	2	Hd,Ad,Ls, Id		3.0	INC2, AG, MOR, PHR
	8	Ddo	99	Mp–		Ad			INC, PHR
	9	Do	1	Fu		A			INC
IV	10	Do	1	Fu		Ad			
	11	Wo	1	FDo		(H)		2.0	MOR, PHR
V	12	Wo	1	Fo		A	P	1.0	
	13	Wo	1	Fo		(A),Art		1.0	DR
VI	14	Ddo	33	F–		A			
	15	Ddo	22	Mau	2	Hd			DR, PHR
VII	16	Ddo	99	F–	2	Hd			PHR
	17	Wo	1	Fo		Hd,Cg		2.5	PHR
	18	Dd+	99	ma.Mp.FDo	2	H,Sc	P	1.0	DV, GHR
VIII	19	Do	1	Fo	2	A	P		FAB2
	20	Do	8	Fu		Art			
	21	D+	7	Fu		An		3.0	MOR, FAB2
IX	22	DdSo	99	F–		Hd			ALOG, PHR
	23	Ddo	99	F–		A			
X	24	Ddo	22	F–		An			
	25	Do	7	F–	2	An			PER

L. Appel

Appendix F

Case 2: Rorschach structural summary

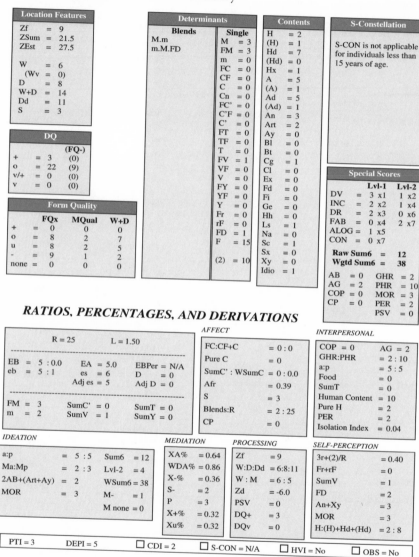

Location Features		
Zf	=	9
ZSum	=	21.5
ZEst	=	27.5
W	=	6
(Wv	=	0)
D	=	8
W+D	=	14
Dd	=	11
S	=	3

DQ		(FQ-)
+	= 3	(0)
o	= 22	(9)
v/+	= 0	(0)
v	= 0	(0)

Form Quality			
	FQx	MQual	W+D
+	= 0	0	0
o	= 8	2	7
u	= 8	2	5
-	= 9	1	2
none	= 0	0	0

Determinants			
Blends	Single		
M.m	M	= 3	
m.M.FD	FM	= 3	
	m	= 0	
	FC	= 0	
	CF	= 0	
	C	= 0	
	Cn	= 0	
	FC'	= 0	
	C'F	= 0	
	C'	= 0	
	FT	= 0	
	TF	= 0	
	T	= 0	
	FV	= 1	
	VF	= 0	
	V	= 0	
	FY	= 0	
	YF	= 0	
	Y	= 0	
	Fr	= 0	
	rF	= 0	
	FD	= 1	
	F	= 15	
	(2)	= 10	

Contents	
H	= 2
(H)	= 1
Hd	= 7
(Hd)	= 0
Hx	= 1
A	= 5
(A)	= 1
Ad	= 5
(Ad)	= 1
An	= 3
Art	= 2
Ay	= 0
Bl	= 0
Bt	= 0
Cg	= 1
Cl	= 0
Ex	= 0
Fd	= 0
Fi	= 0
Ge	= 0
Hh	= 0
Ls	= 1
Na	= 0
Sc	= 1
Sx	= 0
Xy	= 0
Idio	= 1

S-Constellation
S-CON is not applicable for individuals less than 15 years of age.

Special Scores			
		Lvl-1	Lvl-2
DV	=	3 x1	1 x2
INC	=	2 x2	1 x4
DR	=	2 x3	0 x6
FAB	=	0 x4	2 x7
ALOG	=	1 x5	
CON	=	0 x7	
		Raw Sum6 =	12
		Wgtd Sum6 =	38
AB	= 0	GHR	= 2
AG	= 2	PHR	= 10
COP	= 0	MOR	= 3
CP	= 0	PER	= 2
		PSV	= 0

RATIOS, PERCENTAGES, AND DERIVATIONS

R = 25	L = 1.50

EB	= 5 : 0.0	EA	= 5.0	EBPer	= N/A
eb	= 5 : 1	es	= 6	D	= 0
		Adj es	= 5	Adj D	= 0

FM	= 3	SumC'	= 0	SumT	= 0
m	= 2	SumV	= 1	SumY	= 0

AFFECT

FC:CF+C	= 0 : 0
Pure C	= 0
SumC' : WSumC	= 0 : 0.0
Afr	= 0.39
S	= 3
Blends:R	= 2 : 25
CP	= 0

INTERPERSONAL

COP = 0	AG = 2
GHR:PHR	= 2 : 10
a:p	= 5 : 5
Food	= 0
SumT	= 0
Human Content	= 10
Pure H	= 2
PER	= 2
Isolation Index	= 0.04

IDEATION

a:p	= 5 : 5
Ma:Mp	= 2 : 3
2AB+(Art+Ay)	= 2
MOR	= 3

Sum6	= 12
Lvl-2	= 4
WSum6	= 38
M-	= 1
M none	= 0

MEDIATION

XA%	= 0.64
WDA%	= 0.86
X-%	= 0.36
S-	= 2
P	= 3
X+%	= 0.32
Xu%	= 0.32

PROCESSING

Zf	= 9
W:D:Dd	= 6:8:11
W : M	= 6 : 5
Zd	= -6.0
PSV	= 0
DQ+	= 3
DQv	= 0

SELF-PERCEPTION

3r+(2)/R	= 0.40
Fr+rF	= 0
SumV	= 1
FD	= 2
An+Xy	= 3
MOR	= 3
H:(H)+Hd+(Hd)	= 2 : 8

PTI = 3	DEPI = 5	☐ CDI = 2	☐ S-CON = N/A	☐ HVI = No	☐ OBS = No

176

Constellations table

S-Constellation (Suicide Potential)	PTI (Perceptual-Thinking Index)
S-CON is not applicable for individuals less than 15 years of age.	☐ (XA% [0.64] < 0.70) and (WDA% [0.86] < 0.75) X-% [0.36] > 0.29 (Sum Level 2 Special Scores [4] > 2) and (FAB2 [2] > 0) ((R [25] < 17) and (WSum6 [38] > 14*)) or ((R [25] < 16) and (WSum6 [38] > 18*)) ☐ (M- [1] > 1) or (X-% [0.36] > 0.40) 3 Total

DEPI (Depression Index)	CDI (Coping Deficit Index)
Positive if 5 or more conditions are true: (FV + VF + V [1] > 0) or (FD [2] > 2) (Col-Shd Blends [0] > 0) or (S [3] > 2) ☐ (3r + (2)/R [0.40] > 0.56* and Fr + rF [0] = 0) or (3r + (2)/R [0.40] < 0.38*) (Afr [0.39] < 0.53*) or (Blends [2] < 4) ☐ (SumShading [1] > FM + m [5]) or (SumC' [0] > 2) (MOR [3] > 2) or (2xAB + Art + Ay [2] > 3) (COP [0] < 2) or ([Bt+2xCl+Ge+Ls+2xNa]/R [0.04] > 0.24) 5 Total	☐ Positive if 4 or more conditions are true: (EA [5.0] < 6) or (AdjD [0] < 0) ☐ (COP [0] < 2) and (AG [2] < 2) (Weighted Sum C [0.0] < 2.5) or (Afr [0.39] < 0.53*) ☐ (Passive [5] > Active + 1 [6]) or (Pure H [2] < 2) ☐ (Sum T [0] > 1) or (Isolate/R [0.04] > 0.24) or (Food [0] > 0) 2 Total

HVI (Hypervigilance Index)	OBS (Obsessive Style Index)

☐ Positive if condition 1 is true and at least 4 of the others are true:
 	
(1) FT + TF + T [0] = 0
-- 	
☐ (2) Zf [9] > 12
☐ (3) Zd [-6.0] > +3.5
☐ (4) S [3] > 3
    (5) H + (H) + Hd + (Hd) [10] > 6
☐ (6) (H) + (A) + (Hd) + (Ad) [3] > 3
    (7) H + A : Hd + Ad [9:13] < 4 : 1
☐ (8) Cg [1] > 3
	(1) Dd [11] > 3
	☐ (2) Zf [9] > 12
	☐ (3) Zd [-6.0] > +3.0
	☐ (4) Populars [3] > 7
	☐ (5) FQ+ [0] > 1
	-- 	
	☐ Positive if one or more is true:
	
	☐ Conditions 1 to 5 are all true
	☐ Two or more of 1 to 4 are true and FQ+ [0] > 3
	☐ 3 or more of 1 to 5 are true
	   and X+% [0.32] > 0.89
	☐ FQ+ [0] > 3 and X+% [0.32] > 0.89

NOTE: '*' indicates a cutoff that has been adjusted for age norms.

L. Appel

Summary

Functional somatic symptoms (FSS) or psychosomatic phenomena are defined as physical symptoms of unknown source affecting 10%–30% of children and adolescents (Beck, 2008). Since empirical research shows considerable heterogeneity in the clinical presentation, course, and outcome of FSS in adolescents, this article illustrates that similar psychosomatic symptoms in adolescents might in fact reflect different psychopathological states. This understanding is based on Winnicott's (1971) conceptualization as applied by Ogden (1986) to different psychopathological states, viewing these states in terms of collapse of potential or transitional space between reality and fantasy. Following Smith (1990), this conceptualization is presented by Rorschach protocols of two adolescents with psychosomatic disorders. The cases are analyzed using cognitive variables derived from the Rorschach CS (Exner, 2003) and the Reality-Fantasy scale (Tibon, Handelzalts et al., 2005), a Rorschach index that assesses adaptive use, creation, and preservation of potential space between reality and fantasy.

Both patients were 14-year-old adolescents. They were referred to consultation due to complaints of abdominal pain classified as meeting the criteria of Childhood Functional Abdominal Pain (Rome III; Drossman, 2006). The first case illustrated the collapse of the transitional space toward the reality pole, being manifested in alexithymic characteristics of robot-like adaptation to the demands of external reality as well as difficulty identifying and expressing inner reality of both self and others. These characteristics were revealed in the Rorschach in constriction in the cognitive realm: elevated Lambda, few Whole (W) responses, few DQ+ responses, and lowered Zf as well as in the elevated RFS-P. The second case illustrated a tendency to collapse toward the fantasy pole of the transitional space. This state portrays psychotic personality structure, where fantasy is experienced as real as external reality and revealed in the Rorschach in elevated WSum6, elevated level-2, and elevated $X-\%$ as well as lowered RFS-P. Specific treatment attitudes were also suggested for each patient on the basis of this conceptualization.

סיכום

סימפטומים סומטיים פונקציונליים (FSS) או התופעה הפסיכוסומטית מוגדרים כסימפטומים פיזיים ללא פתולוגיה ידועה, וקיימים אצל 30%-10% מהילדים והמתבגרים (Beck, 2008). מכיוון שקיימת שונות משמעותית בתוצאות של מחקרים אמפיריים בהצגה, במהלך ובתוצאות של FSS אצל מתבגרים, מטרת המאמר היתה להדגים שסימפטומים פסיכוסומטיים דומים אצל מתבגרים עשויים לשקף מצבים פסיכופתולוגיים שונים. הבנה זו מבוססת על המשגתו של ויניקוט (1971) כפי שהיא מיושמת על יד אוגדן (1986) לגבי מצבים פסיכופתולוגיים שונים, הרואה מצבים אלה במונחים של קריסת המרחב המעברי או הפוטנציאלי בין מציאות לפנטזיה. בעקבות Smith (1990), המשגה זו מוצגת על ידי פרוטוקולי רורשאך של שני מתבגרים עם הפרעות פסיכוסומטיות. המקרים מנותחים באמצעות משתנים קוגניטיביים הנגזרים מה CS (Exner, 2003), סולם רורשאך (RFS; Tibon et al., 2005) וסולם מציאות-פנטזיה שמעריך יצירה, שימוש אדפטיבי, ושימור של המרחב הפוטנציאלי בין מציאות לפנטזיה.

שני המטופלים היו מתבגרים בני 14, אשר הופנו ליעוץ בעקבות תלונות על כאבי בטן שהוגדרו כעונות על הקריטריון של כאב בטן פונקציונלי בילדות (;Rome III 2006). המקרה הראשון הדגים קריסה של המרחב הפוטנציאלי לכיוון קוטב המציאות, והתאפיין במאפיינים אלקסיתימיים של הסתגלות דמויית רובוט לדרישות המציאות החיצונית, וקושי בזיהוי וביטוי המציאות הפנימית הן, האישית והן זו של אחרים. מאפיינים אלה נחשפו ברורשאך בצמצום בתחום הקוגניטיבי: Lambda מוגבהת, מיעוט תשובות W, מיעוט תשובות DQ+ ו Zf מונמך, כמו גם RFS-P מוגבה. המקרה השני הדגים נטייה לקריסה לכיוון קוטב הפנטזיה של המרחב המעברי. מצב זה מאפיין מבנה אישיות פסיכוטי, אשר בו הפנטזיה נחווית אמיתית כמו המציאות החיצונית, והתגלה ברורשאך על ידי WSum6 מוגבה, level-2 מוגבה ו X-% מוגבה, כמו גם RFS-P מונמך. בנוסף, הוצעו גישות טיפוליות ספציפיות עבור כל מטופל על בסיס המשגה זו.

Résumé

Les symptômes somatiques fonctionnels (SSF) ou les phénomènes psychosomatiques sont des symptômes physiques dont on ignore la source et qui concernent entre 10 et 30% des enfants et adolescents (Beck, 2008). Puisque les recherches empiriques démontrent que la présentation clinique, l'évolution et les conséquences des SSF chez les adolescents sont hétérogènes, cet article à pour objet d'illustrer comment des symptômes psychosomatiques similaires peuvent refléter des organizations psychopathologiques différentes. Notre compréhension est basée sur la conceptualization de Winnicott (1971), suivant son application par Ogden (1986) à différentes organizations psychopathologiques, considérant que celles-ci sont les résultats d'un effondrement d'un espace potentiel ou transitionnel, entre fantasme et réalité. En accord avec Smith (1990), cette conceptualization est présentée à l'aide des protocoles du Rorschach de deux adolescents souffrant de troubles psychosomatiques. Ces cas sont analysés à l'aide des variables cognitives du système intégré du Rorschach (Exner, 2003) et de l'échelle de fantasme-réalité (Tibon, Handelzalts et al., 2005), un indice du Rorschach qui permet d'évaluer l'utilisation adaptative, la création et la préservation d'un espace potentiel, entre fantasme et réalité.

Les deux patients étaient des adolescents âgés de 14 ans. Ils furent envoyés au département de gastro-entérologie suite à des maux d'estomac qui correspondaient aux critères diagnostiques de maux d'estomac fonctionnels infantiles (Rome III; Drossman, 2006). Le premier cas illustrait l'effondrement de l'espace transitionnel vers le pôle de réalité, qui se manifestait par des traits alexithimiques d'adaptation robotisée face à des demandes extérieures et des difficultés à identifier et exprimer sa propre réalité interne ou celle des autres. Ces caractéristiques ont été mises en évidence lors du test du Rorschach par des réductions au niveau de la triade cognitive: Lambda élevé, peu de réponses globales (G), peu de réponses DQ +, un Zf réduit, ainsi qu'un RFS-P élevé. Le deuxième cas montrait une tendance à l'effondrement du côté du pôle fantasme de l'espace transitionnel. Cette organization représente une structure psychotique de la personnalité où le fantasme est vécu comme aussi réel que la réalité extérieure, et qui se révèle au Rorschach par une élévation du WSum6 et Level-2, un X–% élevé, ainsi que RFS-P bas. Sur la base de cette conceptualization, on suggère, pour chaque patient, une attitude thérapeutique à adopter.

Resumen

Los síntomas somáticos funcionales (*Functional somatic symptoms: FSS*) o fenómenos psicosomáticos, se definen como síntomas físicos de origen desconocido y afectan al 10%–30% de niños y adolescentes (Beck, 2008). Puesto que según la investigación empírica estos síntomas muestran una gran heterogeneidad en sus manifestaciones clínicas, presentación, curso y efectos en los adolescentes, el objetivo de este estudio consiste en ilustrar cómo síntomas psicosomáticos similares pueden reflejar diferentes estados psicopatológicos en la adolescencia.

Este enfoque se basa en la conceptualización de Winnicott (1971), aplicada luego por Ogden (1986) a diferentes psicopatologías, observando estos estados en términos de un colapso del espacio potencial o transicional entre la realidad y la fantasía.

Siguiendo a Smith (1990), esta conceptualización aparece en los protocolos de Rorschach de dos adolescentes con trastornos psicosomáticos. Ambos casos se analizan utilizando las variables cognitivas derivadas del Sistema Comprehensivo (CS, Exner, 2003) y la Escala de Realidad-Fantasía (RFS-P, Tibon, Handelzalts et al., 2005), consistente en un índice que evalúa el uso adaptativo, la creación y la conservación de un espacio potencial entre la realidad y la fantasía.

Ambos pacientes tienen 14 años. Se derivaron a consulta por quejas de dolor abdominal persistente que cumplía los criterios de Dolor Abdominal Funcional en la Infancia (Roma III; Drossman, 2006). El primer caso ejemplifica el colapso del espacio transicional hacia el polo de la realidad, con manifestaciones de características alexitímicas, adaptación robotizada a las demandas de la realidad externa y dificultades para identificar y expresar la realidad interna propia y de los demás. Estas características se observan en Rorschach por la constricción en el ámbito cognitivo: Lambda elevado, pocas respuestas Globales (W), escasos DQ + y bajo Zf, así como por una elevación de la RFS-P. El segundo caso ilustra una tendencia al colapso del espacio transicional hacia el polo de la fantasía. Esto refleja una estructura psicótica de personalidad, donde la fantasía se experimenta de forma tan real como la realidad externa y aparece en Rorschach con: elevado WSum6, alto número de Códigos de Nivel-2, elevado X–% y baja RFS-P.

Se sugieren también actitudes terapéuticas específicas para cada paciente, teniendo como base esta conceptualización.

L. Appel

心身症を有する思春期における可能性のある空間の崩壊：2 つの事例研究のロールシャッハ
の例示

　機能性の心身症状（FSS）あるいは心身症現象は原因不明の身体症状によって定義され、
10%〜30%の子どもと思春期がこの疾患にかかっている（Beck,2008）。経験的な研究によ
れば、臨床像、経過、思春期における FSS の結果についてかなりの異質性が示されている
ので、この論文の目的は、思春期の類似した心身症現象が異なった精神病理学的状態を反
映している可能性について例示する事である。この理解は二つの Ogden（1986）によって
異なった精神病理状態に応用された Winnicott(1971)の概念化により基礎づけられており、
現実と空想の間の可能性のある空間あるいは移行空間の崩壊という観点からこれらの状態
を見ている。Smith（1990）を受けて、この概念化を、心身症を示している二人の思春期
のロールシャッハプロトコルにより報告する。これらの事例はロールシャッハ包括システ
ム（Exner,2003）による認知の変数と、現実と空想の間の可能な空間の適用と、創造と維
持を査定するロールシャッハの指標である現実−空想尺度（Tibon ら,2005）をもちいて分
析がなされた。
　患者は二人とも 14 歳であった。彼らは子どもの機能的腹痛（Rome,III:2006）の基準に
該当すると分類される腹痛の訴えによりコンサルテーションに紹介されてきた。第一のケ
ースは現実の極の方向への移行空間の崩壊として例示され、外的な現実の要求に対してロ
ボットのように適応するという失感情的な特徴と、自己と他者の両方について内的現実を
同定し、言葉で表現することの困難さが明らかにされた。これらの特徴はロールシャッハ
における認知の領域の圧縮として現れている：高いラムダ、少ない全体（W）反応、少ない
DQ+反応、低い Zf、同様に高い RFS-P。第二のケースは移行空間の空想の極の方向への崩
壊の傾向として例示された。この状態は精神病人格構造を描き出しており、そこでは空想
は外的な現実と同じくらいに現実的に体験されており、ロールシャッハにおける高い
WSum 6、高い level- 2反応、高い X-%、そして低い RFS-P としてあらわれていた。また、
この概念化にもとづいてそれぞれの患者には特定の治療態度が提案された。

Rorschachiana 32, 183–198
© 2011 Hogrefe Publishing

DOI: 10.1027/1192-5604/a000021

Original Article

Role of Color on the Production of Responses in Children's Rorschach Protocols

Danilo Rodrigues Silva

Faculty of Psychology, University of Lisbon, Portugal

Abstract. Previous studies have shown that, while color has the property to increase the production of responses to the Rorschach, such an effect is not present in children's protocols. Based on a review of the literature, the author highlights the characteristic of high reactive demand of the subject to color stimulus and traces its evolution to the preoperational period, where color nominations and the incongruent use of color, especially of pure color, are frequent. With the entry in the period of concrete operations such responses become rare or even disappear. In turn, the mean number of responses to color cards decreases between 5 to 6 and 11 years, and their form quality goes down as well. The cause of this change is the emergence and development of logical thinking. Given the intensity of color stimulus, the child does not yet have the equipment that will allow her to later integrate color and object as they really are.

Keywords: color, Rorschach, children

Introduction

Many questions have been asked and remain unanswered about the objective reasons why the Rorschach works for adults or about the real potential of the cards in terms of the responses they elicit. However, many more questions arise with the Rorschach when used with children, not only because far fewer studies have been carried out in this area, but also because its field of application is inherently mutable and is naturally dependent on advances in developmental psychology.

Before dealing with some specific aspects of the Rorschach, let us review the two areas on which research has been done: The first concerns the use of the Rorschach and the other the Rorschach instrument itself. The latter includes studies that help to validate the Rorschach as an instrument for psychological evaluation as well as those dealing with the complexity of its valences and their respective impact on the individuals to whom it is applied.

It is generally recognized that the characteristics of the Rorschach used with adults are different from the ones when used with children. Its principles of administration and interpretation cannot simply be transferred from one group to the other, and the study and interpretation of each protocol is ineffective if there is no knowledge of the child's psychological development. The Rorschach has traditionally been considered usable with children from the age of 3, though some proposes its use from the age of 2 – and there are even studies of its use with children under the age of 1 (Boekoldt, 1996). Leichtman (1996), the author of an excellent book on the Rorschach with children, proposes the take into account three different stages by means of which the differentiating characteristics of protocols obtained with the youngest children (those aged between 2 and 6 to 7 years old) can be shown. Stage I covers the years up to the age of 2 whose protocols consist of responses repeated from card to card, with no attention being paid to the obvious differences between them, *perseveration stage*; or from the age of 2 and a half, a new form of perseveration called *modified perseveration*, where the child shows some concern with finding traces of the blot that justify the percept presented is observed. Stage II, called the *confabulation stage*, covers the period between 3 and 5 years of age and is characterized by the occurrence of confabulatory responses, or rather responses based on some part or aspect of the blot, but are extended to include areas that are larger or cover the whole blot. Stage III corresponds to the period between the ages of 5 and 7 during which the Rorschach, as an instrument of evaluation, attains the level of efficiency required and found in its current use.

The fact that a type of protocol can be obtained at Stage III that traditionally considered to have interpretative validity does not mean that there are no more indicators of development. In fact, as well as the possibility of observing continuing improvement in the way the allotted task is approached and carried out after this age, it remains to determine the proportion of the number of responses localized in the whole blot or in parts thereof. There is also a constant increase in human movement responses, with a reduction in the number of pure color responses

(C) and primary color responses (CF), which is nearly always compensated by an increase in the number of secondary color responses (FC). These are important aspects to keep in mind when analyzing and interpreting a child's protocol.

In this study, we propose to highlight a new aspect that has developmental characteristics and that has not been studied so far and whose meaning and scope have therefore not been defined: the significance of the role of color in the production of Rorschach responses in children between the ages of 5 to 6 and 11 to 12.

Color and Perception in Children's Rorschach Responses

Let us begin by stressing the meaning generally given to color in the Rorschach. Although this is not universally accepted, the main systems of this method consider color to be linked to affect, the paradigmatic variable that indicates the presence or expression of affect in a protocol. Its predominance in the characterization of the object seen, the pure chromatic element, or one associated with a shape, or a dominant shape with which the chromatic element is associated, indicates the quite obvious presence of the affective-emotional component in the act of giving the response. This general statement may have many nuances as pointed out by Chabert (1997). The number of responses given to cards VIII, IX, and X also forms a variable called the Affective Ratio (Afr), a ratio that provides a comparison between the number of responses given to these three chromatic cards and the number of responses given to the remaining ones, which mediates in the characterization of the affective-emotional component. Previous studies with three groups of 20 Portuguese children of both sexes, aged 6, 9, and 11 years, show that the value of Afr decreases slightly between the ages of 6 and 11, with median values of 0.54, 0.52, and 0.54 at 5 to 6, 9 to 10, and 11 to 12 years of age (Silva & Marques, 2008a), respectively, indicating that the presence of the affective dimension is more evident at 6 years of age than in later years. This is in line with data from developmental psychology, and it is all the more true if a reduction in this number is accompanied by an increase in the value of R, the total number of responses per protocol. If the value of R increases and the number of responses to the colored cards decreases, it is not surprising that the number of responses given to the cards in their achromatic version increases too. These elements are reinforced by the results of normative data from Portuguese children, whose *Afr* values between 6 and 10 years of age are as follows: 0.59 for an average number of responses (R) of 22.71; 0.53 for an R of 25.25; 0.51 for an R of 24.55; 0.52 for an R of 25.73; 0.55 for an R of 24.00 (Silva & Dias, 2007, pp. 135–139). Although neither the decrease in the values of *Afr* nor the increase in the R averages are regular and accentuated in Portuguese normative data, they enable us to support the data from our studies carried out on the effect of color in the production of responses in children, an effect that leads to a reduction in the importance of color in responses in favor of the achromatic cards.

But the meaning of the color determinant in relation to the affect is not its only function in the essentially perceptive task on which the response is based. Another valence recognized for color is its importance as a component for the perception of the outside world and, among other things, as a way of delimiting and differentiating objects. The present study is primarily concerned with this perceptive dimension.

For a better contextualization of the theme under study, let us begin by showing some of the elements related to the perception of color with aspects that are important for the Rorschach responses. Color appears as one of the properties of five of the ten Rorschach cards: as red on Cards II and III, frequently called the red cards; and multicolored or pastel colors on Cards VIII, IX, and X, generally known as the colored cards. From a developmental perspective, color seems to be a stimulating quality that could be said to impose itself irresistibly to the subject leading to the idea that the subject is attracted by color (Meili-Dvoretzki, 1956; Shapiro, 1960). These studies tell us that children react to color from infancy. This is something that we all easily find, and this is why all of the objects designed to be used with babies such as toys, clothing, soap holders, brushes, etc., are made in soft colors, obviously to avoid hurting or irritating the baby.

What seems to be happening in these age groups is not an attraction to color, but an irresistible passive reaction because of the nature of the actual stimulus of light. The nervous system is not yet completely mature and is unable to react to this stimulus in any other way. Furthermore, children react more intensely to colors when they are shinier or less saturated. Many studies show that children tend to identify objects primarily by color in early infancy. Meili-Dvoretzki (1956) states that when children up to the age of 6 or 7 are confronted by geometrical figures with no meaning and have to classify them, the main criterion adopted for classification is color.

However, if the material for classification has its own meaning as recognized by the child, then it is the shape rather than the color which is adopted as a criterion – and this criterion is adopted from as early as 3 to 4 years of age. This is what happens when babies recognize the feeding bottle by its shape, but react intensely to colorful and luminous stimuli when the shapes hold no meaning for them (Meili-Dvoretzki, 1956). Thus, up to the age of 3, in terms of Rorschach, a child has very little interest in color, given that the colored inkblots have absolutely no meaning for the child.

From the age of 3, however, responses start to appear with particular colors. These are registered, on the one hand, as responses of naming a color and, on the other hand, as responses of Color without shape (Pure C). Meili-Dvoretzki (1956) observed, however, that not all of the Pure C's are of the same kind. In the 3 to 5 age group, the effect of the color sometimes causes the child to associate it with a particular object, as in the response "a blue sun," though this object may have its own specific color.

This pattern of unspecified C shows the schematic method of concept formation, in which one quality or one part of an object serves as criterion for the entire concept. Here the child not only disregards the form, but also the specific color, and for this reason this C is more primitive than the usual Pure C, which is characterized merely by the absence of consideration for form (Meili-Dvoretzki, 1956, p. 152).

Both in the case of naming the color and in the latter case of using the color in an unspecified manner, it is difficult to identify when the color indicated coincides with that of the object referred to, and what we have here are responses which would be a sign of intellectual deficiency or deterioration, or clear signs of thought disturbance, if they were given by older subjects. According to Meili-Dvoretzki (1956), these responses of unspecified Pure C disappear at the age of 6. In any case, they are the first attempt by the child to deal with the urgency of the stimulus. Related with this and other points of our study is a short but very suggestive article by Boekholt (2000).

We also note the importance of color in determining responses in cases of thought disturbance. This is clear in classification and object-grouping tasks, in which the subjects are unable to distance themselves from the stimuli and adopt an approach toward them that is too close and well-defined, consequently giving in to the irresistible lure of color and neglecting the conceptual component – or pushing it into second place (Chabert, 1997; Kleiger, 1999; Leichtman, 1996; Meili-Dvoretzki,

1956). If we consider the results of the studies on thought disturbance, two important aspects come to mind: The first is that color has a greater impact when thinking is disorganized; the second is a consequence of this and shows that such results highlight passive behavior with respect to visual stimuli which is linked to the preeminence of the color element.

There is yet another phenomenon that incontrovertibly shows the role of color in the perception of external reality and the way it evolves during the child's development. In a chapter that is essential reading for a perceptive understanding of the color response in the Rorschach, Shapiro (1960) considers the question of color perception in people who were born blind. He states:

> In the earliest visual experiences of these previously blind people, there is a remarkable deficiency in form vision. Not only is there an initial incapacity to recognize forms (on the basis of anticipated transfer from previous, nonvisual, familiarity) which would not be so surprising to us, but there is an extraordinary difficulty in this initial phase in *learning* to identify forms or in learning to "see" forms of any degree of complexity. (Shapiro, 1960, p. 166)

In contrast to this great difficulty in the perceptive construction of form, the recognition of color is almost immediate. The subjects feel overwhelmed by the abundance and variety of visual impressions they are receiving, "the most gross and diffuse sensations of light and color, movement, figure, and background. The sensations are often of unusual vividness and brilliance, frequently actually painful" (Shapiro, 1960, p. 167). As a result, the process leading to the common perception of objects is complex, slow, and even painful. In this respect, it is again worth quoting Shapiro:

> During this same critical period, in the course of the patient's efforts toward an adequate visual orientation, it is observed that *object identifications* often tend to be made, at first, on the basis of color. There appears, in other words, to be a development which very likely consists over several overlapping phases, from identification of objects at first on the basis of their most conspicuous and gross visual aspects to later perceptual identification primarily in terms of more abstract form qualities. (1960, 167–168)

All of the studies to which we have just referred allow a clear distinction to be made between two kinds of visual experience, one passive and immediate and the other active and constructive. In terms of the Rorschach, this visual experience of color manifests itself in various ways, the best known being the naming of color, with the code *Cn*, for pure color *C*, for color with form in second place *CF*, and for form followed by the color *FC*. This is not the moment to ponder the significance of

Table 1. Averages for color determinants in normative data for Portuguese children aged 6 to 10 (*N* = 86 + 69 + 75 + 66 + 61)

Determinants	6	7	8	9	10
FC	1.08	1.19	1.11	1.27	1.34
CF	1.27	0.99	0.96	1.23	1.10
C	0.63	0.58	0.33	0.39	0.10
Cn	0.04	0.00	0.01	0.00	0.00

these codes; suffice to say that, from a developmental perspective, they correspond to the journey made from a period during which color coerces and constrains to another in which it contributes to the delimitation and enrichment of form.

On the other hand, it is still pertinent to note that the importance or the emphasis lent to color tends to decrease from the age of 6 onward, as may be seen generally and specifically in normative data of Portuguese children between the ages of 6 and 10 (Silva & Dias, 2007). Table 1 shows how the averages of the determinants in which color predominates, that is to say *C* and *CF*, decrease stepwise between the extremes of age, except for 9-year-olds – findings which are repeated in the North American norms of Exner and Weiner (1995, p. 7). Also, averages of *FC* tend to rise progressively as is also found in Exner and Weiner (1995, p. 7).

The Inhibitory Effect of Color
in Children's Rorschach Responses

Our previous studies indicated that, color does not determine the increase in responses to the colored cards (cards VIII, IX and X) in children's protocols as it does in adult protocols. In three studies carried out with Portuguese children of 5 to 6, 9 to 10, and 11 to 12 years of age, using those standard Rorschach cards and their achromatic version with samples of 40 children (20 of each sex) (Silva, 2002, 2009a; Silva & Marques, 2008b), there were no significant differences between the average responses obtained with the one or the other version, though a slight tendency may be observed toward an increase in the average of responses to the achromatic version of the cards among children aged between 5 to 6 and 11 to 12.

Why does the importance of color appear to decline in the responses given by children between the ages of 6 and 11?

We are now in a better position to reflect on this issue. It seems clear that any response to Rorschach falls to some extent within what is in current psychology textbooks called the resolution of perceptive problems. In one of these volumes, there is a figure with the caption *Perceptive Enigmas* and the following question: "What objects are represented here?" (Gleitman, Fridlund, & Reisberg, 2003, p. 316). In the text, the author discusses how the response to this question entails a series of that operations that correspond to the different phases of a problem-solving strategy. Equipped with their own expectations garnered from previous knowledge and experience, subjects elaborate a response hypothesis they then seek to test, repeating these operations until finding the satisfactory response. There is no other way of finding a response to Rorschach's first question *What might this be?*, the difference being that there is no correct response.

From this perspective, going back to some of the data already referred to, particularly about what might be described as an antagonistic property in the stimulus situation, between the demands of the color component, which require an immediate reaction, and those implied by the question cited above, which involve a search and the attentive and concentrated application of the subject to the blots, we find here a possible cause for the reduction of responses in this age group: Children faced with a problem-solving situation in which there are different solutions competing with each other have great difficulty responding, both in terms of quantity and of quality.

Access to specific operations and to logical thinking also prevent children from reacting to color the way they have done up to that point, pointing to the colored blots, calling them by name or associating them with objects whose color is not the same as its natural one. The new mental instrument with which they see and address reality imposes demands the child recognizes and knows and cannot evade. Children are not yet properly equipped to confront color without difficulty, particularly in the problematic situation of finding a response that is appropriate to what has been asked. Meili-Dworetzki's observation is comprehensible when from among the different reactions to color at the Rorschach, he chooses to indicate the "Rejection of colored cards due to irritation with the color" (1956, p. 154), from the age of 8.

Thus, it is reasonable to say that, for this age group, color makes it difficult to satisfy what is asked for in the Rorschach instructions from a

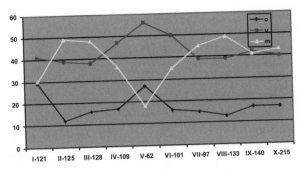

Figure 1. Approximate percentages of the number of entries with each Rorschach card, codified as Form Quality, *o*, *u* and –, in the total sample of Portuguese children of both sexes from 6 to 10 years of age.

perceptive-cognitive perspective, an aspect that may lead to a reduction in the production of responses to colored cards. Data that seems to reinforce this response hypothesis are related to the quality of the responses, as presented in the study of Portuguese normative data. The exact number of those responses per card is not available yet, but we do have the graph representing the percentage of entries for each card from the Form Quality perspective, and for all responses that constitute the reference table for the codification of the Form Quality of the responses to the Rorschach in Portuguese children between the ages of 6 and 10 (Silva, 2009b). Figure 1 gives us an objective approximation of each level of FQ (Silva & Dias, 2007).

When we analyze the graph (Figure 1), we notice that the lowest percentage of entries with each card is related to the Ordinary or Common Form Quality –*o*. Note, however, that these entries correspond to the highest number of responses given, because responses *FQo* correspond to the most frequently indicated percepts. If we look at the line representing the percentages of entries classified as *FQ–*, we conclude that the cards in which these percepts are most frequent are Cards II and III, red cards, and Cards VII, VIII, IX, and X. Thus, of the six cards with the highest percentage as *FQ–* entries, between 40% and 50%, five contain color. Furthermore, the values of *F–* that occur in cards II and III, those that contain red, the most saturated color, are among the three with the highest levels of perceptive distortion. It is not possible to use this data to affirm categorically that color is responsible for the highest number of responses of poor Form Quality for this age period: In each card and for each individual there are multiple causes of unsuccessful perception; in the thematic area under study here, these data still assume particular importance and are consistent indicators. The rise of the level of complexity, caused by the presence of color on the stimulus, increases the perception difficulty and is an important source of misperception in

191

children. This also suggests that children have not yet reached the level of perceptual development that enables them to integrate the color when responding to Rorschach without great difficulty.

Final Remarks

From a mainly perceptive-cognitive perspective, the phenomenon of the reduction in the production of responses deriving from the presence of color in the colored cards is explained by the property of the color stimulus representing such a level of intensity for the young child. An immediate reaction is restrained and is not susceptible to dilation, particularly with stimuli devoid of meaning, as in the case of Rorschach inkblots. Only when children pass into the stage of concrete operations or develop logical thinking do they slowly begin to acquire the means to face and deal with the chromatic requirements of the stimuli, specifically when there is avoidance thereof, which results in a slight and continued reduction in the number of responses to colored cards up to the age of 11 in favor of the achromatic cards.

It has been said that color in Rorschach is connected to affect, that color is a symbol of affect and emotion, and that color indicates their place and intensity in the life of the individual. The question is whether color assumes this same meaning in Rorschach when used with children. In this respect, let us quote Rausch de Traubenberg, who after declaring that she would not talk about the relationship between color and emotion in children and refused to apply the adult model of mental functioning to them, with Boizou (Rausch de Traubenberg & Boizou, 1977), wrote about the way they would approach color responses:

> We will talk about color responses, their interpretative meaning and value in their different dimensions: qualitative interest, subjective attraction or elaboration of representations, different types of elaboration, the character of the provoked emotional tonality experienced or the neutral nature of reactions, the expressive or defensive quality of the behaviors assumed or of their qualitative attitudes. A distinction will be made between reactions to the appearance of pastel colors and to those which involve gray and white. (Rausch de Traubenberg & Boizou, 1977, pp. 46–47)

This position finally considers the effect of color in the protocol of each child, but does not interpret in only one sense, the sense of a connection or means of expression of affect, an attitude that is in tune with the diversity of reactions that may arise from color stimulus in the age group under study. It is significant that in their book these authors make no use of RC%, the equivalent code of Afr. This work underlines the perceptual nature of the act of responding to the Rorschach, particularly in the cards in which color is present. It draws attention to the likelihood that the presence of color, as a demanding stimulus imposed on the subject, competes with the demands of perceptual-cognitive skills being developed in the child and thus determines the inhibition of response production. It shows once again how cautious one should be in addressing issues of child Rorschach from the knowledge of adult Rorschach.

Acknowledgments

This study was supported by Centro de Investigação em Psicologia da Universidade de Lisboa, Fundação para a Ciência e Tecnologia.

References

Boekholt, M. (1996). Fondements pulsionnels de l'expérience visuelle: regard a travers de la genèse du processus Rorschach [Instinctual foundations of visual experience: A look through the genesis of the Rorschach process]. *Psychiatrie de l'Enfant, 39*, 537–579.

Boekholt, M. (2000). En guise d'écho: De l'affect à la pensée à travers le Rorschach des jeunes enfants [As an echo: From affect to thought through young children's Rorschach]. *Psychologie Clinique et Projective, 6*, 255–264.

Chabert, C. (1997). *O Rorschach na Clínica do Adulto* [The Rorschach in adult clinical testing]. Lisboa: Climepsi Editores.

Exner, J. E., & Weiner, I. B. (1995). *The Rorschach: A comprehensive system, Vol. 3: Assessment of children and adolescents* (2nd ed.). New York: Wiley.

Gleitman, H., Fridlund, A. J., & Reisberg, D. (2003). *Psicologia* [Psychology]. Lisboa: Fundação Calouste Gulbenkian.

Kleiger, J. H. (1999). *Disordered thinking and the Rorschach theory, research, and differential diagnosis.* Hillsdale, NJ: Analytic Press.

Leichtman, M. (1996). *The Rorschach: A developmental perspective.* Hillsdale, NJ: Analytic Press.

Meili-Dvoretzki, G. (1956). The development of perception in the Rorschach. In B. Klopfer (Ed.), *Developments in the Rorschach technique, Volume II: Fields of application* (pp. 101–176). New York: Harcourt Brace.

Rausch de Traubenberg, N., & Boizou, M.-F. (1977). *Le Rorschach en Clinique Infantile*

D. R. Silva

L'Imaginaire et le Réel chez l'Enfant [Rorschach in clinical testing: The imaginary and real in children]. Paris: Dunod.

Shapiro, D. (1960). A perceptual understanding of color response. In M. A. Rickers-Ovsiankina (Ed.), *Rorschach psychology* (pp. 154–201). New York: Wiley.

Silva, D. R. (2002). The effect of color on productivity of Card X of the Rorschach. *Rorschachiana, 25,* 123–135.

Silva, D. R. (2009a). Consideraciones sobre la evolución de la variable Proporción Afectiva del Rorschach entre los 5 y 16 años [On the evolution of the Rorschach affective ratio variable from 5 to 16 years of age]. *Investigaciones Psicológicas, 14*(1), 103–113.

Silva, D. R. (2009b). *Form quality table of Rorschach responses – ordinary (o), unusual (u) and minus (–) –, based on a sample of 400 Portuguese children of both sexes and with 6 to 10 years of age.* Unpublished manuscript, Universidade de Lisboa, Portugal.

Silva, D. R., & Dias, A. M. (2007). Rorschach Comprehensive System Data for a sample of 357 Portuguese children at five ages. *Journal of Personality Assessment, 89*(Suppl. 1), S131–S141.

Silva, D. R., & Marques, L. G. (2008a). A cor e o efeito inibitório de respostas no Rorschach de crianças [Color and its inhibitory effect on children's Rorschach R.]. *Psychologica, 48,* 5–24.

Silva, D. R., & Marques, L. G. (2008b). L'effet de la couleur sur la production de réponses au Rorschach chez des enfants non consultants. Une étude génétique [The effect of color on the production of responses in non-patient children's Rorschach]. *Psychologie clinique et projective, 14,* 221–233.

Danilo Rodrigues Silva
Faculty of Psychology
University of Lisbon
Alameda da Universiodade
1649-013 Lisboa
Portugal
Tel. +351 217943600
Fax +351 217933408
E-mail Danilo@fpce.ul.pt

Summary

This study proposes to present an explanation for the phenomenon found in previous studies with children, that color does not determine an increase in the production of responses as it does in adult Rorschach protocols. Studies of the role of color in responses to Rorschach and the types of these responses reveal the intense nature of that stimulus faced with which the incipient perceptive-cognitive activity of the subject proves to be incapable

194

of reacting appropriately. The subject feels the action, is unable to resist it and consequently reacts with primitive types of response such as naming the color, the incongruous combination of color and shape or pure color responses. Those types of response are no longer acceptable or become less frequent once the child has passed into the period of concrete operations or logical thinking. Furthermore, the task of problem solving, as a response to Rorschach, becomes doubly complex when the stimulus of color is present, for an immediate reaction is required for color, and moderation or delay for problem solving. This situation causes conflict which is solved when the child decides to ignore the color stimulus and choose the strategy of problem solving or logical thinking. This decision would explain the reduced production of responses to the colored cards, when compared to the production of responses to achromatic cards. The disturbing effect of the color stimulus seems to make itself felt in the formal quality of the responses, and is found to be poor with the colored cards more often than with the achromatic cards.

Resumo

O presente estudo pretendeu apresentar uma explicação ao fenômeno identificado em estudos anteriores com crianças, nos quais se observou que a cor não determina o aumento da produção de respostas como ocorre nos protocolos de adultos. Estudos sobre o papel da cor nas respostas do Rorschach e os tipos dessas respostas revelam a natureza intensa deste estímulo diante do qual a atividade perceptiva-cognitiva do sujeito se mostra incapaz de reagir de modo adequado. O indivíduo experimenta a ação, mostra-se incapaz de resistir e, por isso, reage por meio de modos primários de respostas, tais como nomeação de cor pura, combinação incongruente entre cor e forma ou respostas de cor pura, sem forma. Esses tipos de resposta se tornam menos freqüentes com a entrada da criança no inicio do período das operações concretas ou do pensamento lógico. Por outro lado, a tarefa de solucionar problemas, como resposta ao Rorschach, se torna duplamente complexa quando se apresenta o estímulo cor, uma vez que este requer uma reação imediata, enquanto que a solução de problemas demanda moderação ou postergação da reação. Esta situação gera um conflito que é resolvido no momento em que a criança decide ignorar o estímulo cor e escolhe a estratégia de solução do problema ou faz uso do pensamento lógico. Tal decisão poderia explicar a produção reduzida de respostas às pranchas coloridas em comparação com a das pranchas acromáticas. O efeito perturbador do estímulo cor parece se fazer presente na qualidade formal das respostas, sendo esta mais frequentemente ruim nas pranchas coloridas do que na maior parte das pranchas acromáticas.

Résumé

Cette étude se propose de présenter une explication du fait révélé par des recherches antérieures selon lesquelles la couleur n'a pas, aux protocoles de Rorschach des enfants, l'effet d'augmentation de la production de réponses qu'on trouve chez les adultes. Des études sur le rôle de la couleur dans les réponses au Rorschach et sur les modalités de telles réponses montrent la nature intense de ce stimulus, face auquel l'activité perceptivo-cognitive naissante de l'enfant se révèle incapable d'une réaction adéquate. Le sujet en souffre l'action, ne peut lui résister et par conséquent il réagit avec des réponses primitives telles que la nomination de couleur ou les combinaisons incongrues de forme et couleur. Ces types de réponses cessent d'être acceptables ou deviennent moins fréquentes avec l'entrée de l'enfant dans le stade des opérations concrètes ou de la pensée logique. Par ailleurs, la tache de solution de problèmes, en tant que réponse au Rorschach, devient, dans cette nouvelle phase, doublement complexe vue la présence du stimulus couleur, car celui-ci demande une réaction immédiate alors que la solution de problèmes demande de la pondération, de la dilation. Cette condition est à l'origine d'un conflit qui ne trouve sa solution que quand l'enfant prend la décision d'ignorer le stimulus couleur et choisit la stratégie de la solution de problèmes ou de la pensée logique. Une telle décision expliquerait la réduction des réponses aux planches couleur par comparaison à la production des réponses données à la plupart des planches achromatiques. Il paraît aussi que l'effet troublant du stimulus couleur se laisse percevoir dans la qualité formelle des réponses. En effet, cette qualité formelle tend à être plus fréquemment mauvaise aux planches couleur qu'aux planches achromatiques.

Resumen

Este estudio pretende presentar una explicación del fenómeno identificado en estudios anteriores con niños, según el cual el color no determina el aumento de la producción de respuestas como ocurre en los protocolos de adultos. Estudios sobre el papel del color en las respuestas al Rorschach y los tipos de estas respuestas revelan la naturaleza intensa de este estímulo delante del cual la actividad perceptivo-cognitiva del sujeto se muestra incapaz de reaccionar de forma adecuada. El sujeto experimenta su acción, no puede resistirle y en consecuencia reacciona con modos primarios de respuestas como la nominación del color, la combinación incongruente entre color y forma o repuestas de color pura, sin forma. Estos tipos de respuesta se tornan menos frecuentes con la entrada del niño en el periodo de las operaciones concretas o del pensamiento lógico. Por otro lado, la tarea de la solución de problema, como respuesta al Rorschach, se torna duplamente compleja cuando se presenta el estímulo color, pues este último requiere una reacción inmediata mientras la solución del problema pide moderación o dilación de la reacción. Esta situación origina un conflicto que es resuelto en el momento en que el niño decide ignorar el estímulo color y escoge la estrategia de la solución de problema o del pensamiento lógico. Tal decisión podría explicar la producción reducida de respuestas a las láminas coloridas en comparación con la de las láminas acromáticas. El efecto perturbador del estímulo color parece hacerse sentir en la calidad formal de las respuestas, siendo esta más frecuentemente mala en las láminas coloridas que en la mayor parte de las acromáticas.

D. R. Silva

子どものロールシャッハプロトコルの反応生成おける色彩の役割

本研究の目的は、以前になされた子どもにおける研究で見出された現象、成人のロールシャッハプロトコルにおいてそうであるのだが、色彩は反応生成の増加の決定要因にはならないという現象に説明を提示することである。ロールシャッハに対する反応における色彩の役割についての研究およびこれらの反応のタイプは、直面する刺激の強烈な性質を明らかにしており、被験者の最初の知覚－認知活動が適切に反応することができなくなることを説明することができる。被験者はその活動を感じ、それに抗うことができず、結果として、色彩命名反応や不調和な色彩と形の結合した反応や純粋色彩反応などの未分化なタイプの反応で対応してしまう。このタイプの反応は子どもがいったん具体的操作期あるいは論理的思考の時期に到達してしまうともはや受け入れがたいものであり、それほど見られなくなる。さらに、ロールシャッハに対する反応のような問題解決の課題は、刺激に色彩が入っている場合に二重に複雑になる、というのは、問題解決を調節して、あるいは遅らせて、色彩に対する早急な反応をすることが要求されているからである。この状況は、子どもが色彩刺激を無視して、問題解決あるいは論理的思考というストラテジーを選択した時に解決されうる葛藤を引き起こす。この決定は、無彩色カードに対する反応生成に比較して、色彩カードにおける反応数の減少が生じることを説明するであろう。色彩刺激の妨害効果は反応の形態質において明らかになるようで、無彩色図版においてよりも有彩色図版において貧困になることが見出されている。

Rorschachiana 32, 199–222
© 2011 Hogrefe Publishing

DOI: 10.1027/1192-5604/a000022

Original Article

The Rorschach in Brazilian Children

Normative Data From a 9- to 11-Year-Old Nonpatient Sample

Renata Loureiro Raspantini, Suélen Fernandes,
and Sonia Regina Pasian

*Faculty of Philosophy, Sciences and Letters of Ribeirão Preto,
Universidade de São Paulo (FFCLRP-USP), Brazil*

Abstract. This study explores the normative patterns of children's responses to the Rorschach. A total of 180 Brazilian children between 9–11 years were selected for the study, presenting indicators of typical development and equally distributed in terms of gender, age, and school origin. Participants were assessed individually, using a child development questionnaire, the Raven's Progressive Matrices Test, and the Rorschach Method (French Approach). The Rorschach protocols were analyzed by three independent judges. To date, 140 protocols have been coded, with their data being reported in average results. Productivity and rhythm indicators: R = 16.1; TLm = 17.2s; TRm = 33.4s. Apprehension modes: G = 44.3%; D = 33.0%; Dd = 22.0%. Determinants and formal quality: F% = 63.1%; F +% = 76.7%; F + ext% = 76.3%. Most evocated contents: A% = 57.5%; H% = 21.4%. Predominant affective reaction styles were studied. Although partial, the present results are promising as they provide an update of existing normative date for children between the age of 9 and 11. This study can help further the sociocultural understanding of the use of the Rorschach test with Brazilian children.

Keywords: children, norms, psychological assessment, personality, Rorschach

Introduction

The Rorschach method is one of the most widely disseminated and used projective techniques worldwide. Adequate analysis of a person's performance on the Rorschach, however, implies the existence of adequate reference parameters for interpretation. Information is particularly needed regarding how test variables are distributed in a population (Fuster, 2008; Güntert, 2000; Hamel & Shaffer, 2007; Meyer, Erdberg, & Shaffer, 2007; Pasian, 1998, 2002; Salcuni, Lis, Parolin, & Mazzeschi, 2007; Silva & Dias, 2007; Weiner, 2001).

Anastasi and Urbina (2000) discussed the need for objective systemization of Rorschach parameters, stating that, in order to describe a person's personality structure, it is necessary to indicate the group this person belongs to as well as to outline individual, idiographic traits. Hence, normative variability and evolution must be taken into account and consider various factors such as group composition as well as time period and sociocultural variations. Complying with these criteria is fundamental in the case of the Rorschach. Thus, up-to-date and adequate normative patterns should be developed in different contexts and sociocultural conditions (Hamel & Shaffer, 2007; Matsumoto, Suzuki, Shirai, & Nakabayashi, 2007; Meyer et al., 2007; Valentino, Shaffer, Erdberg, & Figueroa, 2007).

In agreement with the international discussion about psychological assessment guidelines, Fuster (2008) asserts that the Rorschach method can be applied in most populations and cultures. However, as proposed by the International Test Commission (ITC, 2000), a careful adaptation procedure must be performed. Such procedure is necessary because the normative tables of this technique cannot be applied to all populations, that is, technical parameters may not reliably represent groups with different geographic and socioeconomic characteristics. Accordingly, Van de Vijver (1999) stresses the importance of developing norms for the Rorschach method, in order to support its use in the different contexts where proper research was carried out, leading to more solid psychometric foundations.

In this context, researchers in different countries have made concerted efforts to develop and update Rorschach norms. Based on the systemization of their results, such studies endorse the importance of further research with different population groups, so that professionals can be provided with representative data regarding the persons they are trying to understand, as pointed out by several authors who noticed differences in normative data related to specific cultural and socioeconomic standards in the investigated regions (Boscán & Penn, 1999; Matsumoto et al., 2007; Meyer et al., 2007; Pires, 1999; Silva & Dias, 2006, 2007).

The annals of the XIX International Congress of Rorschach and Projective Methods (held by the International Rorschach Society – ISR, in July 2008) reveal intense involvement in the development of normative studies. Bagbag (2008) carried out a study in Tunisia; Fernandez and Pardillo (2008) developed norms for the Rorschach in the Cuban context; the same was done in France (Andronikof, Chudzik, & Gillaizeau, 2008), Japan (Matsumoto et al., 2008), Italy (Lis, Salcuni, Parolin, Di Riso, & Laghezza, 2008) and Brazil (Gattas, Brunoni, Sasaki, Bueno, & Parsons, 2008; Lelé, 2008a; Villemor-Amaral et al., 2008; Yazigi, Ribeiro, & Semer, 2008). These studies reveal that normative research is a concern in several contexts and countries, especially when differing results were observed between study samples and the classical literature on this projective technique.

In order to know Brazilian normative research in further detail, the authors surveyed the studies presented at the most recent scientific event held by the Brazilian Association of Rorschach and Projective Methods (ASBRo) in October 2008. The studies identified (Fernandes & Pasian, 2008; Lelé, 2008b; Nascimento, Brunoni, Sasaki, Bueno, & Parsons, 2008; Raspantini & Pasian, 2008; Ribeiro, Yazigi, & Semer, 2008; Souza & Duarte Junior, 2008) were based on the Rorschach Comprehensive System (CS) and the French Approach, confirming the different technical possibilities of this projective test.

Based on the Rorschach Comprehensive System, Nascimento et al. (2008) presented the preliminary results of a normative study, analyzing the protocols of 30 adolescents from a total sample of 120 nonpatients from the Brazilian state of São Paulo. According to those authors, data collected up to the conclusion of the study show some similarities with the results found in a sample of adults from the same region as well as with a sample of Italian adolescents. Nascimento et al. (2008) highlight, however, that results are preliminary and demand more systematic analysis before any conclusions can be drawn. Ribeiro et al. (2008), in turn, carried out a normative Rorschach study with the CS based on 211 children from Cuiabá (Brazilian state of Mato Grosso's capital) ranging from 7 to 10 years old. For sample composition purposes, the children's parents were given the Child Behavior Checklist (CBCL) in order to assess possible participants' problems of social competence and identify behavior disorders. Next, Raven's Progressive Matrices test was administered to the children selected by the CBCL, so as to exclude children with low intellectual ability. For the final presentation, the participants were divided into four age groups. Considering the mean productivity rates, the average number of responses (R) by subgroup were 15.9 (7-year-olds), R = 16.6 (8-year-olds), R = 16.2 (10-year-olds), and R = 16.7 for 11-year-olds.

Based on the French Approach, Fernandes and Pasian (2008) present-ed initial results of a study involving 180 children between 6 and 8 years of age from a city in the country region of the Brazilian state of São Paulo. Lelé (2006, 2008b) showed empirical evidence from a research with 100 male and female adults between 18–36 years in the Brazilian state of Minas Gerais (MG), with no critical psychiatric or psychological antecedents and different education levels. The results showed that vol-unteers gave specific popular answers, confirming the need for specific research in this area. Raspantini and Pasian (2008) also briefly presented preliminary results of Rorschach norms in a group of 180 9–11-year-old children from public and private schools, living in a city in the country region of São Paulo. Such data are presented here, following the presen-tation of more robust results and a deeper analysis of the protocols. In the Brazilian northern region, Souza and Duarte Junior (2008) assessed 506 adults living in Belém (Brazilian state of Pará's capital), between 18 and 50 years old, in order to analyze the popular answers produced in this sociocultural context. Their results show similarities and differences compared to data from other Brazilian states, emphasizing the impor-tance of periodically reviewing normative studies.

This conjuncture demonstrates the lack of research on normative Ror-schach data for the Brazilian child population. Despite some Brazilian researchers' efforts (Barreto, 1955; Fernandes & Pasian, 2008; Jacque-min, 1976; Resende, Rezende, & Martins, 2006; Ribeiro et al., 2008; Viana Guerra, 1958; Windholz, 1969), Rorschach research in children is still insufficient and may not adequately represent contemporaneous behavior standards, mainly when considering the speed of sociocultural and environmental changes.

The most recent normative Rorschach study with children in the Bra-zilian context and based on the French Approach is the work by Jacque-min (1976), developed more than three decades ago. In this sense, a question arises: Are these norms technically adequate for the psycholog-ical assessment of children in the current sociocultural context?

In light of this question, the present study aimed to elaborate norma-tive Rorschach data for children between 9 and 11 years old, who had had a mainstream basic education in a city of the country region of the Brazilian state of São Paulo. The authors intended to develop evaluation norms for children in this age range, in order to support analytic and interpretative processes based on this projective technique, considering the current sociocultural reality.

202

Method

The present psychometric study used a cross-sectional strategy of a representative group of nonpatient children, in a specific age range. Therefore, a quantitative methodology was adopted, with both descriptive and analytic-inferential objectives. Various psychological instruments were used to measure our variables.

Participants

The total sample included 180 male and female children, between 9 and 11 years old, studying in public and private schools from a city in the country region of the Brazilian state of São Paulo. The sample was equally composed in terms of sex, age, and socioeconomic and cultural profiles. It is known that such variables are acknowledged by international literature to influence the construction and elaboration of personality characteristics, being central when examining data related to the pattern of Rorschach's responses. For this reason, the study subdivided the participants using such sociodemographic variables, so that their effect on the results could be explored.

However, it must be noted that, given the complexity and diversity of the strategies available for assessing socioeconomic and cultural statuses, the authors opted for considering school origin as the most representative element for such variables. In this sense, public-school participants are assumed to represent low-economic-level Brazilian children, while private school participants are assumed to represent average-high-level to high-economic-level Brazilian children. Such were the contrasting conditions of the groups in terms of economic level.

Although such classification may be limited, this criterion has been adopted in everyday research practice and has proved effective for identifying participants' economic level. In addition, self-report data on this issue are not simple to collect. Social desirability can bias the presentation of such information, leading to an unreal appreciation of reality as effectively experienced by individuals.

In order to achieve the objectives designed for the present study, the following selection criteria were considered: (1) no indicators of intellectual limitation as measured by the results of Raven's Progressive Colored Matrices Test and (2) no signs of critical psychopathological or psychiat-

Table 1. Sample ($n = 140$) characteristics in function of gender, age and school origin variables

Gender	School origin				Total
	Public school		Private school		
Age	Female	Male	Female	Male	
09 years	6	–	15	15	36
10 years	–	15	15	14	44
11 years	15	15	15	15	60
Total	21	30	45	44	140

ric previous circumstances in personal development, as assessed via a questionnaire filled in by participants' parents and/or tutors. Hence, the final sample consisted of children who displayed typical developmental milestones for their age range and school status.

In this research, data for a partial sample of 140 participants are presented, distributed in function of the variables: gender, age and school status, as shown in Table 1.

Measures

Research Project Presentation Letter. Document with information regarding the study's objectives, elaborated by the authors and presented for coordinators or directors whose schools were chosen for data collection. Based on such a document, researchers' insertion in such schools was formally authorized by directors.

Term of Free and Informed Consent. Document sent to parents and/or tutors of the invited participants, so that the former could register their agreement to include their children in the study.

Child Development Questionnaire. This questionnaire was elaborated for the present study in order to complement participants' selection; it included questions regarding child's personal and academic development. The questionnaire was answered by the child's parents and/or tutors.

Raven's Colored Progressive Matrices (Angelini, Alves, Custódio, Duarte, & Duarte, 1999). A minimum performance compatible with the percentile above 25 (level III–), classified as lower medium level, was assumed as an inclusion criterion.

Rorschach's Psychodiagnostic test. In this study, the interpretative framework of the Rorschach's French Approach was adopted, as proposed by

Ombredane and Canivet and presented by Anzieu and Chabert (1987; see also Rausch de Traubenberg, 1990, for an improvement of such framework). Such methodology was approved for use in Brazil by the Federal Psychology Council, which regulates such area's professional exercise in the same country.

Procedure

Data Collection

The research proposal was approved by the Ethics Committee for Research Involving Human Beings of Faculty of Philosophy, Sciences and Letters of Ribeirão Preto – University of São Paulo (FFCLRP-USP) as complying with technical and ethical guidelines scientific research in the Brazilian context, which include secrecy and freedom to take part of the research and to leave it at any time with no repercussions.

The directors of public and private schools received a letter presenting the research project. Participants' parents and/or tutors received a Term of Free and Informed Consent to formalize their agreement and to authorize including their children in the sample.

All psychological assessment instruments were applied individually at the participants' schools. After a brief rapport, Raven's Colored Progressive Matrices Test was applied, according to its manual (Angelini et al., 1999), as well as Rorschach's Psychodiagnostic test, following the technical-scientific framework of the French Approach proposed by Anzieu and Chabert (1987) and Rausch de Traubenberg (1990).

Result Analysis

In order to select participants who met criteria for inclusion, data surveyed by the Child Development Questionnaire were evaluated considering the basic criterion that the child had not undergone psychiatric, neurological and/or psychological treatment nor been prescribed psychotropic drugs in the previous year.

The results of Raven's Colored Progressive Matrices test were examined according to its technical framework, using the analytic standards of Angelini et al. (1999). Children scoring a percentile of 25 or less, i.e., whose intellectual efficiency level was considered inferior to the population's average level, were not included in the sample.

The coding of the Rorschach protocols followed the technical-scientific framework of the French Approach described by Rausch de Traubenberg (1990). For the technical adequacy of Rorschach analysis, three judges coded each of the 140 protocols in a blind and independent process, for a subsequent reliability check. The judges were psychologists with prior experience in psychodiagnostics and on the Rorschach itself, who nevertheless received specific training for this task. The protocols were presented with no personal information; only data regarding age, gender, school origin, and a register number was displayed. The reference material for response coding available for the judges was the atlas developed by Jacquemin (1976), which is the last Brazilian study on norms for Rorschach of children based on the French Approach.

After protocol coding, the reliability index was calculated by the judges in four response categories (localization, determinant/formal quality, response content, and banalities), according the orientations of Weiner (1991) and Fensterseifer and Werlang (2008). To this end, 36 Rorschach protocols were randomly selected from which agreement percentages were calculated for each response according to the categories above. Results from such calculation showed high agreement indices (99% agreement for localization, 92% agreement for determinant, 97% for content, and 93% for banalities), providing an adequate reliability to the current empirical data.

Based on the coding by the judges, performed for all 140 cases, a classification of responses was elaborated from the consensus of the judges' evaluations. Agreement among the judges was declared when at least two of them attributed a similar classification for each category (localization, determinant, content, and popular) for each response in the protocol. When such consensus was not achieved, the first author made a new classification, considering all previous evaluations and the discussion of such responses with the other authors of the present study.

After this step, the final codings of all protocols were inserted in a databank, from which both descriptive and inferential analyzes were performed. For statistical purposes, the significance level adopted was $p \leq .05$. The following procedures were done:

1) Descriptive statistics (mean, standard deviation, median, minimum, and maximum values) of the main variables of the French Approach of the Rorschach method ($n = 140$).

2) Comparison of sample's average results with prior normative parameters (Jacquemin, 1976), using Student's t-test for one sample. Means comparison as performed by the t-test is done with data attending criteria for normality. However, that was the only technical strategy for result comparison, once prior normative data (Jacquemin, 1976) were available only as average results.

3) Kolmogorov-Smirnov's test (K-S) to delimit normal distribution for the Rorschach variables investigated. Because this hypothesis has not been confirmed, a nonparametrical strategy had to be applied for the inferential analyses of the results in function of sex, age, and school origin of the children under assessment. Thus, Mann-Whitney's U-test was adopted to analyze two independent variables, gender and school origin. Kruskal-Wallis test for k independent samples was used to compare age subgroups. The goal of such analyses was to examine the possible effect of each of the variables (age, gender, and school origin) on the participants' performance on the Rorschach, as presented above.

Results

Initially, data were organized based on the descriptive analysis of the main variables in the Rorschach's French Approach (see Table 2). All classification codes follow the technical glossary presented in Rausch de Traubenberg (1990).

The set of Rorschach's productivity variables indicated good associative and interpretative ability for children between 9 and 11 years, who on average gave 16 responses to the test. Additional responses (RA), refusals (Rec), and denials (Den) were practically absent, so that no indicators of massive repression were found. Rhythm-related indicators (LT and RTa) suggested steady reactive and elaborative processes, which confirmed the good general productivity of participants. This finding was expected, as participants composed a normative sample, selected according to criteria compatible with typical development for their respective age.

As to the stimulus' area selected for interpretation, global apprehensions (G) were predominant, followed by responses from stimuli' details (D) and focused on small details (Dd). Responses localized in Dbl were scarcely referred to in the response pool; no responses classified as Do were found along participants' sample.

R. L. Raspantini et al.

Table 2. Descriptive statistics of children's (*n* = 140) performance on Rorschach variables (French approach). (*SD* = standard deviation)

Variable	Mean	SD*	Median	Minimum	Maximum
R	16.1	7.7	14.0	9.0	65.0
RA	0.4	0.7	–	–	3.0
Refusal	0.1	0.5	–	–	3.0
Denial	0.1	0.3	–	–	2.0
TLm	17.2	10.8	14.8	3.4	59.1
TRm	33.4	11.6	31.0	14.2	76.5
G	6.3	2.9	6.0	2.0	17.0
D	5.6	3.9	5.0	–	20.0
Dd	4.1	5.3	3.0	–	47.0
Dbl	0.1	0.4	–	–	3.0
Do	–	–	–	–	–
F+	7.6	3.9	7.0	2.0	27.0
F+/–	0.0	0.1	–	–	1.0
F–	2.7	3.2	2.0	–	21.0
K	1.0	1.3	1.0	–	6.0
kan	1.5	1.6	1.0	–	7.0
kob	0.1	0.4	–	–	2.0
kp	0.1	0.4	–	–	2.0
FC	1.5	1.7	1.0	–	9.0
CF	0.6	0.9	–	–	5.0
C	0.0	0.2	–	–	2.0
FE	0.7	0.9	–	–	4.0
EF	0.3	0.6	–	–	4.0
E	0.0	0.2	–	–	1.0
FClob	0.0	0.0	–	–	–
ClobF	0.0	0.0	–	–	–
Clob	0.0	0.0	–	–	–
A	7.2	3.5	7.0	1.0	21.0
(A)	0.6	0.9	–	–	5.0
Ad	1.3	1.9	1.0	–	13.0
(Ad)	0.1	0.4	–	–	2.0
H	1.8	1.8	1.0	–	9.0
(H)	0.7	0.9	–	–	5.0
Hd	0.8	1.7	–	–	13.0

Variable	Mean	SD*	Median	Minimum	Maximum
(Hd)	0.2	0.5	–	–	2.0
Anat	0.5	0.8	–	–	5.0
Sg	0.0	0.2	–	–	1.0
Sex	0.0	0.0	–	–	–
Obj	1.3	1.7	1.0	–	11.0
Art	0.1	0.4	–	–	3.0
Arq	0.2	0.5	–	–	3.0
Simb	0.1	0.3	–	–	2.0
Abst	0.1	0.3	–	–	2.0
Bot	0.6	0.8	–	–	3.0
Geo	0.3	0.8	–	–	6.0
Nat	0.0	0.1	–	–	1.0
Pais	0.2	0.6	–	–	3.0
Elem	0.0	0.2	–	–	2.0
Frag	0.2	0.5	–	–	3.0

Considering response determinants, it was observed that the large majority were solely determined by form (F%), leaving little room for determinants associated with affective and imaginative elements, that is, related to movement (K), color (C), or shading (E). Among these, K responses of any subtype (human, animal, or object) stood out, followed by color responses (either chromatic or achromatic) and shading ones. Such data suggest that most of the participants restricted themselves to formal elements of the stimuli, formulating mostly low-elaboration responses.

As for responses determined only by their formal quality (respectively, F+, F– and F+/– for good, bad, and imprecise formal quality, respectively), a closer look at their distribution reveals the predominance of F+, followed by F–, and a small percentage of F+/–. This distribution suggests an adequate perceptive precision level in the group of children under analysis, an expected performance of the present, normative sample.

The distribution of movement-determined responses shows a higher frequency of small movement determinants (kan, kob, kp) than the large ones (K). The participants' internal dynamistic resources (associated with K-determined responses) may still be very immature and only partially developed, limiting the possibilities of abstraction and reflexive attitudes in their current stage of life.

With respect to color-related determinants, FC was more predominant

Table 3. Simple frequency and percentage distribution of children (*n* = 140) in function of the affective reaction style (TRI) and the formula of latent tendencies (TL)

Affective reaction style	TRI		TL	
	f	%	f	%
Introversive	27	19.3	59	42.1
Extratensive	37	26.4	4	2.9
Evitative (coartative/coartated)	73	52.1	75	53.6
Ambitent	3	2.1	2	1.4

than CF and C, indicating adequate integration of rational (i.e., form-related) elements and affective (color) ones. Such integration can also be observed in shadowing-related determinants, since FE responses were also more frequent than EF and E.

Response contents comprised animal (A) and human (H) ones in the large majority of children's interpretations. Object-content responses frequencies came in third following the first two categories mentioned above.

Finally, to complete the general picture of the present sample's average performance on the Rorschach, the authors analyzed the variables related to emotional functioning and affective control, i.e., the Affective Reaction Style (TRI) and the Formula of Latent Tendencies (TL). These results are shown in Table 3.

The results show the clear predominance of the evitative style (also referred in French Approach as coartative-coartated type) in both TRI and TL, indicating that most of the children reacted to the Rorschach in an inhibitory way, suggesting use of a restriction of affective expression. This finding can also be understood as evidence that children tend to experience affection in daily life in a repressive way, in association with internal strategies of impulse coercion. These characteristics are theoretically expected for the age range under analysis, considering participants' developmental and mental elaboration needs, according to the Rorschach's French Approach.

Discussion

The elaboration process of normative data for projective techniques is a complex task, broadly presented and discussed in the specific literature of this scientific field (Azoulay et al., 2007; Fuster, 2008; McGrew, 2009; Meyer et al., 2007; Ritzler, 2009; Weiner, 2001).

Jacquemin (1976) worked in the Brazilian context particularly on the Rorschach's French Approach, performing a normalization study of 480 male and female children between 3 and 10;11 years, studying in public and private schools of Ribeirão Preto (country region of the Brazilian state of São Paulo). For data analysis purposes, such a sample was divided into two subgroups, 3–6-year-old children (Group I), and 7–10;11-year-old children (Group II). Because the present study's sample consisted of 9–11-year-old children, the preliminary data reported here were compared to the main results of Jacquemin's (1976) Group II, as an orienting strategy for result discussion. This was done in light of the interpretative, comparative approach of the present study, considering prior Brazilian normative references based on the Rorschach's French Approach. This discussion is important for pointing out the evidences of normative references' adequacy for such context or the need for their technical review.

As for Rorschach productivity, the present results are lower than the ones reported by Jacquemin (1976; average of 16.1 answers, compared to 18.8 in the earlier study). An analysis of the apprehension type shows some differences between the current results and the evidence presented by the above-mentioned author. An important variation was found for location G (44.3% vs. 38.9% in the earlier research), D (33.0% vs. 45.8%) and Dd (22.0% vs. 13.7%). Despite such differences, these results suggest that both samples showed Rorschach indicators of adequate apprehension of global and relevant details of reality, which confirms adaptation expectancies of the participant's sociocultural context. As mentioned above, both studies assessed nonpatient children of typical development. Nevertheless, the empirical evidence reported herein indicated that children at times tended to capture the stimuli in a general and superficial way (predominance of G), confining themselves to the minutiae of the stimuli (high frequency of Dd), compared to the 1970s sample. Such findings confirm the necessity of reviewing normative references of the Rorschach (French Approach) with Brazilian children of the age range reported herein and reinforce the practical contribution of such data.

With respect to responses with solely formal determinants (F%), relevant differences are observed between the two studies: Jacquemin (1976) found 70.2% for the formal determinant (F%) vs. 63.1% in the present research. Such indexes suggest that the children assessed in the present study may be performing a smaller rational investment when interpreting reality, compared to children from the 1970s sample. Such results reaffirm the

211

importance of elaborating new reference standards for Rorschach's French Approach in this age range for the Brazilian context.

A look at the response content shows that animal (57.5%) and human (21.4%) contents prevailed in the present study. This tendency agrees with the results of the 1970s research, in which animal and human contents were also the most evoked ones, with frequency levels of 56.0% and 16.0%, respectively. Such results seem to follow findings from other investigations on the Rorschach performance of school-age children. However, not all of these studies were carried out using the framework of the French Approach, as illustrated by the study of Meyer et al. (2007).

An international normative study using the framework mentioned was carried out by Azoulay et al. (2007), who aimed to develop Rorschach norms for use in France. 287 nonpatient participants took part in the study, including teenagers and adults (ranging from 13 to 25 years), equally divided in three age subgroups, social/professional category (three subgroups), and sex, allowing for intra- and intergroup comparisons. The main average results reported were R = 25.8; G% = 43.3; D% = 43.6; Dd% = 10.2; Dbl% = 2.9; F% = 61.3; F+% = 65.2; H% (including subcategories) = 20.4; A% (including subcategories) = 47.1. Although the age range of the present study does not allow for comparisons with the data from Azoulay et al.'s (2007), this study is reported as an illustration of the methodological concerns of the French Approach regarding technical standards used interpretative processes using the Rorschach method, a concern that motivated the present scientific investigation.

Finally, the results presented here may still change, given that it consisted of the analysis of only 140 protocols from a sample of 180 children. Therefore, the present data must be seen as preliminary, albeit as an important tendency for new normative standards for the Rorschach method (French Approach) for children between the age of 9 and 11 and belonging to a Brazilian sociocultural context. Although limited in its population representativeness (a convenience sample, although carefully selected), the empirical evidence herein reported constitutes a clear demonstration of the need for an improvement of psychological assessment instruments. Such concern also strengthens the orientations and requirements of the Brazilian Federal Psychology Council (CFP, 2003) and the International Test Commission (ITC, 2000) for the development of adequate norms for different groups in a range of contexts.

References

Anastasi, A., & Urbina, S. (2000). *Testagem psicológica* (7a ed.) [Psychological testing, 7th ed.]. Porto Alegre: Artmed.

Andronikof, A., Chudzik, L., & Gillaizeau, I. (2008). Caractéristiques des Rorschach d'adolescents [Rorschach characteristics in adolescents]. In L. Nijssens & L. Cohen (Eds.), *Proceedings, 19th International Congress of Rorschach and Projective Methods* (p. 176). Leuven, Belgium: ISR.

Angelini, A.L., Alves, I.C.B., Custódio, E.M., Duarte, W.F., & Duarte, J.L.M. (1999). *Matrizes progressivas coloridas de Raven: Escala especial* [Raven's Colored Progressive Matrices: Special scale]. Manual. São Paulo: CETEPP.

Anzieu, D., & Chabert, C. (1987). *Les méthodes projectives* (8a ed.) [The projective methods, 8th ed.]. Paris: Presses Universitaires de France.

Azoulay, C., Emmanuelli, M., Rausch de Traubenberg, N., Corroyer, D., Rozencwajg, P., & Savina, Y. (2007). Les données normatives françaises du Rorschach à l'adolescence et chez le jeune adulte [French normative Rorschach data for adolescents and young adults]. *Psychologie Clinique et Projective, 13,* 371-409.

Bagbag, F. (2008). Tunisian children Rorschach. In L. Nijssens & L. Cohen (Eds.), *Proceedings, 19th International Congress of Rorschach and Projective Methods* (p. 53). Leuven, Belgium: ISR.

Barreto, A.P. (1955). O Psicodiagnóstico aplicado à criança [Psychodiagnosis applied to children]. *Neurobiologia, 111*(28), 169-182.

Boscán, D.C., & Penn, N.E. (1999). The Rorschach test: A Mexican sample using the Comprehensive System. In S. Luyten, M. Hildebrand, B. Leunissen, C. Ruiter, I. Verduyin, V. Vogel, & M. Wieland (Eds.), *Proceedings, 16th International Congress of Rorschach and Projective Methods* (p. 12). Amsterdam, Netherlands: ISR.

Conselho Federal de Psicologia (CFP). (2003). *Resolução 2002/2003.* Brasilia, DF: Author. Retrieved from http://www.pol.org.br

Fensterseifer, L., & Werlang, B.S.G. (2008). Apontamentos sobre o status científico das técnicas projetivas [Notes on the scientific status of projective techniques]. In A.E. Villemor-Amaral & B.S.G. Werlang (Eds.), *Atualizações em métodos projetivos para avaliação psicológica* (p. 15-33). São Paulo: Casa do Psicólogo.

Fernandez, P., & Pardillo, J. (2008). Listado de respuestas populares en cuba: Un estudio de normalización transcultural con el Rorschach [List of popular responses in Cuba: A cross-cultural, Rorschach normative study]. In L. Nijssens & L. Cohen (Eds.), *Proceedings, 19th International Congress of Rorschach and Projective Methods* (p. 136). Leuven, Belgium: ISR.

Fernandes, S., & Pasian, S.R. (2008). Crianças diante do Psicodiagnóstico de Rorschach: Especificidades de desempenho no interior de São Paulo [Children facing the Rorschach method: Performance specificities in the country region of São Paulo]. In S.R. Pasian, E.T.K. Okino, S.R. Loureiro, & F.L. Osório (Eds.), *Anais, 5. Encontro da Associação Brasileira de Rorschach e Métodos Projetivos* (pp. 205-220). Ribeirão Preto, Brasil: ASBRo.

Fuster, P.J. (2008). Adaptar el Rorschach (SC) a las diferentes poblaciones: Un estudio generalizable desde la población española [Adapting the Rorschach (CS) to different populations: A generalizable study based on the Spanish population]. In L. Nijssens & L. Cohen (Eds.), *Proceedings, 19th International Congress of Rorschach and Projective Methods* (p. 135). Leuven, Belgium: ISR.

Gattas, R. S., Brunoni, G. R., Sasaki, T. N. D., Bueno, R. R., & Parsons, T. G. (2008). Preliminary results of a normative study of the Rorschach Comprehensive System in a nonpatient Brazilian adolescent sample. In L. Nijssens & L. Cohen (Eds.), *Proceedings, 19th International Congress of Rorschach and Projective Methods* (p. 52). Leuven, Belgium: ISR.

Güntert, A. E. V. A. (2000). Técnicas projetivas: o geral e o singular em avaliação psicológica [Projective techniques: The general and the singular in psychological assessment]. In F. F. Sisto, E. T. B. Sbardelini, & R. Primi (Eds.), *Contextos e questões da avaliação psicológica* (pp. 77–85). São Paulo: Casa do Psicólogo.

Hamel, M., & Shaffer, T. W. (2007). Rorschach Comprehensive System data for 100 nonpatient children from the United States in two age groups. *Journal of Personality Assessment, 89,* 174–182.

International Test Commission (ITC). (2000). *International guidelines for test use.* Retrieved from www.intestcom.org/itc_projects.htm

Jacquemin, A. A. (1976). *O teste de Rorschach em crianças brasileiras* [The Rorschach test in Brazilian children]. São Paulo: Vetor.

Lelé, A. J. (2006). Resultados de 100 psicodiagnósticos de Rorschach em mineiros [Results of 100 Rorschach protocols in people from the Brazilian state of Minas Gerais]. In N. A. Silva Neto & D. M. Amparo (Eds.), *Anais, 4. Congresso Nacional da Associação Brasileira de Rorschach e outros métodos projetivos* (pp. 87–99). São Paulo, Brasil: Vetor.

Lelé, A. J. (2008a). La diversite de resultats dans les modes d'apprehension: comparaison des donnees normatives au Rorschach [The diversity of results in apprehension modes: Comparison among normative Rorschach data]. In L. Nijssens & L. Cohen (Eds.), *Proceedings, 19th International Congress of Rorschach and Projective Methods* (p. 153). Leuven, Belgium: ISR.

Lelé, A. J. (2008b). Estudo preliminar de dados normativos brasileiros no Rorschach no estado de Minas Gerais [Preliminary study of Brazilian normative Rorschach data in the state of Minas Gerais]. In S. R. Pasian, E. T. K. Okino, S. R. Loureiro, & F. L. Osório (Eds.), *Anais, 5. Encontro da Associação Brasileira de Rorschach e Métodos Projetivos* (p. 107). Ribeirão Preto, Brasil: ASBRo.

Lis, A., Salcuni, S., Parolin, L., Di Riso, D., & Laghezza, L. (2008). Rorschach Comprehensive System Data of sample of nonpatient children from Italy: Aged 5–7 years. In L. Nijssens & L. Cohen (Eds.), *Proceedings, 19th International Congress of Rorschach and Projective Methods* (p. 51). Leuven, Belgium: ISR.

Matsumoto, M., Morita, M., Suzuki, N., Tsuboi, H., Hatagaki, C., & Shirai, H. (2008). Application of Rorschach for Japanese children: What the Rorschach means for Japanese children. In L. Nijssens & L. Cohen (Eds.), *Proceedings, 19th International Congress of Rorschach and Projective Methods* (p. 315). Leuven, Belgium: ISR.

Matsumoto, M., Suzuki, N., Shirai, H., & Nakabayashi, M. (2007). Rorschach Comprehensive System Data for a sample of 190 Japanese nonpatient children at five ages. *Journal of Personality Assessment, 89,* 103–112.

McGrew, K. (2009, July). *The art and science of intelligence test development: Theory, tools, tips and troubles.* Presentation given at the IV Congresso Brasileiro de Avaliação Psicológica e V Congresso da Associação Brasileira de Rorschach e Métodos Projetivos e XIV Conferência Internacional de Avaliação Psicológica: Formas e Contextos, Campinas, São Paulo, IBAP. Retrieved from http://www.ibapnet.org.br/congresso2009/material/testdevhandouts.pdf

Meyer, G. J., Erdberg, P., & Shaffer, T. W. (2007). International reference samples for the Rorschach Comprehensive System. *Journal of Personality Assessment, 89,* 201–216.

Nascimento, R. S. G. F., Brunoni, G. R., Sasaki, T. N. D., Bueno, R. R., & Parsons, T. G. (2008). Resultados preliminares de um estudo normativo com o Sistema Compreensivo do Rorschach em uma amostra de adolescentes não-pacientes brasileiros [Preliminary results of a normative study on the Rorschach (Comprehensive System) in a sample of Brazilian nonpatient adolescents]. In S. R. Pasian, E. T. K. Okino, S. R. Loureiro, & F. L. Osório (Eds.), *Anais, 5. Encontro da Associação Brasileira de Rorschach e Métodos Projetivos* (pp. 189–204). Ribeirão Preto, Brasil: ASBRo.

Pasian, S. R. (1998). *O Psicodiagnóstico de Rorschach: um estudo normativo em adultos da região de Ribeirão Preto* [Rorschach's Psychodiagnostic test: A normative study in adults from the region of Ribeirão Preto]. Unpublished doctoral dissertation, Universidade de São Paulo, Ribeirão Preto, Brazil.

Pasian, S. R. (2002). Atualizações sobre o Psicodiagnóstico de Rorschach no Brasil: Breve panorama histórico [Updates on Rorschach's Psychodiagnostic test in Brazil: A brief historical panorama]. *Psico-USF, 7*(1), 43–52.

Pires, A. A. (1999). The Rorschach normative study in Portugal. In S. Luyten, M. Hildebrand, B. Leunissen, C. Ruiter, I. Verduyin, V. Vogel, & M. Wieland (Eds.), *Proceedings, 16th International Congress of Rorschach and Projective Methods* (p. 101). Amsterdam, Netherlands: ISR.

Raspantini, R. L., & Pasian, S. R. (2008). Psicodiagnóstico de Rorschach em crianças brasileiras de nove a onze anos de idade: dados preliminares [Rorschach's Psychodiagnostic test in Brazilian children between 9 and 11 years old: Preliminary data]. In S. R. Pasian, E. T. K. Okino, S. R. Loureiro, & F. L. Osório (Eds.), *Anais, 5. Encontro da Associação Brasileira de Rorschach e Métodos Projetivos* (pp. 221–237). Ribeirão Preto, Brasil: ASBRo.

Rausch de Traubenberg, N. (1990). *La pratique du Rorschach* [The practice of Rorschach] (6th ed.). Paris: Presses Universitaires de France.

Resende, A. C., Rezende, T. C., & Martins, L. D. (2006). Estudo normativo do Rorschach para crianças goianienses: Dados preliminares [Normative study of the Rorschach for children from the Brazilian state of Goiás: Preliminary data]. In N. A. Silva Neto & D. M. Amparo (Eds.), *Anais, 4. Congresso Nacional da Associação Brasileira de Rorschach e outros Métodos Projetivos* (pp. 124–135). São Paulo, Brasil: Vetor.

Ribeiro, R. K. S. M., Yazigi, L., & Semer, N. L. (2008). Estudo normativo do método de Rorschach Sistema compreensivo em crianças de Cuiabá [Normative study of the Rorschach Comprehensive System Method in children from Cuiabá]. In S. R.

R. L. Raspantini et al.

Pasian, E. T. K. Okino, S. R. Loureiro, & F. L. Osório (Eds.), *Anais, 5. Encontro da Associação Brasileira de Rorschach e Métodos Projetivos* (p. 55). Ribeirão Preto, Brasil: ASBRo.

Ritzler, B. (2009, July). *Empirical foundations of the Rorschach Comprehensive System*. Presentation given at the IV Congresso Brasileiro de Avaliação Psicológica e V Congresso da Associação Brasileira de Rorschach e Métodos Projetivos e XIV Conferência Internacional de Avaliação Psicológica: Formas e Contextos, Campinas, São Paulo. Retrieved from http://www.ibapnet.org.br/congresso2009/material/html

Salcuni, S., Lis, A., Parolin, L., & Mazzeschi, C. (2007). Rorschach Comprehensive System Data for two samples of nonpatient children from Italy: 75 aged 5–7 years and 148 aged 8–11 years. *Journal of Personality Assessment, 89*, 85–90.

Silva, D. R., & Dias, A. M. (2006). Questões de desenvolvimento a propósito das normas portuguesas do Rorschach para crianças [Developmental issues in Portuguese Rorschach norms for children]. *Revista Iberoamericana de Diagnóstico e Avaliação Psicológica, 1*(21), 47–59.

Silva, D. R., & Dias, A. M. (2007). Rorschach Comprehensive System Data for a sample of 357 Portuguese children at five ages. *Journal of Personality Assessment, 89*, 131–141.

Souza, A. M. D. R., & Duarte Junior, A. P. (2008). As respostas banais de sujeitos paraenses ao teste de Rorschach: Uma análise comparativa. [The popular answers of subjects from Pará to the Rorschach test: A comparative analysis]. In S. R. Pasian, E. T. K. Okino, S. R. Loureiro, & F. L. Osório (Eds.), *Anais, 5. Encontro da Associação Brasileira de Rorschach e Métodos Projetivos* (pp. 170–177). Ribeirão Preto, Brasil: ASBRo.

Valentino, M. A., Shaffer, T. W., Erdberg, P., & Figueroa, M. (2007). Rorschach Comprehensive System Data for a sample of 42 nonpatient Mexican American children from the United States. *Journal of Personality Assessment, 89*, 183–187.

Van de Vijver, F. (1999). Projective testing. *European Journal of Psychological Assessment, 15*, 63.

Viana Guerra, C. (1958). As respostas de crianças de três a oito anos ao Psicodiagnóstico de Rorschach [The responses of children between 3–8 years old to Rorschach's Psychodiagnostic Test]. *Boletim do Instituto de Psicologia, 8*(3–4), 20–31.

Villemor-Amaral, A. E., Yazigi, L., Primi, R., Nascimento, R. S. G. F., Semer, N. L., Meyer, G. J., & Viglione, D. J. (2008). Comparing location areas and frequency of responses in the Rorschach Comprehensive System considering a Brazilian sample and American data. In L. Nijssens & L. Cohen (Eds.), *Proceedings, 19th International Congress of Rorschach and Projective Methods* (p. 110). Leuven, Belgium: ISR.

Weiner, I. B. (1991). Editor's note: Interscorer agreement in Rorschach research. *Journal of Personality Assessment, 56*, 1.

Weiner, I. B. (2001). Considerations in collecting Rorschach reference data. *Journal of Personality Assessment, 77*, 122–127.

Windholz, W. H. (1969). *Rorschach em crianças: a pesquisa* [Rorschach in children: The research]. São Paulo: Vetor.

Yazigi, L., Ribeiro, R., & Semer, N. L. (2008). Normative study of the Rorschach

Comprehensive System in Brazilian children. In L. Nijssens & L. Cohen (Eds.), *Proceedings, 19th International Congress of Rorschach and Projective Methods* (p. 52). Leuven, Belgium: ISR.

Sonia Regina Pasian
Department of Psychology
Faculty of Philosophy, Sciences and Letters of Ribeirão Preto
University of São Paulo
Avenida dos Bandeirantes, 3900 – Monte Alegre
14040-901 Ribeirão Preto/SP
Brazil
Tel. +55 16 3602-3785
E-mail srpasian@ffclrp.usp.br

Summary

In agreement with international standards for the improvement of psychological assessment instruments, projective methods have been studied in several contexts. Among such instruments, the Rorschach method stands out: Despite its importance for personality assessment, studies are still needed that address especially the development and the updating of norms for its use. Researchers from different countries have carried out studies in this direction, while also stressing that more research is necessary for different population groups in order to offer professionals representative data, especially regarding child development. In Brazil, where this need has been observed, the present study aimed to elaborate the normative patterns of children's responses to the Rorschach. 180 children (9–11 years old) were selected for the study, presenting indicators of typical (nonpathological) development and equally distributed in terms of sex, age, and school origin (private or public). All participants were from a city in the State of São Paulo (Brazil) and were authorized by their parents/tutor to participate in the study. They were assessed individually using a child development questionnaire, the Raven's Progressive Matrices Test, and the Rorschach method. Data from the Rorschach were collected and coded according to the French Approach. Later, the Rorschach protocols were analyzed by three independent judges, with the final classification for each response being done using judges' consensus. To date, 140 protocols have been coded, and their data are included here.

The average results were as follows: productivity and rhythm indica-

R. L. Raspantini et al.

tors: R = 16.1; TLm = 17.2s; TRm = 33.4s; apprehension modes: G = 44.3%; D = 33.0%; Dd = 22.0%; determinants and formal quality: F% = 63.1%; F+% = 76.7%; F+ ext% = 76.3%; most evocated contents: A% = 57.5%; H% = 21.4%; predominant affective reaction style: evitative (co-arctation). Although only partial, the present results are promising as updated normative references for the Rorschach (French Approach) for 9–11-year-old children. Considering the lack of such studies and the specificities of the Brazilian sociocultural contexts, they allow for an adequate use of the Rorschach.

Resumo

Em concordância às diretrizes internacionais de aprimoramento dos instrumentos de avaliação psicológica, os métodos projetivos têm sido objeto de estudo e intensa pesquisa em diferentes contextos. Dentre esses métodos, destaca-se o Psicodiagnóstico de Rorschach que, apesar de constituir importante estratégia de avaliação da personalidade, ainda exige investigações científicas. Pesquisadores de diferentes países têm concentrado esforços no desenvolvimento e na atualização de normas para o Rorschach e reafirmam, a partir da sistematização de seus resultados, a importância de que mais estudos nesse sentido sejam realizados em diversos grupos populacionais, a fim de que os profissionais possam contar com dados representativos dos indivíduos que queiram compreender, o que se torna ainda mais premente na avaliação do desenvolvimento infantil. Esta necessidade técnica também se faz presente no contexto do Brasil, justificando a presente investigação. Desse modo, este trabalho objetivou elaborar padrões normativos do Rorschach para crianças brasileiras de nove a 11 anos de idade. Para tanto, foram selecionados 180 estudantes desta faixa etária, com indicadores de desenvolvimento típico, distribuídos equitativamente em função do sexo, idade e procedência escolar (escolas públicas ou particulares), residentes em uma cidade do interior do Estado de São Paulo/Brasil e devidamente autorizados a participar da pesquisa por seus pais e/ou responsáveis. Os instrumentos utilizados para coleta de dados foram: a) Questionário Informativo sobre desenvolvimento das crianças, preenchido pelos pais e/ou responsáveis; b) Teste das Matrizes Progressivas Coloridas de Raven; c) Psicodiagnóstico de Rorschach, aplicados individualmente às crianças, em adequadas condições para avaliação psicológica. Os dados do Rorschach foram colhidos e codificados de acordo com a

Escola Francesa. Posteriormente, os protocolos do Rorschach foram analisados por três examinadores independentes, com experiência prévia na técnica projetiva e que receberam treinamento específico para este trabalho, chegando-se a uma classificação final de cada resposta a partir do consenso entre estas análises independentes, garantindo a devida precisão aos resultados. Até o presente momento, 140 protocolos do Rorschach foram codificados, os quais compõem os dados aqui apresentados. Os resultados médios, em termos de produtividade e ritmo, foram: R = 16,1; TLm = 17,2 segundos e TRm = 33,4 segundos. Em relação aos modos de apreensão, as seguintes proporções médias foram encontradas: G = 44,3%, D = 33,0% e Dd = 22,0%. No que concerne aos determinantes e qualidade formal, os dados médios foram: F% = 63,1%, F+% = 76,7% e F+ ext% = 76,3%. Os conteúdos mais evocados foram A% = 57,5% e H% = 21,4%. O estilo de vivência afetiva predominante foi o evitativo (coartativo). Embora parciais, estes resultados mostraram-se promissores como atuais referências normativas do Rorschach (Escola Francesa) para crianças escolares de 9 a onze anos de idade, tendo em vista a carência de estudos desta natureza e as especificidades do contexto sócio-cultural brasileiro, podendo favorecer a adequada utilização do Método de Rorschach.

Résumé

En accord aux lignes directrices internationales d'amélioration des instruments d'évaluation psychologique, les méthodes projectives ont fait l'objet d' études et d'intenses recherches dans différents contextes. Parmi ces méthodes, nous trouvons le test de psychodiagnostique du Rorschach, qui établi une importante stratégie d'évaluation de la personnalité, mais qui malgré cela, nécessite encore des recherches scientifiques. Les chercheurs de différents pays ont concentré leurs efforts sur le développement et la mise à jour des normes pour le Rorschach et réaffirment, à partir de la systématisation de leurs résultats, de l'importance de mener des études supplémentaires pour divers groupes de population, de sorte que les professionnels peuvent compter sur des données représentatives des individus qui' ils veulent comprendre, ce qui est encore plus important lorsqu'il s'agit d'évaluer des enfants en développement. Cette nécessité technique est aussi présente dans le contexte du Brésil, justifiant la notre étude. Ainsi, cette recherche a tenté d'établir des standards normatifs du Rorschach pour des enfants brésiliens âgés de 9 à 11 ans. Pour cela, nous avons sélectionné 180 écoliers de cette fourchette d'âge, dont le stade de développement est typique, répartis par sexe, âge et l'école d'origine (écoles publiques ou privées), vivant dans une ville de l'État de São Paulo (Brésil) et dont les parents ou tuteurs ont consenti à leur participation. Les instruments utilisés pour la collecte de données ont été: a) un questionnaire nous informant sur le développement des enfants, rempli par les parents et/ou tuteurs; b) le test des matrices progressives de Raven; c) le test du Rorschach, appliqué individuellement aux enfants dans des conditions appropriées pour l'évaluation psychologique. Les données du Rorschach ont été recueillies et codées en accord avec l'école française. Ensuite, les protocoles de Rorschach ont été analysés par trois observateurs indépendants ayant une expérience dans les techniques projectives et qui ont reçu une formation spécifique pour ce travail, permettant un classement final de chaque réponse basé sur un consensus interjuge. À ce jour, 140 protocoles de Rorschach ont été codées, ce qui repésentent les données présentées ici. Les résultats moyens, en termes de productivité et rythme sont: $R = 16,1$; $TLm = 17,2$ secondes et $TRm = 33,4$ secondes. En ce qui concerne les modes d'appréhension, les proportions moyennes suivantes ont été trouvées: $G = 44,3\%$, $D = 33,0\%$ et $Dd = 22,0\%$. En ce qui concerne les déterminants et la qualité formelle, les données moyennes ont été: $F = 63,1\%$, $F+ = 76,7\%$ et $F+ ext = 76,3\%$. Les contenus les plus souvent évoquées ont été le $A = 57,5\%$ et le $H = 21,4\%$. Bien que partiels, ces résultats se sont montrés prometteurs comme les références normatives actuelles du Rorschach (école française) pour les écoliers de 9 à 11 ans, compte tenu de l'absence d'études de cette nature et les spécificités du contexte socioculturel brésilien. Nous espérons que cette étude va encourager l'utilisation appropriée de la méthode de Rorschach.

Resumen

Los métodos proyectivos han sido objeto de estudio e intensa investigación, en diferentes contextos, en concordancia con las directrices internacionales para el mejoramiento de los instrumentos de Evaluación Psicológica. Entre dichos métodos se destaca el Psicodiagnóstico de Rorschach, el cual, a pesar de constituir una importante estrategia para evaluación de la personalidad, todavía exige mucha investigación científica. Investigadores de distintos países han concentrado esfuerzos en el desarrollo y actualización de normas para el Rorschach y reafirman, a partir de la sistematización de sus resultados, la importancia de que más estudios en ese sentido sean realizados en diversos grupos poblacionales. Esto permite que los profesionales cuenten con datos representativos de los individuos que quieran comprender, algo preeminente en la evaluación del desarrollo infantil. Esta necesidad técnica también se hace presente en el contexto de Brasil, lo que justifica la presente investigación. Este trabajo pretendió elaborar estándares normativos de Rorschach para niños brasileros de nueve a once años de edad. Para esto fueron seleccionados 180 estudiantes con indicadores de desarrollo típico, distribuidos equitativamente en función de sexo, edad y procedencia escolar (escuelas públicas o privadas), residentes en el interior del estado de Sao Paulo, Brasil, debidamente autorizados por sus padres o responsables para participar en la investigación. Los instrumentos utilizados para la colecta de datos fueron: a) cuestionario informativo sobre desarrollo de los niños, contestado por los padres y/o responsables; b) test de las Matrices Progresivas Coloridas de Raven y c) Psicodiagnóstico de Rorschach. Los dos últimos fueron aplicados individualmente a los niños, en condiciones adecuadas para la evaluación psicológica. Los datos de Rorschach fueron colectados y codificados de acuerdo con la Escuela Francesa. Posteriormente, los protocolos del Rorschach fueron analizados por tres examinadores independientes, con experiencia en la técnica, que además recibieron un entrenamiento específico para este trabajo. Se llegó así a una clasificación final de cada respuesta a partir del consenso entre estos análisis independientes, lo que garantizo la debida precisión de los resultados. Hasta el momento, 140 protocolos de Rorschach han sido codificados y componen los datos aquí presentados. Los resultados medios, en términos de productividad y ritmo, fueron: $R = 16,1$; $TLm = 17,2$ segundos e $TRm = 33,4$ segundos. Con relación a los modos de aprensión, las siguientes proporciones medias fueron halladas: $G = 44,3\%$, $D = 33,0\%$ e $Dd = 22,0\%$. En lo que concierne a los determinantes y la calidad formal, los dados medios fueron: $F\% = 63,1\%$, $F+\% = 76,7\%$ e $F+ \text{ext}\% = 76,3\%$. Los contenidos más evocados fueron: $A\% = 57,5\%$ e $H\% = 21,4\%$. El estilo de vivencia afectiva predominante fue el evitativo (coartativo). Aunque parciales, estos resultados se mostraron promisorios como referencias normativas actuales de Rorschach (Escuela Francesa) para escolares de 9 a 11 años de edad, en vista de la carencia de estudios de esta naturaleza y de las especificidades del contexto sociocultural brasileño, lo que puede favorecer el uso adecuado del Método de Rorschach.

221

R. L. Raspantini et al.

ブラジルの子どものロールシャッハ反応：9-11歳児の非患者の標準データ

心理学的なアセスメントの道具の向上のための国際的基準に賛成して、投映法はいくつかの文脈で研究されてきている。これらの道具の中で、パーソナリティアセスメントにとって重要性であり、研究が必要とされており、それを利用するための基準の開発や更新に取り組んでいるものとして、ロールシャッハ法は目立っている。さまざまな国々の研究者がこの方向性における研究を実行し続けており、同時に彼らは専門家に典型となるデータを提供するためには異なった集団に対するさらなる研究が、特に子どもの発達を評価する際には、必要であることを強調している。ブラジルにおいては、同様の必要性が述べられており、この研究はロールシャッハ法に対する子どもの標準的な反応のパターンを詳しく示すことを目的としている。180名の典型的な発達（病理を有していない）を示していて、性別や年齢、学校種（公立か私立か）が均等になるように調整された子ども（9歳〜11歳）がこの研究のために選び出された。すべての参加者がサンパウロ（ブラジル）州の地方区のある街から選ばれ、両親や後見人からこの研究に参加することが正当であると認められた。参加者は個別にアセスメントされ、子どもの発達質問紙、Raven の Progressive Matrices Test、ロールシャッハ法が用いられた。ロールシャッハのデータは French Approach にもとづいて収集され、コード化された。その後、ロールシャッハプロトコルは 3 人の独立した判断によって分析され、それぞれの反応の最終的な分類はこの判断の一致によっておこなわれた。これまで、140 のプロコトルがコード化され、それらのデータがここに報告されている。平均は以下のような結果となった。生産性とリズムの指標：R=16.1；LTa=17.2s；RTa=33.4s。把握型：G=44.3%；D=33.0%；Dd=22.0%。決定因と形態水準：F%=63.1%；F+%=76.7%；F+ext%=76.3%。最も頻出した反応内容：A%=57.5%；H%=21.4%。不完全ではあるが、こういった研究が欠如していることや、ロールシャッハ法の適切な使用を認めるようにブラジルの社会文化的文脈の特殊性を考慮すれば、この結果は 9-11 歳の子どもの（French Approach の）ロールシャッハ法の標準資料としてアップグレードされることが請け合れている。

Rorschachiana 32, 223–251
© 2011 Hogrefe Publishing

DOI: 10.1027/1192-5604/a000023

Original Article

Projective Kit for Early Childhood (P. K. E. C.)

A Projective Tool for Research and Clinical Assessment

Pascal Roman[1], Mathilde Dublineau[2], and Camila Saboia[3]

[1]*University of Lausanne, Switzerland,* [2]*Université Lumière, Lyon 2, France,*
[3]*Université Paris-Diderot, France*

Abstract. This article highlights, on the one hand, the relevance of the Projective Kit for Early Childhood – a projective play test – in the dual prospect of research practice, and of clinical practice, on the other hand, considering a form of continuity between both these processes, as stressed by C. Chabert (1995). First, a brief introduction to this unique test in the field of psychopathology in young children serves to assess the relevance of this projective device in clinical practice and research. Then we successively present the test's implications in actual clinical research, involving an evaluation of the psychoaffective dynamics of children with West syndrome (a form of epilepsy occurring in infants from the early stages of life, which impairs their development and frequently leads to psychopathological pictures in the autism spectrum) and as part of a clinical consultation process focused on the problem of depression.

Keywords: projective test, children, play, West syndrome

The P. K. E. C. – An Invitation to Play

The P. K. E. C. (Roman, 2004, 2005) is a projective play test for children from 6 months to 4 years of age. Among projective tests, it finds its place in the continuum of tests given to children. Specifically, in relation to play tests, it is administered earlier than the Sceno Test (Von Staabs, 1962) aimed at children from 3 or 4 years old. The P. K. E. C. thus complements an array of devices to assess the psychoaffective dynamics of children and may be envisaged in addition to tests aiming at assessing cognitive development such as the Brunet-Lézine test (Brunet & Lézine,

1951). In a way, the P. K. E. C. opens up an experimental system to observe the child's play, which, contrary to observations according to Bick (1964) whose objective is to accompany an infant or young child's mental processes through observation, relies on an explicit invitation to symbolize.

The P. K. E. C. puts forward a free-play situation using standardized material (see attached list of play material). This free-play situation is initiated by offering the material and inviting the child to play on a play mat[1], accompanied by an adult relative if applicable. From the psychologist's point of view, this situation triggers a clinical observation mechanism that relies on the psychologist's ability to simultaneously accompany the child's play in a nondirective and kindly manner, and to gather the necessary data to subsequently draw up a play observation report. This play observation serves as support for the objectivizing of the processes mobilized by the child during symbolization work. One might say that the child is therefore placed in an experimental situation of playing under someone's gaze, "alone in the presence of another" (Winnicott, 1958).

The play situation is thus introduced by an instruction (see footnote) with the essential intent of authorizing the child to play, and of supporting the child in the game. The psychologist intervenes little, and only to invite the child to explore the devices in a case of significant inhibition (on the mode of object-presenting, in reference to Winnicott, 1957).

The material at the child's disposal is standardized[2] and offers various solicitations in terms of sensoriality, motor mobilization and/or eliciting fantasy expression. The material of the P. K. E. C. test consists of familiar objects from the child's universe: balls, dolls, stuffed animals, play tea set, telephone, building blocks ... This material carries an identifiable function for the child in a project of play (on the imitation mode), but also gives a large place to the imaginary in its utilization (on the translation mode). The presence of the objects in the P. K. E. C. is based on the choice of making available to the child a diversity of solicitations on the sensoriality, motor and fantasy modes, and to allow each child to enroll in the play, whatever their age, motor skills and register of psycho-affective development may be (test designed for children from 6 months to 4 years old).

---

1 The material's provision comes with the following instruction: "See all these toys – you can play with them any way you like."
2 For a full presentation of the test please refer to the Test Manual (in French) (Roman, 2004).

True to the spirit of projective tests, beyond the material's own latent solicitation, the P. K. E. C. involves a whole range of latent inducements, on which the analysis of observed play is based. These inducements cover a large spectrum, both from the point of view of identity stakes (testing the material's consistency and its structuring potential) and that of identificatory stakes (relying on the material's *figurative* elements).

Hence, it is understood that this test – like any projective test involving the subject's creativity – assesses the child's symbolization potential: The P. K. E. C. may thus be considered as a "symbolizing device" ("dispositif à symboliser") (Roman, 1997). This device forces the child's symbolization potentials from the beginning – under the terms of the clinical instrument involved – of a free-play area for the child which may be *potentially transitional*. Indeed, it is in relation to the hurdle represented by proposing the test (offering the material, giving an instruction and analyzing the observed play) that the P. K. E. C. is likely to trigger this transitional potential.

Finally, it should be specified that

– the test material and administration are subject to a methodology guaranteeing a form of neutrality in how the psychologist presents the test (suppression of the psychologist's desires regarding the material provided and the way in which it is put forward),

– analysis of play observations (objectification of the movements governing play expression based on identification of the toys chosen and how they are involved in the game) also obeys a rigorous methodology.

Play observations are subject to a three-fold examination (on the methodology, see Roman, 2004):

– Identification of the test objects used by the child,

– Consideration of how the child handles the play elements (contact, manipulation, assembly, scene-staging)[3]

– Scoring of play processes (Boekholt, 1993; Roman, 2004), which reveal the defense mechanisms used by the child. Indeed, in her work on the dynamics of mental functioning in very young infants, Boekholt stresses the benefits of mapping this, as defense mechanisms are considered for their contribution to personality development (Klein,

---

3 Object handling modes: Contact (CTCT), Manipulation (MAN), Association (ASS), Scene-Staging (SCS).

1934, 1940) rather than as a stabilized mechanism for personality organization.

Beyond the formalization (deconstruction) of the mental movements governing child's play, these various tools for analytical assessment allow an actual objectivation of the child's subjective positions[4], as expressed in the temporality of the playtime, where children set their own pace[5]. Crossanalysis of these formal assessment data – and putting the child's play and the test's latent inducements (fantasy generation) into perspective – opens up a field for clinical interpretation to assess children's mental functions.

Clinical Research into the West Syndrome

The P. K. E. C. projective test was used in the framework of research for the P. I. L. E. project (International Program for Child Language, Hôpital Necker (Paris), headed by Prof. Bernard Golse), the objective of which is to study body language and interaction prior to verbal expression of various cohorts of babies at risk. This occurs along five complementary lines: *interactive, developmental, psychodynamic, attachment,* and *psychopathological*, from age 3 months to 4 years. We restricted our study to babies suffering from West syndrome, an early form of epilepsy potentially leading to autistic disorders (in 7% to 33% of cases). In the framework of the PILE program, the study of this cohort was supervised by Dr. Lisa Ouss-Ryngaert. We used the P. K. E. C. projective tool particularly to assess psychodynamic aspects in children from 15 to 18 months, repeating the test at 24 and 36 months[6]. The analytical assessment of the P. K. E. C. was conducted based on a single test filmed in the PILE project's video booth (*Aube de la Vie*). The scoring of play processes (see above) and material handling modes was performed based on the observation report, which served to identify the various play organizers

---

4   The establishment of benchmark data based on an experimental survey of 140 children serves to position each individual subject in relation to a group standard, which naturally remains relative.
5   The only restriction in this respect is the maximum playtime set at half an hour.
6   At the time of writing, the data regarding ages 24 and 26 months had not yet been analyzed.

among the various categories retained in the methodology. It should be stressed that when the child displays difficulties in engaging in the test's proposed play, due to external and specific reasons such as tiredness, hunger, or the collateral impact of medication taken on the day of the test, we then proposed a new test at a later date and analyzed the test in which the child gave the *best* performance. This procedure helped us to better identify whether the child's refusal to engage in play was a temporary state or due to the child's own mental functioning. The children's play as observed by the P. K. E. C. may highlight possible symbolization disorders in children affected by West syndrome inasmuch as this test provides indicators of a gap in the cathexis of symbolic play between children. In this context, the notion of play is taken as a "revelator" of the child's object organization.

Within the cohort of 16 babies with West syndrome, three groups were distinguished for the purposes of illustration: West children presenting autistic traces (WA), those with a developmental delay (WD), and those without autistic traces or developmental delay, referred to as "West normal" (WN) (see Table 1). The classification of WA children was based on the PREAUT early detection grid (Crespin, Laznik et al., 2006) applied to the children in the study at age 9 months and subsequently confirmed by the CARS (Childhood Autistic Rating Scale, Schopler et al., 1980) at ages 2, 3, and 4 years. For the assessment of developmental aspects, we administered the Brunet Lézine test to the children in the PILE research at ages 12, 18, 24, and 36 months. For sake of comparison, we also studied a control group consisting of 7 "healthy" children without chronic medical pathology. While analyzing these findings, we also referred to the control group babies surveyed by Roman (2004, 2005) to back up our results.

Quantitative Analysis

The quantitative analysis of these data (P. K. E. C. scores based on consideration of play processes, on the one hand, and of the material's handling mode on the other) and the qualitative assessment (child's mode of involvement in play) are presented successively. The quantitative data analysis was performed by statistician C. Lalanne (Inserm Paris).

The quantitative assessment takes into account the cathexis of play processes, then the child's handling mode.

Table 1. Age when taking the P. K. E. C., developmental age on that occasion and individual scores in the P. K. E. C.

Children	Actual age	Developmental age	Identification of play processes								Handling modes				
			NP	SM	RC	RE	EI	IF	OC	Tot	CTc	Mnp	Ass	Msc	Total
West Autistic															
WA1	28M4J	7M27J	30	20	12	0	2	0	0	64	5	2	0	0	7
WA2	16M20J	7M9J	9	6	7	0	5	0	0	24	2	2	0	0	4
WA3	18M23J	6M12J	9	2	5	0	5	0	0	21	2	0	0	0	2
WA4	21M21	12M6J	12	24	4	1	0	0	0	41	2	5	1	0	8
West Delay															
WD1	35M22J	23M18J	4	23	23	4	2	0	6	62	2	7	4	2	10
WD2	18M5J	11M21J	7	24	21	2	3	0	5	59	1	7	3	2	10
WD3	16M8J	8M15J	9	28	12	0	6	0	0	55	7	4	0	0	11
WD4	18M26J	8M 18J	5	12	11	0	4	0	1	33	5	5	0	0	13
WD5	17M25J	8M 3J	8	14	16	0	2	0	1	41	8	3	0	0	9
West Normal															
WN1	14M19J	13M12J	6	25	8	2	1	0	0	41	2	7	3	1	13
WN2	15M10J	14M27J	3	25	15	2	3	0	2	50	2	3	3	0	7
WN3	18M12J	15M21J	5	29	9	2	1	0	4	49	5	4	2	1	12
WN4	17M23j	13M27J	5	25	22	1	0	0	2	55	2	4	2	0	9
WN5	16M	11 m24J	9	27	11	0	1	0	0	48	8	2	0	0	11
WN6	15M11J	14M12J	9	24	22	2	2	0	3	67	4	6	2	1	13
WN7	15M16J	12M6J	2	23	22	2	0	0	2	51	3	7	1	2	11

Note. Processes scored with the P. K. E. C.: NP = processes used outside play with the material; action directed toward the material; RC = processes resorting to a relationship with the material; SM = sensorimotor processes – the test; ER = processes resorting to external reality; AI = processes resorting to avoidance and inhibition; who attends resorting to imagination and fantasy; OC = processes resorting to objectivity and control. Handling modes: CTc = Contact, Mnp = Manipulation, Ass = Association, Msc = Scene-Staging.

Play Processes

In order to analyze and interpret the results, we retained the score for each play process, then expressed it as a percentage of the total number of processes in the test. In other words, the ratios shown in Table 2 indicate the relative contribution of each process indicated in Table 1.

When reviewing both Table 2 and Table 3, one observes that most play processes observed across $n = 16$ subjects consist of sensorimotor processes (an average of 42% (Table 2) vs. 62% in the experimental survey on a random (nonclinical) sample (see Roman 2004, 2005) and 55% in the PILE control group (Table 3) and of recourse to a relationship with the clinician and the mother (average 28% vs. 17% in the experimental survey on a random sample and 23% in the PILE control group). One also sees an increase in the AI process (6% vs. 1% in the experimental survey on a random sample and 1% in the PILE control group) as well as a decrease in the OC process (3% vs. 8% in the experimental survey on a random sample and 7% in the PILE control group).

Handling Modes

In order to analyze and interpret the results, we retained the score showing the frequency of a handling mode and then expressed it as a percentage of the total number of handling modes. In other words, the ratios shown in Table 4 indicate the relative contribution of each handling mode.

Among the handling modes observed in children with a West syndrome, one observes a majority of handling by contact (43% vs. 24% in the PILE control group) and by manipulation (41%). The association is lower than in the control group (12% vs. 19% in the PILE control group), and scene-staging virtually inexistent (4% vs. 15% in PILE children).

To conclude the quantitative analysis, one may say that there are several differences in the data collected from children suffering from West syndrome and from random children:

– The play processes observed are mainly sensorimotor, though less frequent than in the control group. However, there is also an increase in recourse to a relationship with the clinician and the mother (RC) and in the AI (avoidance – inhibition) process, and a decrease in the OC (objectivity – control) process.

– Handling modes are dominated by contact (with a higher incidence

Table 2. Distribution of play processes for the cohort (n = 16), in relation to all processes (last column)

Children West Autistic	NP (%)	SM (%)	RC (%)	ER (%)	AI (%)	IF (%)	OC (%)	Total No.
WA1	46.90	31.20	18.80	0.00	3.10	0.00	0.00	64
WA2	33.30	22.20	25.90	0.00	18.50	0.00	0.00	24
WA3	42.90	9.50	23.80	0.00	23.80	0.00	0.00	21
WA4	29.30	58.50	9.80	2.40	0.00	0.00	0.00	41
West Delay								
WD1	6.50	37.10	37.10	6.50	3.20	0.00	9.70	62
WD2	11.30	38.70	33.90	3.20	4.80	0.00	8.10	59
WD3	16.40	50.90	21.80	0.00	10.90	0.00	0.00	55
WD4	15.20	36.40	33.30	0.00	12.10	0.00	3.00	33
WD5	19.50	34.10	39.00	0.00	4.90	0.00	2.40	41
West Normal								
WN1	14.30	59.50	19.00	4.80	2.40	0.00	0.00	41
WN2	6.00	50.00	30.00	4.00	6.00	0.00	4.00	50
WN3	10.00	58.00	18.00	4.00	2.00	0.00	8.00	49
WN4	9.10	45.50	40.00	1.80	0.00	0.00	3.60	55
WN5	18.80	56.20	22.90	0.00	2.10	0.00	0.00	48
WN6	14.50	38.70	35.50	3.20	3.20	0.00	4.80	67
WN7	3.90	45.10	43.10	3.90	0.00	0.00	3.90	51
Average for each process	18.60	41.99	28.25	2.12	6.07	0.00	2.98	47.56

Table 3. Control group reference data for play processes

	NP %	SM %	RC %	ER %	AI %	IF %	OC %	Total
T1	10.00	64.00	18.00	0.00	0.00	0.00	8.00	50
T2	10.70	46.40	32.10	1.80	1.80	0.00	7.10	56
T3	10.90	56.40	20.00	7.30	0.00	0.00	5.50	55
T4	9.20	50.80	27.70	4.60	0.00	0.00	7.70	65
T5	7.80	62.50	18.80	4.70	0.00	0.00	6.20	64
T6	7.60	53.00	22.70	6.10	4.50	0.00	6.10	66
T7	11.60	52.20	20.30	7.20	1.40	1.40	5.80	69
Moy.	9.69	55.04	22.80	4.52	1.11	0.21	6.63	60.71

Table 4. Distribution of handling modes for the cohort ($n = 16$), in relation to all handling modes (last column)

Children West Autistic	Contact (%)	Manipulation (%)	Association (%)	Scene-staging (%)	Total No.
WA1	71.40	28.60	0.00	0.00	7
WA2	50.00	50.00	0.00	0.00	4
WA3	100.00	0.00	0.00	0.00	2
WA4	25.00	62.50	12.50	0.00	8
West Delay					
WD1	13.30	46.70	26.70	13.30	10
WD2	7.70	53.80	23.10	15.40	10
WD3	63.60	36.40	0.00	0.00	11
WD4	50.00	50.00	0.00	0.00	13
WD5	72.70	27.30	0.00	0.00	9
West Normal					
WN1	15.40	53.80	23.10	7.70	13
WN2	25.00	37.50	37.50	0.00	7
WN3	41.70	33.30	16.70	8.30	12
WN4	25.00	50.00	25.00	0.00	9
WN5	80.00	20.00	0.00	0.00	11
WN6	30.80	46.20	15.40	7.70	13
WN7	23.10	53.80	7.70	15.40	11
Average for each process	43.20	40.62	11.72	4.24	9.38

Table 5. Control group reference data for handling modes

Age	Contact (%)	Manipulation(%)	Association (%)	Scene-staging (%)	Total
T1	37.50	56.20	0.00	0.00	16
T2	37.50	31.20	18.80	12.50	16
T3	20.00	40.00	20.00	20.00	15
T4	43.80	31.20	12.50	18.80	16
T5	6.20	37.50	25.00	12.50	16
T6	12.50	50.00	25.00	18.80	16
T7	10.00	35.00	35.00	20.00	20
Avg.	23.93	40.18	19.46	14.64	16.43

231

Table 6. Median of scores obtained in the PKEC by babies affected by West Syndrome

PKEC	Median of play processes (50% of children score below the median and 50% above)								Median of handling modes (50% of children score below the median and 50% above)				
	NP	SM	RC	ER	AI	IF	OC	Tot	CTCT	MAN	ASS	SCS	Total choice
WN	5	25	15	2	1	0	2	50	3	4	2	1	11
WD	7	23	16	0	3	0	1	55	5	5	0	0	10
WA	10.5	13	6	0	3.5	0	0	32.5	2	2	0	0	5.5

than in random children) and manipulation, with a small contribution of association and scene-staging.

Qualitative Analysis

The task is to compare the occurrence of specific play processes and handling modes between the various groups of West children (Table 6), the children of the PILE program control group and Roman's group of "random" babies (Roman 2004, 2005).

In order to gain a global understanding of the play organization of West children across the various groups, rather than for each individual child as detailed above, we have represented the occurrence of each aspect of play in Table 6 below. We deliberately chose to work with medians rather than relative frequency or average because of the significant age variability between the children in each group. This lack of data is explained by the difficulty in administering the P.K.E.C. to the survey's children at the appointed age because of the usual problems linked to the subjects' availability in the framework of longitudinal research.

Play Processes

The high frequency of certain play processes in relation to the control group raises hypotheses on these children's mental functioning considered from a psychoanalytic point of view.

Nonplay Processes (NP)

Within the cohort of children affected by West syndrome, one observes that the *sickest* children – those with autism or autistic risk (in **bold** in the table above) – tend to present a higher score in the NP process: WA1 = 47%, WA2 = 33%,

WA3 = 43%, WA4 = 30% vs. an average frequency of 19% in West babies (Table 2).

This may be explained by the fact that these children find it difficult to make contact with the play objects. They show a developmental delay evidenced by scores in the Brunet-Lézine test which are much lower in the hand-eye coordination than the posture control field (WA1: BL postural = 44, BL coordination = 19; WA2, BL P = 52, BL C = 44; WA3, BL P = 39, BL C = 29; W 20, BL P = 66, BL C = 54). This problem with fine coordination, often resulting in delayed handling of the objects, may influence these children's ability to access symbolic play.

For instance, child WA1 is unable to achieve a drive cathexis of the object. This failure subsequently leads to stereotyped movements (which might call up the cathexis of autistic objects as described by Tustin, 1981) and to a total inability to use the object in a creative and symbolic fashion (object usage as described by Winnicott, 1957): She takes the duck and knocks it on the mat while bending her body in a swinging motion, then does the same with the baby bottle. In child WA4, behaviors suggesting stereotyped observation can also be observed (she takes up each object and beats herself on the head in a repetitive way).

This issue of the inability to use objects is particularly present in children affected by West syndrome with autistic disorders. This indicates early signs of symbolization disorders (Roman, 2004).

This issue of the inability to use an object is particularly present in children affected by West syndrome with autistic disorders. In the example above, one observes that both these WA children display a refusal to engage in the test's proposed play. In fact, their play is marked by repetitive explorations without any intentionality in discovering the play objects. On the other hand, West children with a developmental delay, despite psychomotor limitations, make real efforts to overcome these and to engage in exploring the objects of the test. For instance, after several unsuccessful attempts, WD1 picks up the phone and, with the clinician's help, takes it up to the ear and ends up pretending to have a telephone conversation with someone.

In this context we are able to suggest that the data assessed through the P. K. E. C. offer a fine analysis of the quality of children's play, thus uncovering major aspects of the child's mental functioning up to the detection or confirmation of traces of an ongoing autistic organization.

The median of the NP play process in the group of autistic and autistic risk children of this cohort is 10.5, whereas children with a developmental delay (WD) score an average of NP = 7, slightly above the median of

233

children categorized as "normal" (WN) in this cohort: NP = 5 (Table 6), which is close to the scores found in the random children surveyed by Roman (NP = 4).

This does not seem related to developmental delay, as a comparison of the scores obtained for play processes between autistic children and the younger children in the Roman group, closer to the developmental age of autistic children (6–11 months), shows an average of 3 vs. 10.5 for autistic children (Table 6). This therefore appears to be a pattern of object exploration dynamics specific to autistic or children at risk of autism, which seems to be confirmed by the results subsequently obtained at ages 24 and 36 months[7]. These findings served to confirm the existence of a specific pattern for autistic children and the existence of a "mere" gap for children with a development delay, who end up displaying the same pattern as children without delayed development, albeit at a different stage.

When the clinician draws the child's attention to engage the child in play by presenting certain toys (*object presenting* by Winnicott, 1957), the reaction of certain children like WA2 and WA3 is to refuse the object or even contact with the clinician. This is validated by the low frequency of the *SM* process (sensorimotor, revealing an action directed toward the material) as well as of the *RC* process (resorting to a relationship with the clinician) in these children – with a marked tendency to RC3 processes (see below).

Sensorimotor Processes (SM)

Within the cohort of children with West syndrome, one observes a low frequency of the SM process (action directed toward the material) in autistic West children. Children WA2 and WA3 are located below the average occurrence of 42%. This gap is even more obvious when considering the average for the SM process: West "normal" (WN = 25), West "delay" (WD = 23), and West "autistic" (WA = 13). For these children with autistic risk, the figures vary between 6 and 29, whereas for the cohort in the control groups, the occurrence is higher (from 26 to 40).

This difference may be explained by these children's sensorimotor limitation which impairs them more in object exploration.

Compared to the control group, these SM processes are globally lower

---

7 This analysis was recently completed by one of the authors, Camila Saboia, as part of her PhD thesis (Université Paris-Diderot, January 2011, unpublished).

in children with West syndrome than in the control groups (55% in the PILE Group) (Tables 2 and 3).

Processes Resorting to the Clinician (RC)

Within the cohort of children with West syndrome, the RC process is less frequent in autistic or autistic risk babies: The RC median is WN = 15, WD = 16, and WA = 6. In the latter group, the nature of calls on the clinician is rather characterized by RC3 (insistence on boundaries and delineation of space; need for inducement). This represents intermittent intervention by the clinician to engage the child in play. Autistic children with West syndrome therefore find it more difficult to explore the toys and to interact with the clinician or the relative attending the test, further compounding their inability to play (NP).

However, in autistic children with West syndrome, the process appears to be closer to the control groups West = 28% (Table 2), Témoin PILE = 23% (Table 3). One may conclude that on the whole West children resort to the clinician more, but not those who are autistic. In children affected by West syndrome, resorting to the clinician might generally be construed as a form of need for support in exploring the material (RC initiated by the child as a form of appeal), whereas in WA children this would be more of a need to re-engage them in play (RC initiated by the clinician), because of their repeated refusal to engage in the test, highlighting the degree of their mental retreat.

Processes Resorting to Objectivity and Control (OC)

Within the cohort of children affected by West syndrome, the OC process is well represented by the children's interest in exploring movement: emptying and filling the boxes, building and rebuilding Lego constructions, imitating everyday gestures. The OC process highlights children's ability to control external reality, i.e., the *illusion of omnipotent control over objects* (Winnicott, 1957). This should probably be understood in relation to the child's psychoaffective maturation, inasmuch as the child starts to distinguish external reality from internal reality, which opens up the construction of object permanence.

For children with West syndrome, one observes that the occurrence of OC processes in children with autistic risk is nonexistent: average OC = 0 (Table 6), whereas in other children, occurrences varies according to each child's level of mental organization. Thus, the highest score was that of child WD1 due to a much more advanced age, despite psychomotor delay. However, for other children, such as WN3 or WN6, whose development is good, the scores are higher. For WN children OC = 2, and for WD children OC = 1.

Compared to the control groups, babies with West syndrome present a lower resort to OC processes than the control groups: 3% in babies with West syndrome (Table 2) vs. an average occurrence of 5% in random children of the experimental survey and 6% in the PILE Group (Table 3).

Processes Resorting to External Reality (ER)

Within the cohort of children affected by West syndrome, ER processes represent play such as "taking the glass in the toy tea set and pretending to drink" or "taking the baby bottle to feed the doll." This process shows the child's first attempts at bodily representation and the ability to distinguish outside from inside (container/content). One observes that, like the OC processes, ER processes are more frequent in children with a West syndrome considered as "normal" (WN). For these processes, the median is 2 – a similar result to that found in the random children of the experimental survey. Autistic children, on the other hand, display an exploration in the primitive spectrum which is restricted to the oral or sound exploration of objects; the median for autistic or autistic risk children is 0.

Compared to the control groups, in children affected by West syndrome one observes a frequency below the average for the random children of the experimental survey (2% for West children (Table 2) and 4% for random children (Table 3).

Avoidance – Inhibition Processes (AI)

Within the cohort of children affected by West syndrome, the median for the AI process is slightly higher for autistic children (WA = 3.5 in relation to children with a delay WD = 3) (Table 6), whereas for children considered "normal" the median is lower (WN = 1) and AI = 0 for the control groups. This highlights the hypothesis according to which an absence of pacing characterizes play exploration in these children, more specifically in those presenting traces of symbolization disorders.

Compared to the control groups, children affected by West syndrome display a high occurrence of the process: AI = 6% (which reveals a restriction of the exploratory activity and therefore of its pace) (Table 2). One notes a variation from 0 to 6, compared to 1 to 3 for the random children in the experimental survey, which leads to a restriction in the

236

choice of objects for these children (from 4 to 13, whereas for random children the choice varies from 16 to 20).

Object Handling Modes

Contact (CTCT)

Within the cohort of children affected by West syndrome, the handling modes of children WA1, WA2, and WA3 was limited to a feeble and fleeting exploration, expressed by the Contact mode, occurring more often than the average frequency in West children (WA1 = 71%, WA2 = 50%, and WA3 = 100%, for an average occurrence of 43%; Table 4). These children favor sensory, touch, and above all sound explorations, with a predominance of the SM7 process(= sensory, touch, sound, olfactory, and kinesthetic explorations): WA2 takes the duck and makes noise; WA1 takes the Lego box and moves his fingers across the Lego blocks to make noise.

Compared to the control groups, the average in babies affected by West syndrome is higher than that in control group babies (43% for West children (Table 4) vs. 24% in PILE children (Table 5)). However, this item is difficult to assess because of its strong interindividual variability.

Manipulation (MAN)

Within the cohort of children affected by West syndrome, the "normal" children manipulate objects twice as much as autistic or autistic risk children (average WN = 4, WA = 2, WD = 5) (Table 6). This slightly higher frequency in the latter group is probably linked to repetitive object manipulation movements with children who find it difficult to explore objects because of motor limitations. However, this repetitive manipulation is different from those in autistic children, whose stereotyped nature seems rather related to a drive discharge. Indeed, children with developmental delay display intentionality in discovering and exploring objects, evidencing drive targeting.

Compared to the control groups, the predominant handling mode in babies affected by West syndrome is Manipulation, the frequency of which is 40% in West babies and thus identical to the average 40% frequency in PILE children group (Tables 4 and 5). The WD children have the highest number of manipulations (the others have a lower number, with an average similar to that of the control group). This might reflect the developmental delay: Children spend more time manipulating the

237

object as an exploratory mode than associating or scene-staging, which call for greater maturity of children global development.

Association (ASS) and Scene-Staging (SCS)

Within the cohort of children affected by West syndrome, the P. K. E. C. protocols for children with a major developmental age delay, around 8 months (WD3 and W1D4) show Association and Scene-Staging modes that are more or less identical to protocols for autistic children (ASS = 0 and SCS = O), i.e., lower than the Roman group (ASS = 2.5, SCS = 0). This is not the case with children with a moderate delay, such as WD8, whose scores for these handling modes are no different from those of children considered as "normal" within this cohort.

These results lead to the hypothesis that children with a developmental delay below a certain age may present play modes close to those of autistic children, particularly in aspects which require psychoaffective organization such as the ability to associate (ASS) and to make-believe (SCS). However, it appears that they then catch up, demonstrating access to the symbolic dimension, despite their psychomotor limitations: This is the case of children WD2 and WD1. The developmental delay dimension therefore seems more important that the autistic disorders.

Compared to the control groups, children affected by West syndrome display fewer ASS (12) and SCS (4) processes than the PILE children (ASS = 19.5 and SCS = 14.5, respectively). WN children seem closer to the profile of the control groups (Table 4 and Table 5).

Choice of Objects

Within the cohort of children affected by West syndrome, in autistic children one observes a limitation of the *total choice of objects*, with a median of 5 vs. a median of 11 for WN children and 10 for WD children (Table 6). This variation supports the hypothesis that autistic West children find it difficult to establish a relationship to the objects, i.e., to be interested in fetching and exploring them (*object-relating*, D.-W. Winnicott, 1957). In the case of WA1, the low occurrence of object choices (7 of a total of 33 objects) may be explained by the child's tendency to take a few objects and retreat into stereotyped movement.

Compared to the control groups, children affected by West syndrome selected considerably fewer objects than did control group children (W = 9 vs. 28 for Roman group and 16.5 for PILE group children). Children

238

with a West syndrome therefore seem to interact less with the surrounding physical world: They engage in stereotyped exploration, whereas other children display a more systematic and less "inquisitive" exploration.

Object Exploration Pace

One observes a lack of pacing in most children of this cohort. This is evidenced by the children's difficulty in moving from one game to another when taking the test. This is even more obvious in some children with autistic disorders, inasmuch as they are less sensitive to the clinician's interventions (object presenting RC3). As already mentioned above, this amounts to an object refusal which will lead to stereotyped movements.

Thus, the analytical assessment of the P.K.E.C. and analysis of all clinical data collected in this framework confirm a gap in symbolic play within the cohort of babies with West syndrome. This difference can be seen between autistic or autistic risk children and the others, even those with a sensorimotor delay and, more generally, in probable gaps between the cohort of children with West syndrome and the control groups. This therefore shows the relevance of a projective clinical approach with populations of children whose organic disorders may become the root of psychopathological developments, whose nature should be assessed as early as possible so as to identify appropriate care.

Clinical Approach to Depression: Move or Sink

Following an overview of the current stakes of perinatal depression, the presentation of a clinical situation with the proposal of the P. K. E. C. test will serve to highlight the relevance of the test in the framework of the child's therapeutic consultation (Winnicott, 1971).

Update on Perinatal Depression

The specificity of clinical research into infant depression is to challenge the clinician in both defining and identifying it due to its polymorphic symptomatology. Golse (2001) confirms the relevance of using the wording "depression" in infant care due to symptomatic analogies with adult care, although he insists on the lack of a structural analogy. Moreover, he warns against the haste with which – further to Green's (1983) work on the effects of maternal depression on child development – practitioners might be tempted to attribute child disorders too directly to the poor quality of maternal care. Indeed, Golse stresses that maternal psychopathology has neither a direct nor a linear impact on the child, if only because this systematically presumes a failure on the part of the third party or parties who could or should have stepped in to protect the child.

This proves to be all the more justified when the task is to reconstruct the infant's life development after the event. Nevertheless, as stressed by a host of studies, it is important to deal with maternal postpartum depression (whose occurrence is about 10% to 20%) as early as possible in order to mitigate the impact of interaction discontinuities which set in the mother-baby relationship.

Since the 1980s, in the wake of the establishment of the deleterious effects of maternal depression on infant development, regardless of any mother-baby separation, there has therefore been renewed interest in perinatal psychiatry. It was child psychiatrists who, through anamnestic analysis, initially found mood disorders and maternal depressions in women consulting them with infants suffering from sleep disorders, digestive tonus disorders (colic, digestive spasms, regurgitation, etc.), or early developmental delay. Cox et al. (Cox & Holden, 1994; Cox, Holden, & Sagovsky, 1987) put forward a method of early detection of postpartum depression which relied on a 10-item screening scale, the Edinburgh Postnatal Depression Scale (EPDS).

Murray et al. (Murray, 1996; Murray & Stein, 1991) demonstrated the effects of maternal depression on the psychoaffective and developmental progress of children whom they observed over a 5-year period.

Poinso et al. (2001) highlighted how difficult it is to care for these families as the mother's symptomatology is often rationalized and concealed. They found that it was not rare for the depression to be felt by the mother in a projective way, with the child becoming the persecutor of the mother or even the whole family with its incessant crying at night.

These projective defenses appear all the more easier to introduce into the mother-baby relationship since, on the one hand, the entanglement of mental apparatuses is particularly conducive to this and, on the other hand, the fantasy of being a bad mother unavoidably emerges when the latter is confronted with a deterioration in the quality of her relationship with her baby. This fantasy, subject alternately to denial and guilt, obstructs calls for care.

Indeed, both guilt and feelings of incompetence are massively observed in the clinical assessment of the mother-baby relationships in the framework of preterm births, defined as deliveries occurring before 37 weeks of amenorrhea. Such births currently represent approximately 7% of all births in France, i.e., 55,000 children per year (AUDIPOG Maternity Units Sentinel Network) and growing by almost 20% from 1995 to 2003[8].

For the parents, a preterm birth represents a series of successive traumas (mourning a full pregnancy, mourning a normal birth, mourning a perfect child) and entails a disruption of their psychoaffective economy and a restructuring of the family equilibrium. Narcissism is tested in both parents, to varying degrees and in different forms. Ferrari (2000) recalls that the separation imposed by a preterm birth arouses mixed feelings in the parents: Love and hate are at their maximum. The mother particularly has ambivalent feelings toward her baby, of love and tenderness as well as hostility from the frustration and suffering imposed by the baby.

The mother's fragilization, coupled with the baby's complex start in life, in a context in which the father is also grappling with his own anxieties, fears, and pain in the face of a depressive situation, leads us to consider such families as presenting a high risk of interactive dysfunction and of triggering a depressive symptomatology.

Maïa and Antidepressive Representations Generated by the P. K. E. C.

In this contribution, the clinical assessment of a child aged 3 years and 6 months is presented in order to understand the symbolization disorders leading the child to preferentially cathect modes of acting in a spectrum which can be qualified as defensive.

Analysis of the P. K. E. C. protocols is particularly interesting in this case to highlight symbolization disorders – and particularly to refine

---

8   This growth is explained by: an increase in the number of births (+4% from 1995 to 2003), multiple pregnancies for which the risk of preterm birth is approx. 50%, an increase in the number of deliveries by cesarean section. Very preterm births (i.e., before 33 weeks of amenorrhea) represent about 1.5% of newborns.

their analysis through the various dimensions (sensoriality, motricity, symbolic expression, expression of connections, onset of transitionality) involved in the test. The P. K. E. C. is proposed by the psychologist with a dual objective in mind: to assess the child's mental functioning and to support symbolization processes based on the development of a play area in which the child may develop her ability to play "alone in the presence of another" (Winnicott, 1958).

Maïa, 3 Years and 6 Months

Maïa is accompanied by her mother. She is introduced as a tyrannical child who cannot bear separation. She was born prematurely at 7 months. Maïa is the second-born to the young couple: A first child, Louis, born at 5 months, died at birth without reanimation. He was subsequently incinerated without burial, which the mother admitted regretting from the onset of the interview. It should be noted that the major problems encountered in both pregnancies radically preclude any plans for further children – Maïa's mother explicitly indicates that another pregnancy might kill her.

Maïa is described as crying a lot in her first months, leading her parents to watch over her 24 h a day, to keep her with them at night, but also to make countless visits to the doctor. In fact, she does not seem to have suffered any specific somatic disorders. She is described as "having done everything early – walking, potty training," while constantly challenging her parents. Indeed, she demonstrates opposition behaviors suggesting emotional disturbance, seems to withdraw from her parents' shows of affection, provokes, shouts ... She makes her parents' life impossible though they cannot imagine being separated from their daughter. Their call for help was prompted by a feeling of being "overwhelmed," as they admit. Maïa's mother describes herself as very involved in her daughter's everyday life, which includes kindergarten since she was 30 months old. However, the mother herself questions the quality of her own involvement, saying that she is "there without being there."

Maïa subsequently attends several consultations in the presence of both parents. Maïa's father also seems helpless in the face of his daughter's demanding nature and admits that he tends to easily give in to her.

The P. K. E. C. is proposed to Maïa on four occasions, at approximately 2-week intervals.

P. K. E. C. – Play Observation 1

Maïa explores the material set out on the play mat. She names the various objects and asks the psychologist what she should do with the building blocks. She takes the baby bottle, turns it upside down and says that there is no milk in the bottle. She takes the bear and kisses it. She then says "I'll be careful not to damage your toys." She assembles the blocks and brings them to the psychologist. She explores the tactile quality of the hard ball and the soft ball.
Maïa takes the hard doll, takes off the nappy ("I'm taking off the knickers") and takes it to a corner of the office which she calls the toilet: "He's going to pooh," then wipes the doll's bottom. Maïa then takes up a soft toy (an orange dog called Mandarin), which is always available in the psychologist's office. She asks the dog's name, as well as her (real) cat's, saying that she would like it to be a girl called Mimi, as she herself would like to be called Mimi, and considers that the psychologist's name might be Maïa. Maïa offers Mandarin the bottle, saying that Mandarin would like to drink from the bottle like a baby. Then Mandarin "poohs everywhere" with great agitation: Maïa makes the dog drop excrements in various places in the office, but particularly on the low table and the psychologist's documents lying there. Playtime ends on a question by Maïa: "Is my mother dead?" (about 20 minutes).

Maïa generally shows herself dissatisfied with the play material, moving from one activity to another without really being able to stage scenes, then exits the play situation proper (leaving the proposed playing framework) by resorting to an object outside the play material. In fact, she has trouble playing in the sense that she cannot engage in the imaginary, but she does handle the material. Everything seems to indicate that she cannot rely on enough inner security to "play in the presence of another."

P. K. E. C. – Play Observation 2

The second game is much shorter, given the lengthy prior meeting in the presence of both her parents, during which Maïa provided much clinical material to work on the suffering underlying her symptoms. In particular, she again questions her name (this time with her parents there), in continuity with the game in the previous session: "My name is Mimi, I'm not Maïa." One hears both the stakes related to the place she, Maïa, occupies as a differentiated subject in her parents' cathexes, and the control dimension she tends to muster in her relationship with her parents by naming herself.

Maïa takes both the hard and the soft dolls and starts feeding them the bottle. The care given during the feeding is rough and Maïa leaves the dolls on the floor while feeding them. She then fetches Mandarin. Mandarin picks up the phone and Maïa asks the psychologist to call in Mandarin's place: The psychologist must "act" as Mandarin according to Maïa's instructions along the game. Mandarin must ask for food – milk of course, brought by the baby bottle, but also fruit juice which Maïa brings in a glass from the tea set she has fetched from the box, and other food which Maïa brings on a plate, with the cutlery to feed Mandarin. Playtime again ends on great excitation for Maïa, translated into Mandarin dropping excrements in various places in the office (about 10 minutes).

243

One may highlight how Maïa introduces control movements into the game: She restricts the number of toys she chooses, and she "directs" the psychologist to act in scenarios that leave but a narrow leeway (restricted play) in relation to her instructions. The oral link is hypercathected, with a need to mediate it. Maïa relies on the psychologist to open up symbolic play.

P. K. E. C. – Play Observation 3

Before the start of the third play session, Maïa's parents indicate that their daughter is starting to be afraid of strangers, which one might see as the onset of a form of organizer in Maïa's psychoaffective development. The parents state that Maïa is back to soiling herself (defecating in her pants), an element the mother had mentioned as an aside during the initial consultation. Maïa's parents can now entrust her to her grandparents, contemplate getting away as a couple for a weekend, which they had not been able to do in several years. They stress that their daughter is "precious" to them.

Maïa introduces herself on a rather seductive mode: wearing a glittery skirt, she winks at the psychologist.

Maïa herself fetches the P. K. E. C. bag for the psychologist to set up the content. She explicitly expresses wanting to play with the psychologist – "with you" – she says. Maïa again stages a meal for Mandarin and Maïa's own soft toy which she has brought to each session. Maïa feeds each toy, either with the bottle or from a plate with a fork, having fetched the material from the tea set box. Access to food is always conveyed through the telephone: Each toy phones the psychologist to tell him what it would like to drink and/or eat. Having fed both toys, Maïa starts organizing to put them down "for a nap" on the blankie. After this rest time, Maïa stages a ball game between both toys, then a game of tag. Maïa is able to play for a while "alone in the presence of the psychologist," but then the game quickly evolves into a form of excitation which again leads to Mandarin dropping excrements outside the area defined as the toilet – albeit in a more restrained fashion (about 15 minutes).

One observes how Maïa resorts to the psychologist's support to deploy her play, then releases herself from this support in a furtive way. However, her ability to keep a reassuring image within herself remains limited, and again leads to excitation.

P. K. E. C. – Play Observation 4

Maïa's parents emphasize their daughter's positive development; she seems to have given up her various ways of forming a tyrannical link to her environment. They are able to express the feeling of better finding their place as parents in a relationship to their daughter to her place as a child (Could Maïa be freed of identification with the dead child? One might think of Salvador Dali, who said he was forced to be a "clown" to free himself of a link to the figure of the dead brother attached to his own name, which had also been given to his stillborn brother some time before his own birth.).

244

Maïa repeats and reproduces the game initiated in the previous session, with the two soft toys that were not part of the P. K. E. C. Both toys call the psychologist in turn, asking for what they wish to eat or drink, and Maïa prepares the bottle, dish, plates, and cutlery. After the meal session, Maïa shows the psychologist that the soft toy has a hole in its tummy (which is true): Supported by the psychologist, she is able to initiate "care" for her toy, which introduces another line of play. From then on, Maïa devotes particular attention to her toy, asking the psychologist to give it the appropriate care, before engaging herself in this task. In this case, no outburst is observed on Maïa's part. As for Mandarin, the dog stops dropping excrements inappropriately (about 12 minutes).

Summoning the nursing figure successively as a professional, then as a maternal figure, allows the expression of a kind of repetition in the transfer of an ambiguous experience, through strongly cathected identification movements.

Trauma and Depression

In Maïa's case we can stress how much her preterm birth – a trauma in itself – rekindled the painful loss of her elder brother in a similar context of prematurity. In addition to the parent-baby link in such traumatic births, there is the issue of how each of the parents mourn the dead child and how this fits into each of their life stories. The hypothesis of post-partum depression in Maïa's mother and its impact on her relationship with her daughter does not evade the father's difficulty in making up for the mother's shortcomings, inasmuch as he himself was grappling with his loss and suspended parenthood. Through her omnipotent and tyrannical behaviors, Maïa is, by calling attention to herself and constantly mobilizing her parents, probably trying to keep them alive and avoid their collapse: She is moving to keep from sinking, but also to avoid her parents' sinking.

Parental depression remains hidden behind tiredness and anger, behind the child's symptoms, but it is lurking in the shadows. Ciccone (2004) submits that a child pushing things to the limit is trying to find what there is beyond the limit. It seems as though the child is uncertain whether the adult ultimately cares for it and really cathects it.

The child's attacks, rejections, and provocations serve to get the parents' attention so as to keep them present/alive. However, these movements call for so much mental energy that the child is little available and too alone to develop enough elaboration and symbolization capacities to allow it to form links in its drive-life. The family finds itself in a system

245

of constant closeness driven by permanent conflict, which prevents the development of a sufficiently effective shield against excitation for Maïa. Control and self-control coexist with drive discharge processes.

The therapy sessions supported by the P. K. E. C. allow the deployment of a transitional area guaranteeing some degree of continuity and enabling Maïa to engage in symbolization processes and to represent herself in the game.

Conclusion

Given the many possible diagnoses from a same symptom in a baby, Golse (2001) stresses the need for the clinician to use countertransference to refine understanding of the disorders observed. Indeed, he advises against overreliance on observation grids, which do not take into account the child's clinical history.

The Projective Kit for Early Childhood offers both a clinical observation tool and support for research through a device that promotes the clinician's availability for transference-countertransference interaction with babies or young children. It puts forward a standardized situation combining a formalized identification of processes with the deployment of a flexible area – an "in-between" position with the child – which constitute the interest and richness of this projective test.

References

AUDIPOG Maternity Units Sentinel Network. http://www.audipog.net/tab-stat.php

Bick, E. (1964). Notes on infant observation in psychoanalytic training. *International Journal of Psychoanalysis, 45,* 558–566.

Boekholt, M. (1993). *Les épreuves thématiques en clinique infantile* [Thematic tests in child clinical practice]. Paris: Dunod.

Brunet, O., & Lézine, I. (1951). *Le développement psychologique de la première enfance* [Psychological development in early childhood]. Paris: E. A. P.

Chabert, C. (1995). Contribution des méthodes projectives dans la recherche en psychologie clinique et en psychopathologie [Contribution of projective methods in the research in clinical psychology and psychopathology]. In O. Bourguignon & M. Bydlowsky (Eds.), *La recherche clinique en psychopathologie* (pp. 95–112). Paris: P. U. F.

Ciccone, A. (2004). *Psychanalyse de l'enfant tyrannique* [Psychoanalysis of the tyrannical child]. Paris: Dunod.

Cox, J.-L., & Holden, J. M. (1994). *Perinatal psychiatry: Use and misuse of the Edinburgh Postnatal Depression Scale*. London: Gaskell.

Cox, J.-L., Holden, J.-M., & Sagovsky, R. (1987). Detection of postnatal depression: Development of the 10-item Edinburgh Postnatal Depression Scale. *British Journal of Psychiatry, 150,* 782–786.

Crespin, G., & Serradet, J.-L. (2006). Évaluation d'un ensemble cohérent d'outils de repérage des troubles précoces de la communication pouvant présager un trouble grave du développement de type autistique. La recherche Préaut [Evaluation of a coherent set of tools for the localization of early commmunication disorders in order to predict developmental disorders of the autistic type. The Préaut research]. *Journal Français de Psychiatrie, 25,* 46–48.

Ferrari, L. (2000). Place de la psychanalyse dans l'accompagnement de l'enfant prématuré et de sa famille [Place of psychoanalysis in the care for a premature child and its family]. *Médecine thérapeutique/pédiatrie, 3,* 311–316.

Golse, B. (2001). Les dépressions chez le bébé: affect, état, structure? [The depressed baby: Affect, state structure?] *Revue française de psychosomatique, 2*(20), 29–45.

Green, A. (1983). Le complexe de la mère morte [The dead mother complex]. In A. Green (Ed.), *Narcissisme de vie, narcissisme de mort* (pp. 222–253). Paris: Minuit.

Klein, M. (1934/1976). Contribution à l'étude de la psychogénèse des états maniaco-dépressifs [A contribution to the psychogenesis of manic-depressive states]. In *Essais de psychanalyse* (pp. 311–340). Paris: Payot.

Klein, M. (1940/1976). Le deuil et ses rapports avec les états maniaco-dépressifs [Mourning and its relation to manic-depressive states]. In *Essais de psychanalyse* (pp. 341–369). Paris: Payot.

Murray, L. (1996, janvier). *L'impact de la Dépression du postpartum sur le développement de l'enfant* [The impact of postpartum depression on child development]. Colloque international de Psychiatrie périnatale, Monaco.

Murray, L., & Stein, A. (1991). The effects of postnatal depression on mother-infant relations and infant development. In M. Woodhead, R. Carr, & P. Light (Eds.), *Becoming a person* (pp. 163–174). London: Routledge.

Poinso, F., Samuelian, J. C., Delzenne, V., Huiart, L., Sparrow, J., & Rufo, M. (2001). Dépression du post partum: délimitation d'un groupe à haut risque dès la maternité, évaluation prospective et relation mère-bébé [Postpartum depression: Delimitation of a high-risk group immediately after birth, prospective evaluation and mother-baby relations]. *La psychiatrie de l'enfant, 442,* 379–413.

Roman, P. (1997). La méthode projective comme dispositif à symboliser [The projective method as a device to symbolize]. In P. Roman (Ed.), *Projection et symbolisation chez l'enfant* (pp. 37–51). Lyon: PUL.

Roman, P. (2004). *La Mallette Projective Première Enfance – Manuel d'utilization et matériel de l'épreuve* [Projective Kit for Early Childhood (P. K. E. C.) – Handbook and test material]. Paris: E. C. P. A.

Roman, P. (2005). La Mallette Projective Première Enfance (MPPE) – Un outil clinique pour l'évaluation de la personnalité du jeune enfant [The Projective Kit for Early Childhood (P. K. E. C.): A clinical tool for the evaluation of a young child's personality]. *Devenir, 15*, 233–259.

Schopler, E., Reichler, R. J., DeVellis, R. F., & Daly, K. (1980). Toward objective classification of childhood autism: Childhood Autism Rating Scale (CARS). *Journal of Autism and Developmental Disorders, 10*(1), 91–103.

Von Staabs, G. (1962). *Le Scéno-test* [Sceno-Test]. Paris: Delachaux & Niestlé.

Tustin, F. (1981). Les objets autistiques [Autistic objects]. In F. Tustin (Ed.), *Les états autistiques chez l'enfant* (pp. 193–220). Paris: Seuil.

Winnicott, D.-W. (1957). *Jeu et réalité* [Play and reality]. Paris: Gallimard.

Winnicott D.-W. (1958). La capacité d'être seul [The capacity to be alone]. In D.-W. Winnicott (Ed.), *De la pédiatrie à la psychanalyse* (pp. 205–213). Paris: Payot.

Winnicott, D.-W. (1971). *La consultation thérapeutique chez l'enfant* [Therapeutic consultations in child psychiatry]. Paris: Gallimard.

Pascal Roman
Department of Psychology
University of Lausanne
Quartier UNIL-Dorigny
Bâtiment Anthropole
1015 Lausanne
Switzerland
E-mail pascal.roman@unil.ch

Summary

The purpose of this article is twofold:
- First, to present the Projective Kit for Early Childhood, a projective play test designed for infants aged 6 months to 3 years. This unique test in the field of clinical practice and psychopathology in young children is presented from the vantage points of its theoretical basis and methodological implications (play material, psychologist's involvement in the test ...) of the actual test as well as of the processing of collected clinical data. Data resulting from observing the children's play are scored in terms of play processes (relying on the work of Boekholt, 1993) as well as of the play materials' handling modes.
- Second, to study the continuity between research practice and clinical practice (Chabert, 1995), highlighting the test's scientific foundations and relevance. A first example involves an evaluation of the psychoaffective dynamics of children with a West syndrome – a form of epilep-

sy occurring in infants from the early stages of life, which impairs their development and frequently leads to psychopathological pictures in the autism spectrum – in the framework of a research project on language development in infants in order to identify milestones in autistic vs. nonautistic mechanisms of relationship to the world through the children's play. The second illustration relies on a clinical consultation process for infants and focuses on the clinical understanding of the problem of depression through a repetition of the test, which paves the way for its use as part of a psychotherapeutic project.

Résumé

L'objectif de cet article est double:
- D'une part, il s'agit de présenter l'épreuve projective de la Mallette Projective Première Enfance, épreuve projective de jeu, élaborée à destination des jeunes enfants, âgés de 6 mois à trois ans. Cette épreuve, unique dans le champ de la clinique et de la psychopathologie du jeune enfant, sera présentée tout à la fois du point de vue de son ancrage théorique et de ses implications méthodologiques (matériel de jeu, disposition du psychologue dans l'épreuve ...), au plan de la passation et au plan du traitement des données cliniques recueillies; en effet, ces données, qui prennent la forme d'une observation du jeu de l'enfant, font l'objet d'une cotation en termes de procédés de jeu (en appui sur les travaux de M. Boekholt, 1993) et en termes de choix et de mode de saisie du matériel de jeu,
- D'autre part, considérant une forme de continuité entre pratique de recherche et pratique clinique (C. Chabert, 1995), il s'agit d'illustrer, dans ces deux champs, l'implication et l'intérêt scientifiques de l'épreuve. Une première illustration porte sur l'évaluation du fonctionnement psychique d'enfants présentant un syndrome de West (une forme d'épilepsie survenant dès les premiers temps de la vie du nourrisson, et qui entrave son développement, avec des évolutions fréquentes vers des tableaux psychopathologiques dans le registre de l'autisme), dans le cadre d'une recherche portant sur le développement du langage chez l'enfant, et permet de construire des repères, au travers du jeu de l'enfant, sur les modalités autistiques versus nonautistiques du rapport au monde; puis, une seconde illustration, qui s'appuie sur une clinique de la consultation du jeune enfant, sera centrée sur la compréhension clinique de la problématique de la dé-

pression au travers d'un dispositif de proposition répétée de l'épreuve qui ouvre la voie à une utilization de celle-ci dans un projet psychothérapeutique.

Resumen

Este articulo tiene une doble objetivo:
- De una parte, consiste en presentar la prueba proyectiva del Maletín Proyectivo de la Primera Infancia, prueba proyectiva de juego, creada y destinada para los niños pequeños, entre los 6 meses y los 3 años. Esta prueba, única en el campo de la clínica y la psicopatología del niño joven, será presentada desde su punto de vista de su anclaje teórico y al mismo tiempo desde sus implicaciones metodológicas (material de juego, disposición del psicólogo en la prueba ...), en el plano de la realización de la prueba y en el plano del tratamiento de los datos clínicos obtenidos. En efecto, estos datos, que toman la forma de una observación del juego del niño, son el objeto de una evaluación en términos de procedimientos de juego (apoyados sobre los trabajos de M. Boekholt, 1993) y en términos de opción y de manera de captar el material del juego.
- De otra parte, considerando una forma continua entre la practica de la investigación y la practica clínica (C. Chabert, 1995), consiste en ilustrar, en estos dos campos, la implicación y los intereses científicos de la prueba. Una primera ilustración conlleva a la evaluación del funcionamiento psíquico de niños que presentan el síndrome de West (una forma de epilepsia que afecta a niños en edades tempranas de la vida, dicho síndrome perjudica el desarrollo y frecuentemente conlleva a cuadros psicopatológicos de espectro autista) en el marco de una investigación sobre el desarrollo del pañal en el niño, y permite construir puntos de referencia, a través del juego del niño, sobre modalidades autísticas versus no autísticas de relación en el mundo. Una segunda ilustración, la cual se apoya en la clínica de la consulta del niño joven, será centrada sobre la comprensión clínica de la problemática de la depresión a través de un dispositivo de proposición repetida de la prueba que abre la vía a la utilización en un proyecto psicoterapéutico.

要約

この論文の目的はふたつある

　ひとつの目的は 6 カ月から 3 歳の乳幼児のために考案された、早期の小児期のための投影法キット、投影的プレイテストを提示することである。幼い子どもの臨床実践や精神病理の領域におけるこのユニークな検査は理論的な基礎や方法論的意義（プレイの用具、検査における心理学者の関与など…）の観点、集められた臨床データの処理をどのようにおこなうかという観点と同様に実際の検査としての観点から提示される。実際、この子どものプレイの観察のからもたらされたデータは、プレイの用具を扱う様式と同様に、プレイのプロセスという観点（B,Boekholt,1993 にもとづく）からスコアされる。

　もうひとつの目的は、研究の実践と臨床実践を間のある種の連続性を考慮しながら、検査の科学的根拠と適合性に光をあてることである。最初の事例には、幼児の言語発達の研究プロジェクトという枠組みにおいて、ウェスト症候群１を有する子どもたちの心理感情的力動の評価を含んでおり、それは子どものプレイを通しての外界との関係する自閉的－非自閉的機制の重要な段階を同定するのに役に立つ。二つ目の事例は、幼児のための臨床コンサルテーションにもとづくものであり、心理療法的プロジェクトの一部としての利用という道を開くための、検査の繰り返しを通じてうつの問題が臨床的に理解されてくるということに焦点が当てられている。

1　ウェスト症候群とは生涯の早期の段階から幼児期に発症するある種のてんかんであり、発達を損ない、しばしば自閉スペクトラムに位置する精神病理を示すことがある。

Instructions to Authors – *Rorschachiana*

Aims and Scope. *Rorschachiana* is the scientific publication of the International Society for the Rorschach. Its aim is to publish scientific work in the field for (and by) an international audience. The journal is interested in advancing theory and clinical applications of the Rorschach and other projective techniques, and research work that can enhance and promote projective methods. All papers published are subject to rigorous peer-review to internationally accepted standards by external relievers and the Society's Board of Assessors, working under the auspices of the experienced international editorial team.

Categories of Papers. *Rorschachiana* is interested in promoting theory, practice, and clinical research in the field of projective methods. The Journal publishes Original Articles dealing with all themes in the research and theory on and the application of projective techniques. A limited number of Case Studies will be considered for publication each year. Case Studies aim to present a specific clinical assessment or therapeutic intervention by examining in depth, and in a holistic manner, various aspects of one or several cases (e.g., comparative case study). They should include: the context of assessment/treatments (e.g., setting, theoretical framework, assessment process, test used); a thorough and detailed description of the case (e.g., reason for referral, presenting problem, background information, socio-demographic data, diagnosis); the central issues/dilemmas/questions raised by the case; case data (e.g., test results, themes of interviews, summary of therapeutic intervention, description of the therapy process); the analysis and interpretation which is based on the case data in the light of the theoretical framework; a discussion on the conflict, theoretical or clinical challenges of the case (e.g., what might have influenced the interpretation); a conclusion which presents the imitations of the study but also considers the implications for wider theoretical and/or research issues.

Submission of Manuscripts. Manuscripts should be first submitted by e-mail to the Editor-in-Chief for initial screening in the format outlined below: Sadegh Nashat, Editor – *Rorschachiana*, Child and Family Department, Tavistock Clinic, 120 Belsize Lane, London NW3 5BA, UK, E-mail rorschach.submission@gmail.com.

Alternatively, upon request, manuscripts may be submitted in duplicate on paper.

The Editor-in-Chief will screen manuscripts in order to ensure that they fall within the aims and scope of *Rorschachiana*. Those that fit will be reviewed by two independent reviewers. All papers will be subject to peer review under the auspices of the Editor-in-Chief and the Editorial Board in terms of their merits, readability, and interest. Unsolicited manuscripts will not be returned to the author(s). Authors are advised to review the *Rorschachiana* Manuscript Submission Checklist before submission, in addition to the advice below.

For more information please visit www.hogrefe.com/journals/rorschach.

Format of Manuscripts. Manuscripts must be written in English with margins of at least 2.5 cm all around (typescript). Every line of the manuscript, without exception, should be typed double-spaced. The right margin of the text should be ragged: do not justify the right margin. The first line of each paragraph should be indented.

Without exception, the entire manuscript should be typed in upper case and lower case Roman letters. Please do not type anything (e.g., the names of the authors) in capital letters.

For emphasis, words or numbers may be set in italics; please do not use bold typeface or underlining. The entire text should be typed in regular paragraphs. Computer techniques for highlighting text and other embellishments should be avoided.

All pages should be numbered beginning with 1. Place the page number and a short version of the title at the top right of each page.

Each manuscript should contain the following, in the correct order:

1. A first title page to include the title of the paper, full name of the author(s), the affiliation of the author(s), the address for correspondence (including e-mail address and telephone and fax numbers, if available). The author who will be responsible for correspondence should be indicated. A word count should also be included.
2. Abstract: should not exceed 200 words; up to 5 key words to be listed alphabetically on the same page. This page should carry the title of the paper but not the author name(s).
3. Main text: not usually to exceed 6000 words and to be clearly organized. A clear hierarchy of headings and subheadings is recommended.
4. Reference citations in the text and in the reference list should follow the conventions listed in the *Publication Manual of the American Psychological Association* (6th edition). Non-English titles should be translated into English in brackets following the original title. The name and volume number of journals and the title of books should be set in italics. All references listed must be mentioned in the text and all references mentioned in the text must be listed in the "References" section. All references cited in the text should appear in an alphabetical list.
5. Footnotes should be avoided if at all possible; if they are unavoidable, then they should be placed at the end of the text, after the references.
6. The positioning of tables or figures should be indicated with the following statement placed in the text at the appropriate place: "Enter Table × about here." Each table or figure should be placed on a separate page after the reference section. Tables and figures should be numbered using Arabic numerals. Figures must be accompanied by a legend; tables should have a brief descriptive title. All tables and figures must be referred to in the text. *Rorschachiana* is printed in black and white only, so that figures should be supplied as greyscale images rather than in color, as either vector graphics (EPS) or high-resolution (300 dpi) bitmap (TIF) images.
7. Summaries should be provided (see section below).

Summaries. The final part of the manuscript is the "Summary" (300 to 400 words), which should be submitted in English, French, Spanish and in the native tongue of the first author. The Editorial Team will prepare a Japanese translation. If the French or Spanish versions of the summary cannot be provided, then please inform the Editor immediately as the Editorial Board will need time to prepare these.

Style. Please use a clear and readable style, avoiding jargon. Technical terms should be defined when first used. It is recommended to use plurals instead of he/she whenever possible: "If a patient is depressed, he or she ..." is better expressed as "When patients are depressed, they ..." American spelling is preferred.

The Editor retains the right to modify the presentation and/or wording of the text whenever necessary.

Cover Letter. Please attach a letter confirming that all authors have agreed to the submission of the article, and that the article is not currently under consideration for publication elsewhere.

Copyright Agreement. By submitting an article, the author confirms and guarantees on behalf of him- or herself and any coauthors that he or she holds all copyright in and titles to the submitted contribution, including any figures, photographs, line drawings, plans, maps, sketches, and tables, and that the article and its contents do not infringe in any way on the rights of third parties. The author indemnifies and holds harmless the publisher from any third-party claims. The author agrees, upon acceptance of the article for publication, to transfer to the publisher the exclusive right to reproduce and distribute the article and its contents, both physically and in nonphysical, electronic, or other form, in the volume to which it has been submitted and in other independent publications, with no limitations on the number of copies or on the form or the extent of distribution. These rights are transferred for the duration of copyright as defined by international law. Furthermore, the author transfers to the publisher the following exclusive rights to the article and its contents:

1. The rights to produce advance copies, reprints, or offprints of the article, in full or in part, to undertake or allow translations into other languages, to distribute other forms or modified versions of the article, and to produce and distribute summaries or abstracts.
2. The rights to microfilm and microfiche editions or similar, to the use of the article and its contents in videotext, teletext, and similar systems, to recordings or reproduction using other media, digital or analog, including electronic, magnetic, and optical media, and in multimedia form, as well as for public broadcasting in radio, television, or other forms of broadcast.
3. The rights to store the article and its content in machine-readable or electronic form on all media (such as computer disks, compact disks, magnetic tape), to store the article and its contents in online databases belonging to the publisher or third parties for viewing or downloading by third parties, and to present or reproduce the article or its contents on visual display screens, monitors, and similar devices, either directly or via data transmission.
4. The rights to reproduce and distribute the article and its contents by all other means, including photomechanical and similar processes (such as photocopying or facsimile), and as part of so-called document delivery services.
5. The right to transfer any or all rights mentioned in this agreement, as well as rights retained by the relevant copyright clearing centers, including royalty rights to third parties.

Online Rights for Journal Articles. Guidelines on authors' rights to archive electronic versions of their manuscripts online are given in the Advice for Authors on the journal's web page at www.hogrefe.com.